LANDSCAPING

THE HARROWSMITH
LANDSCAPING HANDBOOK

EDITED BY JENNIFER BENNETT
ILLUSTRATIONS BY IAN GRAINGE

Canadian Cataloguing in Publication Data

Main entry under title:

The Harrowsmith landscaping handbook

Includes index.
ISBN 0-920656-39-0

1. Landscape gardening.   2. Ornamental
horticulture.   I. Bennett, Jennifer.
II. Harrowsmith.

SB473.H37   1985   635.9   C85-099482-9

Trade distribution by Firefly Books, Toronto

Printed in Canada for:
Camden House Publishing Ltd.
7 Queen Victoria Road
Camden East, Ontario
K0K 1J0

Front Cover: Pierre St. Laurent/Stock Market Inc.
Back Cover: **Left**: Eva Hoepfner
              Right: Derek and Jane Abson/
              Photo/Graphics

The creation of *The Harrowsmith
Landscaping Handbook* depended upon
the work of many people whose names
do not appear elsewhere on these pages.
They include assistant editor David
Archibald; graphic artists Linda Menyes,
Janice McLean and Marta Scythes; copy
editors Mary Patton, Tracy C. Read and
Sharon McFadzean; typesetter Patricia
Denard; proofreader John Archibald;
executive editor Frank Edwards; and
publisher James Lawrence.

Contents

1 In Search Of Paradise

Knots, parterres and the fashionable history of landscaping

By Jennifer Bennett

Landscaping. Can it turn common earth into paradise? Here, living on our suburban lots, in our city townhouses, on our farms or simply with our dreams, we have places that are pretty enough in their own way, with their flowers and bushes and trees. Yet they are only suggestive of what we commonly think of as landscaping: groomed parks, tree-lined avenues and boulevards, topiary and hedges, immaculate, ever-blooming perennial borders designed and maintained by professionals. Intimidation comes easily. What we have is usually passable and certainly home – but it is not paradise.

Yet paradise originally meant garden. The word was used to denote any of the gardens of the Persian King Cyrus the Great, who lived in the sixth century B.C. In the words of the Greek Xenophon, "the Persian King is zealously cared for, so that he may find gardens wherever he goes. Their name is Paradise and they are full of all things fair and good that the earth can bring forth." Which sounds a little like the biblical Paradise, but quite unlike anything a gardening Northerner might expect. "All things fair and good that the earth can bring forth" are the sorts of things that will simply not grow in such a climate, even had we the skill and knowledge to grow them.

But paradise has also been defined simply as "a place of rest and joy," – just one-third of which, incidentally, is set aside for "well-behaved women," according to the Koran – and virtually any garden, with the help of skilful and sensitive landscaping, can be that. What is landscaping? It is the consideration of one's piece of property as a milieu, a vista, a unit whose parts all contribute harmoniously to the whole. Landscaping is art, yet more than art. One can use many of the same principles of design, colour and balance that would be employed on an artist's canvas, but because plants are the most important elements in this medium, time, as well as space, must be considered. The landscape artist must think not only of what is, but also of what will be – a season, a year, 20 years hence. Maintenance is essential; change optional and possible at any time. The landscape has a life of its own.

Much like the other arts, landscaping has long been the subject of changing fashion, reflecting our need to be perceived as up-to-date and either controlling or working with nature. Like that of other fashions, the history of landscaping proceeds virtually hand in hand with the history of leisure time. For aeons, landscaping was affordable to those rich enough to spend time, or hire others to spend time, doing nothing but thinking about the aesthetics of their natural surroundings. Before that, everyone was vitally concerned with controlling and working with nature simply to ensure that there would be enough food.

Although the earliest records of plant cultivation begin about 10,000 years ago, the first decorative gardens do not appear in history until around 2000 B.C. in Mesopotamia, also the rumoured location of the Garden of Eden, Paradise indeed. These gardens were formal and had religious significance, as well as acting as public relations notices for the rulers who created them. Here, plants gathered from other lands could demonstrate, in living colour, the conqueror's dominion. Such was the case in two instances documented during the 12th century B.C. In Egypt, Ramses III planted, along a sacred pathway, flowers gathered from afar, while in Assyria, King Tiglath-pileser I planted "trees that none of the kings, my forefathers, have

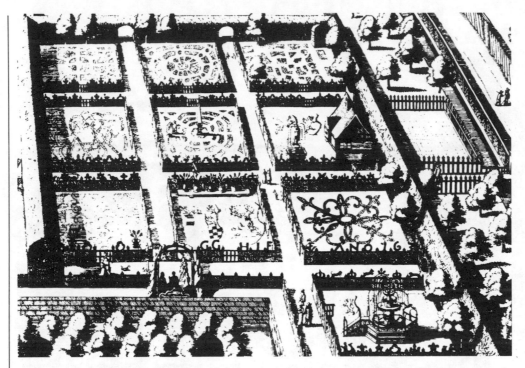

possessed...carried off from the countries I conquered." In the Egyptian gardens, some of these plants were displayed in pots, a custom that was adopted by the ancient Greeks and Romans. The Hanging Gardens of Babylon were even more impressive, resembling, it seems, a living, green ziggurat that advertised the prowess of the king who likely built them around 600 B.C., Nebuchadnezzar. The gardens were described by Strabo, a Greek geographer and historian, as consisting "of vaulted terraces raised one above another." Diodorus, a Sicilian historian who lived, as did Strabo, at the beginning of the Christian era, wrote that the top terrace contained the main garden and "certain engines" that drew water from the Euphrates through hidden conduits to the terraces, a triumph of early irrigation equalled only by the gardens of the Aztecs.

Further east, the powerful message of landscaping was also used by the Emperor Wu Ti who, in his vast second-century-B.C. grounds, exhibited rare plants gathered from throughout the Orient. Bridges, streams, pavilions and man-made hills were structural elements long appreciated in such gardens, where both wealth and restraint were displayed. One Chinese ruler, around 2000 B.C., actually filled a garden pool with rice wine, so that his guests, on the stroke of a gong, could jump out of their boats and imbibe. In the sixth century A.D., Lo-Yang Chia Lang Chi wrote of one Chinese garden: "With its hills and ponds, this garden excelled in beauty many princely pleasure grounds. Here had been built up a number of hills . . . that look as if they had been formed by nature. Within these heights there were double peaks and curving ridges by the side of deep streams and

valleys. There were plenty of tall, leafy trees which afforded protection against the rays of the sun and moon and hanging creepers which did not prevent the mist from creeping in. The paths ran zigzag up the hills and down the valleys." From early times, Orientals also deliberately included large rocks in their gardens to produce an aesthetic and meditative effect that would be refined further by the Japanese in their exquisite Zen Buddhist water or sand gardens and would finally be modified and combined with other techniques in gardens of the 20th-century New World.

It was in early Greece and Rome that the tradition of the very formal European garden first flourished. These geometric plans, with their long, symmetrical perspectives and carefully maintained plants, gave the impression of vast, controlled spaces, and probably, of the great civilizing power of their owners, usually members of the ruling class. The smaller Italian town garden or *villa urbana* contained rectangular beds edged with box or ivy, straight paths and decorative elements such as statues, urns and fountains. Even smaller gardens might be given the illusion of size with a painted backdrop that depicted a garden or landscape.

The Roman classical garden would have a long-lasting influence on western landscaping, but so, too, would the smaller, walled garden. Mediaeval European gardens were often similarly walled, in part simply to protect them from a barbaric world. Here, medicinal and culinary herbs grew along with a few vegetables – turnips, cabbages, onions – and perhaps fruit trees. Gardens of the mediaeval European gentry were more natural, often including arbours and turf seats. Describing the best plan for a "small garden," Petrus de Crescentiis wrote in

Public Archives Canada PA 45762

Yew, box, privet and other co-operative plants were carved into shapes conventional and outlandish in the practice of topiary, one of the landscape fashions that stressed man's dominance over nature. Not to be outdone, some North American gardens, such as this one in Victoria, British Columbia, imitated the Italian idea.

his *Opus Ruralium Commodorum* at the end of the 13th century: "Let the site of the garden be of such a measure as may suit the plants to be permanently grown in it, and it should be planted with fragrant herbs of all kinds, such as rue, sage, basil, marjoram, mint and similarly all kinds of flowers, such as violet, lily, rose, gladiolus and the like. Between the level turf and the herbs let there be a higher piece of turf made in the fashion of a seat, suitable for flowers and amenities; the grass in the sun's path should be planted with trees or vines, whose branches will protect the turf with shade and cast a pleasant refreshing shadow, but in these trees shade will be more sought for than fruit, and therefore they will not need to be dug or manured, which might do harm to the turf." De Crescentiis' gardens of Kings and Lords included a fish pond, such wildlife as "hares, stags, roebucks, rabbits and the like harmless beasts," and "pheasants, partridges, nightingales, blackbirds, goldfinches, linnets and all other kinds of singing birds." There would be "bowers made entirely of leafy trees, in which the King and Queen with the barons and lords may sojourn in dry weather." All grassy areas were, at this time, kept clipped with scythes or grazing animals. Not until 1830 would the lawn mower be invented, causing the lawn to become a focal point and a fetish.

The pleasance, as it was called in England, was a treed garden used for dancing, for such games as "bowls", early lawn bowling, as a place where a knight might woo his lady, or where he might simply retire, with other

The linear perspectives favoured in classical landscapes are still widely used in public parks, such as this example from the early 20th century in Hamilton, Ontario. With its formal outlines defined by topiary, hedges and arches, such a style brings new meaning to William Lawson's 1618 description, ''Nature, corrected by Art.''

gentlemen, for dessert. Here, beds of flowers or herbs were often enclosed in raised beds, edged with wood or stones. John Parkinson, herbalist to King Charles I of England, recommended the use of especially round, white stones ''for durability, beauty of the sight, handsomeness in the work, and ease in the working.'' The mixture of different plants in these beds was ''so comelily and orderly placed in your borders and squares, and so intermingled,'' wrote William Lawson in 1618, ''that one looking thereon, cannot but wonder to see, what Nature, corrected by Art, can do.''

Corrected by Art, Nature could, in fact, do much more. During the 16th century, raised beds had taken the shape of what were called knots, rows of clipped plants that resembled a flattened knot of rope, and were best viewed from a high perspective such as an upper-storey window. Young Queen Elizabeth could amble, in 1564, in the garden of Richmond Palace, where there was a knot divided into four quarters, with a yew tree at the centre. Mazes or labyrinths were larger versions, designed to confuse and entertain any who entered them. In 1603, James I of England ''re-created himself'' in the labyrinth of one garden, with ''bays, rosemary and the like, overshadowing his walk.''

Scent was important in these gardens. Francis Bacon rated garden plants for their pleasant fragrances and decided that ''that which above all others yields the sweetest smell in the air is the violet,'' and next was ''the muskrose, then strawberry leaves dying...then sweetbrier, then wallflowers, then pinks and gilliflowers; then the flowers of the lime-tree; then the honeysuckles....But those which perfume the air most delightfully not passed by as the rest but

Royal Botanical Gardens

being trodden upon and crushed are three; burnet, wild thyme and water-mints. Therefore, you are to set whole alleys of them to have the pleasure when you walk or tread."

There were arbours, sometimes extending the length of a path which they shaded with ivy, honeysuckle, roses, clematis or grapes. A "pleached alley" could be made of trees such as holly, box, yew or linden clipped to overhang and shelter the pathway underneath. With pruning now high style, the technique of topiary (from the Latin *topiarius* – gardener), learned from the Greeks and Romans, brought into fashion plants such as yew, box or privet which could be trained and trimmed to look like balls, pyramids, spires and later, chess pieces or even mounted horses leaping over hedges. Always a controversial practice, topiary fit well into the classical controlled garden, but could easily seem outlandish elsewhere. Besides, like other garden features demanding severe and repeated pruning, it was labour-intensive. Though it had and still has its uses — in Ohio, an arborvitae hedge spells "Dawes Arboretum" for 2,100 feet — topiary, like the knot and the maze, was a fashion for the dedicated, and perhaps the eccentric.

Topiary well suited the Italian Renaissance, which dispensed, in large part, with introspective mediaeval enclosures, creating instead what were virtual theatre sets with stone patios, statues, fountains, lakes, urns and, only incidentally, native trees and shrubs planted in straight lines or geometric curves to echo the architectural themes. Hillsides were terraced. The Italian style spread throughout Europe with mixed results. Jacques Boyceau wrote in 17th-century France, "It tires me inexpressibly when I find every garden laid out in straight lines, some in four squares, others in nine or in six, and nothing different anywhere," while two centuries later, William Robinson, a Scotsman given to prolixity who described the Italian classical garden as "a place of statues and stone-work out of place," wrote, further, that "in English gardens, where any copy of the Italian idea was accepted, the result was disastrous."

PLANTS ACROSS THE WATER

Although in the 17th century various landscape designers such as Lancelot "Capability" Brown urged the replacement of topiary, clipped hedges and geometric beds with winding paths, ponds, curved beds and informal groupings of trees and shrubs, this new, more natural style of landscaping was to be forgotten for almost two centuries while gardeners turned to a more beguiling fashion, the collection of plants from abroad. As European explorers charted new lands and brought home exotic plants, the new species were first the prizes of the rich, who built greenhouses and conservatories to house them, and then, through propagation, the plants took their places in the front gardens of the new middle class. Philip Miller, author of the popular *Gardener's Dictionary,* wrote that between the book's first edition in 1731 and its eighth in 1768, the number of plant species available in England had doubled. John Loudon, who invented an eclectic garden style called Gardenesque, especially to accommodate all the new arrivals, estimated that in 1700 there were about 1,000 non-native plant species available in England, and by 1800 there were about 6,000. Such plants as magnolias, mountain laurels, rhododendrons, azaleas, forsythias and mock-oranges arrived in Europe in the 18th century. After the introduction of Chinese roses, which produced large-bloomed teas when hybridized with the native European types, the introduction of new roses so beguiled France and

Although Jacques Boyceau wrote that "it tires me inexpressibly when I find every garden laid out in straight lines, some in four squares, others in nine or six," a 16th-century Belgian garden did include interesting naturalistic elements, such as a moat that connected the various garden elements and a forest surrounding the whole.

Italy, that by the late 18th century there were almost 1,000 different types. In 1830 one English nursery advertised more than 1,500 different roses. These were often grown in a rosarium, a special bed in which each individual type was displayed on its own so that differences between cultivars could be easily seen.

By 1800 large gardens boasted important collections of orchids, cacti, dahlias, chrysanthemums and ferns. "Rockwork," early rock gardens, displayed trailing or dwarf roses and, later, alpine wildflowers. For almost a century, so many plants poured into Europe from all over the world that wealthy or adventurous gardeners were almost forced to specialize. Those who chose to grow only plants from North America were given peculiar ideas about that newly settled continent. Thus gardening books instructed these gardeners that their soil must mimic a bog or marsh. A misconception about the nature of North American plant life had developed because most plant hunters traversed the New World by river and the specimens they collected were usually found on the riverside or in swamps.

In England, such collecting so overshadowed any other landscaping consideration that after seeing the middle-class gardens there, the Director General of Gardens to the King of Bavaria wrote in 1833, "The immense multitude of plants which, since the commencement of the present century, have been brought from all parts of the world to Europe, and more especially England, supply the landscape gardener with an inexhaustible fund for decorating his grounds. . . . The palette of the landscape painter, if I may so express myself, is now loaded with such a mass of colours and tints, that his

means are superabundant, compared with the work of art he has to create . . . thus I found English gardens a real chaos of unconnected beauties." William and Robert Chambers wrote in their *Chambers's Information for the People* of 1874, "An error not uncommon in deciding what flowers shall be planted, is to select numbers merely for their rarity or novelty, without reference to what will be their appearance when in bloom." By then, the Victorian practice of transplanting tender annuals such as bright red salvia and blue lobelia from the conservatory into frost-free, geometrically shaped beds must have added even more colour to the confusion.

The Dutch, meanwhile, were more orderly, keeping different flowers, and even different colours, within their own beds. One English gardener sniffed, "We ridicule this plan because it exhibits too great a sameness and formality," but William or Robert Chambers said that for his part, "I am disposed to copy the Dutchman; and I would have my bed of hyacinths distinct, my anemones, my ranunculuses, my pinks, my carnations distinct, and even my beds of

hollyhocks, double blue violets, and dwarf larkspurs distinct, to say nothing of different sorts of roses."

NOBLE SAVAGES

But such small arguments distracted the gardener from the fact that a far more important landscaping ground swell was underway. The 19th century brought Romanticism to Europe, a backlash against logic and the Industrial Revolution that saw the adulation of the "noble savage" by English folk who, agape with wonder, took Grand Tours of the Alps and saw, in all their glory, the uncivilized mountain peaks praised by contemporary poets. Landscaping took a full turn away from the rigid designs of the past and toward a simulation of the natural landscape. Mrs. Loudon's *The Ladies' Magazine of Gardening* of 1842 includes a description of "Lady Broughton's rockwork at the Hoole near Chester" wherein Lady Broughton used "a great deal of her time for six or eight years" to create an impressively rugged imitation of the Swiss Alps, complete with valleys, trees and wildflowers. However, "it was a task of greatest difficulty to make it stand against the weather." That almost any amount of work seemed worthwhile in a climate of increasing revulsion against classical landscaping can be understood by comments of the French landscape architect André Parmentier, during the 1820s: "Our ancestors gave to every part of a garden all the exactness of *geometric* forms: they seem to have known of no other way to plant trees, except in straight lines; a system totally ruinous to the beauty of the prospect. We now see how ridiculous it was, except in the public gardens of the city, to apply the rules of architecture to the embellishment of gardens.

"The majestic trunk is now allowed

the liberty of displaying its form, or of following in its vigorous shoots the plan of nature. Gardens are now treated like landscapes, the charms of which are not to be improved by any rules of art."

In North America, where Parmentier published those statements, landscape gardening had had an unusual history. Not only was this virtually virgin land settled by people who already had some idea of garden aesthetics, but it was also settled by people with differing cultural heritages and, therefore, different landscaping backgrounds. Canadian and American settlers brought seeds and cuttings with them, not only for grains and vegetables, but also for favourite flowers — hollyhocks, pinks, lilies, irises, peonies — as well as shrubs such as lilacs and roses. M.L. Borowsky writes in *Plants from Ukraine in Canada* that Ukranian immigrant farmers brought soil from their native land, along with seeds and roots of their favourite herbs and flowers. "These plants often served medicinal purposes, were used to ornament dwellings during traditional festivals and their aromas became an integral part of the culture-conditioning process started in infancy." These imported plants also served to decorate the yard and garden of the new home, which may well have sat in a field of newly burned stumps, or by the dirt road of a young city. Here, the immigrants responded to the tales of visitors from the Old World and found new gardening ideas during their own trips abroad.

Certainly North Americans were slow to respond to Old World trends. By the late 18th century, knots and their associated mazes and leafy ornaments were utterly passé in Europe, although George Washington might have thought his American garden quite *au courant* in 1799, when a visiting English architect

The use of geometric, symmetrical models, the application of ''the rules of architecture to the embellishment of gardens,'' was deplored by André Parmentier everywhere but in public parks. At the Macoun Memorial Garden in Ottawa, a geometric, architectural foreground is softened by a background of mixed trees and shrubs.

reported, "I saw here a parterre stripped and trimmed with infinite care into the form of a richly flourishing fleur-de-lis, the expiring groan, I hope, of our grandfathers' pedantry." (The word *parterre*, meaning "on the ground," first came into use in the 16th century. It denotes a section of garden, often divided from other elements by a hedge, fence or wall and usually featuring interesting design elements close to the ground.) Far from expiring, however, Washington's fleurs-de-lis have been replanted to re-create the president's

beloved garden at Mount Vernon for today's tourists. Simple knot gardens for the display of herbs have also experienced a small, recent revival. The Parisian André Parmentier, who lived in the United States for only six years, until his death in 1830, had a great influence on a population still struggling to bring its new land into submission. An essay published in his own nursery catalogue was republished in Thomas Fessenden's widely available *The New American Gardener* of 1843. Parmentier was clearly an advocate of the new

naturalistic style: "For where can we find an individual sensible to the beauties and charms of nature, who would prefer a *symmetric* garden to one in modern taste; who would not prefer to walk in a plantation irregular and picturesque, rather than in those straight and monotonous alleys, bordered with mournful box, the resort of noxious insects?"

Some of Parmentier's observations indicated the excesses of the time: "As to tombs and cemeteries, I should wish to banish them entirely from gardens . . . Whilst on this subject, I will mention an anecdote of the celebrated Kent, architect of the English gardens, which will show to what extent this mania may be carried. He built a tomb in a park, and, to make the place still more gloomy, planted around it dead and mutilated trees; but, notwithstanding the celebrity he had acquired, he was loaded with ridicule, and forced to displace the trees."

GERTRUDE JEKYLL

While, in this time of green revolution, the designs of Capability Brown were being revived, a new spirit of vitality pervaded English landscaping in the ideas of Gertrude Jekyll, who, in bringing the instincts of the artist to the craft of landscaping, had a lasting influence on gardens great and small. Born in 1843, she wrote at least 14 books on gardening and landscaping. She confessed in 1899 that she would "lay no claim to . . . botanical knowledge, or even to knowing the best practical method of cultivation; but I have lived among outdoor flowers for many years, and have not spared myself in the way of actual labour, and have come to be on closely intimate and friendly terms with a great many growing things, and have acquired certain instincts which, though not clearly defined, are of the nature of useful knowledge."

What Jekyll did unintentionally was demonstrate that gardening, and even garden design, could be done well by ordinary people. One did not require university training or years of apprenticeship in order to become "closely intimate" with plants. What one did need to create a harmonious landscape was a fresh consideration of the shapes and colours of plants, both in sun and shade, their appearance alone and with one another. This was not, of course, the first time that plant colour had been considered. In the 17th century, Sir Henry Wotton had written of the English garden of Sir Henry Fanshaw that the owner "did so precisely examine the *tinctures* and *seasons* of his flowers that in their *settings*, the *inwardest* of which that were

14

to come up at the same time, should be always a little *darker* than the *outmost,* and so serve them for a kind of gentle shadow."

But Jekyll was different. She planted, for instance, an entirely bronze, red and purple border at Hidcote Manor, one of her most famous English gardens, where purple-leaved maples and plums, purple sandcherries, red day lilies and dahlias, roses and potentillas produced a subtle yet spectacular display. Jekyll also planted an entirely white-blooming garden, another all pink. There were also beds of mixed colours, some formal, some more natural. "It is not enough to cultivate plants well," she wrote in her book *Wood and Garden,* "they must also be used well. The servant may set up the canvas and grind the colours, and even set the palette, but the master alone can paint the picture. It is just the careful and thoughtful exercise of the higher qualities that makes a garden interesting, and their absence that leaves it blank, and dull, and lifeless."

Jekyll's influence, combined with the work of many other gardeners and landscape designers from various backgrounds, has produced a 20th-century style that allows for anything at all, provided it is in its proper place. *Garden Design* (Prentice-Hall, Scarborough, 1984), a recently published book that features the work of several outstanding North American designers, includes photographs of gardens ranging from the starkly modernistic to the traditionally Oriental, in styles that vary from classical to natural. In this century, the rock garden has increased in popularity, as has the domestication of more alpine plants. New fertilizers and herbicides have turned the lawn into an object of worship. Swimming pools, children's swing sets, picnic tables and barbecues may be the fountains,

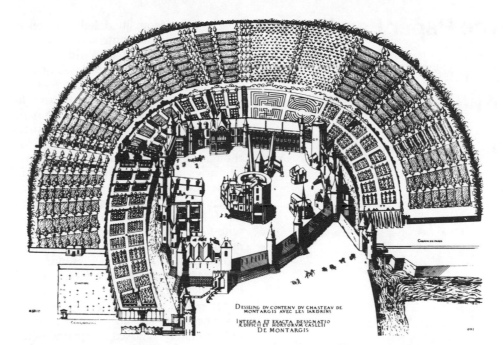

DESSEING DV CONTENV DV CHASTEAV DE MONTARGIS AVEC LES IARDRINS
INTEGRA ET EXACTA DESIGNATIO
AEDIFICII ET HORTORVM CASELLI
DE MONTARGIS

bowling greens, turf seats and statues of the 20th-century landscape.

Today's amateur landscape designer may be limited by time, climate, space and finances, but is at liberty to choose what he or she likes from any of the gardening styles of the past, or even to invent a new style. We can buy plants whose ancestors grew continents away, or cultivars that have been bred for more interesting colour or shape, greater hardiness or disease resistance. Native plants may be used. As long as the garden is pleasant and functional, its plants suited to the designer's needs, limitations and desires, then it can be said to be properly landscaped. As Gertrude Jekyll once wrote, ". . . the best purpose of a garden is to give delight and to give refreshment of mind, to soothe, to refine, and to lift up the heart in a spirit of praise and thankfulness."

A paradise is not impossible, even for the Northern gardener, in spite of the unwieldy stuff with which he or she works: a lack of expertise; a climate that too often brings frost instead of warmth, or rain instead of sun, or sun instead of rain; too little land for what one wishes to grow, or too much land for the time one can spend with it; dogs and cats and children, all bent on making a playpen of paradise; the skepticism of neighbours; the gardener's lack of patience; his or her lack of money. It is possible, nevertheless, to create "a place of rest and joy." Beauty can be gleaned from the beasts of cleared forest, shaded backyard, desert or quagmire. Beauty has, indeed, a practicality of its own. A place to relax, play games and meditate, to have picnics and pick flowers and fruit, to enjoy sun, shade and rain can be as nurturing as a garden planted only to feed the body.

Jennifer Bennett is an Associate Editor of Harrowsmith *Magazine and the author of the* Harrowsmith Northern Gardener *(Camden House, 1982)*

2 | The Paper Landscape

A great garden begins with a great plan

By Laura Berman

"The most exquisite delights of sense are pursued in the contrivance and planning of gardens," Sir William Temple wrote in his *Miscellanea* of 1692. He maintained that landscapes "with fruit, flowers, shades, fountains and the music of birds that frequents such happy places, seem to furnish all the pleasures of the several senses . . . . " Those thoughts are just as true almost three centuries later, when the planning of a garden can still produce as much pleasure as the well-planned garden itself. All the gardens I most enjoy, whether designed by myself or by others, appeal to "the several senses," providing a balanced, harmonious mixture of visual, aural, olfactory and even gustatory delights.

But such a garden, unless its creation was absolutely serendipitous — and unfortunately, landscapes treated with that approach tend to look disjointed and unbalanced — depends upon careful planning. The novice landscape designer must take into consideration not only aesthetic principles and the characteristics of individual plants and garden structures, but also the microclimate of the yard — its own peculiar environmental conditions. The designer then draws rough maps of the property, followed by increasingly sophisticated renderings of the area and its proposed landscaping. The ultimate aim, a visually interesting and exciting yard that is well planned to accommodate a variety of activities, will be a pleasure to use and to care for if sufficient planning time has been taken at the outset.

To begin, the gardener must very carefully assess the needs and requirements of all who will use the yard, now and in the future. The more specific these assessments are, the better. The decision that the children will want to use the yard for play and that the landscaper will entertain occasionally and grow a vegetable garden is not enough. What kind of play activities will be involved? Sandbox? Badminton? Swimming? Will there be outdoor cooking? How much food should be produced from a vegetable garden, berry bushes or fruit trees? Are there particular views that should be emphasized? Others best hidden?

Initially, the landscape construction will be fairly time consuming, but if it is well designed and constructed, yearly maintenance thereafter may involve only a little pruning, weeding and planting. The more the gardener thinks about it now, the easier it will be to design a landscape that will suit his or her needs, both now and in the future.

The first step in the analysis is the creation of what is known as a base plan, an accurate map, drawn to scale, of the property, including the house and other features such as a garage, driveway, storage shed, fences, walls, trees and such. If a surveyor's or architect's drawing already exists, so much the better, but if not, do not lose hope. Most properties can easily be drawn to a scale of either 1/4 inch to 1 foot or 1/8 inch to 1 foot, on the appropriate 1/4 inch- or 1/8-inch-grid graph paper. Use a tape measure at least 50 feet long, and ask someone to assist with the measuring. The first drawing, done outdoors, will be rough, but a neater copy can be made indoors later.

First take the outside dimensions of the property, and then locate the house within the property lines, taking note of its exterior features — windows, doors, downspouts, meters, hose connections, air conditioners and anything else that might affect the landscape design — and measuring their distance from the house corners. Then locate and measure other

which professionals should be consulted. For instance, retaining walls, regardless of height or construction materials, require some drainage. A strip of gravel directly behind the wall, with small spaces or weepholes at 6-foot intervals along the wall base, will usually be enough to prevent water from collecting behind the wall and weakening it. Improperly built walls are not only expensive to replace, but safety hazards as well.

MICROCLIMATE

The base plan should also include all available information on the microclimate, which includes notations of the sun's path across the yard, areas of long-lasting shadow, the prevailing wind direction, the location of frost pockets (low-lying areas where cold air collects), approximate maximum and minimum temperatures, soil quality and quantity and areas with drainage problems. The microclimate of each yard is unique, influenced not only by the location of the property, but also by the shape and height of the house, the topography of the land, trees in the yard and close to it, and many other factors. Microclimate notations are best made on an overlay of tracing paper, in order to keep the base plan uncluttered, as it will be used extensively during the design phase of the landscape.

To assess the average minimum and (less important) maximum temperatures of the property, it is not necessary to purchase a minimum-maximum thermometer. General climatic information can be obtained from a local weather office or from zone maps. The latter, however, provide only a rough estimate of the local conditions. It is quite possible to live in zone 5 and be able to grow plants rated for zone 6 in a sheltered corner, although the reverse is

features, relating them to something whose location is known, probably the house. For any large trees, give the dimensions of the canopy or branch spread as well as the diameter of the trunk about 6 to 10 inches off the ground. With the help of utilities, the township or the municipality, determine the location and identity of sewers, phone cables, overhead wires and such. Monetary and convenience costs can be high if they are damaged.

Note changes of ground level as well. This can be done with a series of planks, or more easily, with a string level, a carpenter's level strung through with a cord, which is then stretched from the top of the slope to the bottom. Raise the instrument until it is level, measure the distance from the cord to the ground at the base of the incline and divide this amount by the horizontal length from

top to bottom to give the percentage of slope. For instance, a 2 percent slope falls 2 feet for every 100 feet, or 1 foot for every 50 feet of distance. This is a normal slope for a lawn, barely perceptible to the eye as anything but flat, but sufficient, if all other factors are normal, to provide adequate drainage. In fact, a slope of 1.5 to 10 percent is acceptable for areas of grass or ground cover and 3 to 5 percent is the preferred slope for planting beds. Lawn grades of up to 25 percent are acceptable but will not be easy to maintain. Shrubs will have difficulty establishing themselves on a slope greater than 10 percent.

Gardeners faced with grading problems should consult a landscape architect or an engineer. Terracing can render a precipitous incline usable, but the building of terraces and retaining walls is, in most cases, a matter about

Agriculture Canada

more likely, that low-lying cold areas will turn a supposed zone 5 yard into zone 4. Nevertheless, knowing the climatic zone and the average minimum temperature of the yard makes the choice of sufficiently hardy shrubs and trees much easier. Many nursery catalogues include zone notations for woody species.

Of all the microclimate features, the soil is the easiest to control. A soil high in organic content and nutrients is so essential to the growth of healthy plants that any time spent improving soil quality will contribute more to the eventual success of the plants than anything else. Soil has two main components: particles of inert rock, and particles of decayed organic matter, or humus. The size, shape and amount of the rock particles influence the soil's ability to retain water, while the organic matter contains the nutrients required by the plants for growth. The mixture of rock particles and organic matter that is topsoil may be virtually nonexistent or as deep as 2 feet on a particular site. The more the better. New homes in subdivisions often have very little good topsoil. Although the land may once have been agricultural, in the process of development the topsoil was likely either stripped off and sold or compacted so severely by large machinery that it is no longer loose and airy. In such situations, new topsoil may have to be purchased, an expensive venture that could cost about $6 a cubic yard, delivered.

Beneath the topsoil is the subsoil, which contains very little organic matter. It is essentially bedrock on its way to becoming topsoil, and so is much harder than the topsoil. Especially hard subsoil, hardpan, which may have been caused by the passage of heavy machinery, by the weight of overlying buildings or even by being walked on for a long time, may be so solid that water cannot percolate through it and delicate roots cannot penetrate it. Hardpan underlying an area to be planted must be broken up, although it can be useful underneath a proposed structure that requires compacted subsoil – a paved sitting area, a driveway, storage shed or path.

Humus, the organic component of the soil, contains all the nutrients that plants need. It aerates the soil and, because it retains moisture like a sponge, makes it more drought-resistant. The most valuable asset of any garden, it is worth whatever time and effort is necessary to ensure that it is present in plentiful supply. Humus is really more a process than a product, a substance that is in a continual state of decay and augmentation by new organic material. Plant and animal wastes break down into humus which is taken up in a soluble form by other plants and animals and then returns to be broken down yet again. In nature, plants limit their population to what can be supported by the existing humus – a population that is very large in a rainforest jungle, where heat and moisture speed the process of decay and growth. In a colder Northern garden, the conversion process is much slower, so fewer plants can be supported on the same area. Gardeners who want lush plant growth in the North must supply the soil with an abundance of already decayed humus.

The easiest, cheapest and most effective way of improving the topsoil with humus is to produce compost, which can either be dug into the soil or raked lightly onto already existing planting beds. The compost should be

Plant populations in nature are limited by soil quantity and quality, but in the cultivated landscape, a gardener can coax a dense population of normally noncoexistent species to flourish by tending the soil as carefully as the plants.

19

The standard reference for this book, the Canadian climatic zone map has been divided into areas of roughly similar growing conditions. Lower numbers indicate progressively cooler areas that will support only increasingly hardy plant species. Landscape gardeners who choose plants described as hardy enough for their own or a cooler zone will suffer the fewest losses from frost damage and winterkill.

Western Canada

Eastern Canada

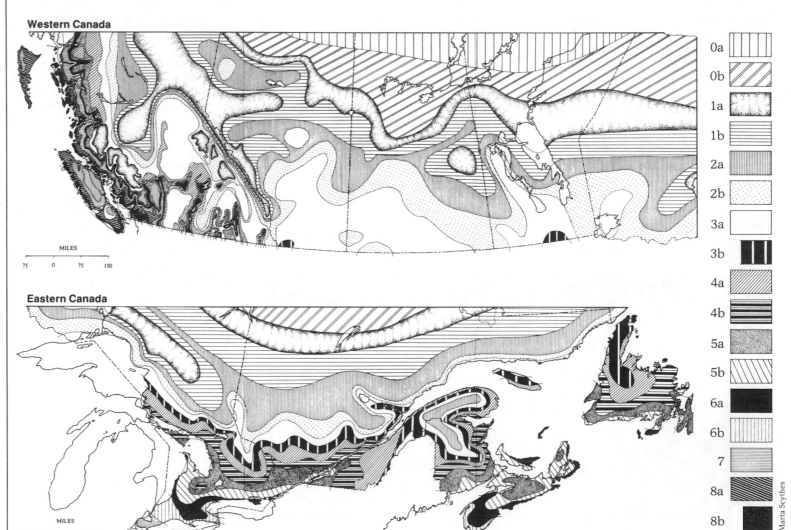

MILES
75 0 75 150

0a
0b
1a
1b
2a
2b
3a
3b
4a
4b
5a
5b
6a
6b
7
8a
8b

Marta Scythes

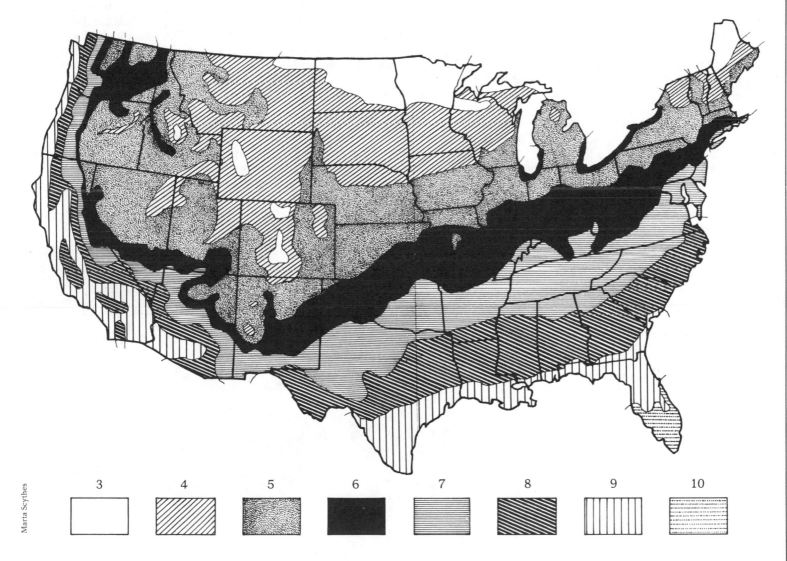

Although similar to the Canadian map (facing), the United States Department of Agriculture climatic zone map, which also indicates warmer areas with higher numbers, defines zones only by their average minimum winter temperatures. Although this and the Canadian system are the references used by most plant books and nurseries, other regional maps with different zoning systems do exist.

3 4 5 6 7 8 9 10

Marta Scythes

made in a structure of some sort, perhaps just four posts supporting chicken wire, or a three-sided brick enclosure. Where wildlife is a problem, give it a ventilated cover. A properly made and frequently turned compost pile should not smell at all. In the city, construct a neat compost pile with a lid to help allay the fears of the neighbours.

The compost itself is made of three components: plant wastes, both coarse and fine (but be careful of weeds that may tyrannize the pile), kitchen wastes such as eggshells and coffee grounds, and topsoil. A fourth possible additive is manure or blood meal, both of which have a high nitrogen content that will speed composting and add nutrients to the finished fertilizer. Layer the ingredients as they become available, keeping the pile moist. Allow it to sit for two or three weeks, then fork the pile over. Repeat turning it about once a month until it is crumbly and well mixed, which takes about three months in warm weather or as long as a year in less temperate circumstances. Shredding all the ingredients will greatly speed composting. Do not make the mistake of thinking that you will not need a compost pile. Even gardeners lucky enough to inherit a soil rich in humus will need to replace the amount that is used up by the plants every year, or the soil will be steadily depleted.

Another way of adding humus to the soil is the application of a yearly layer of organic mulch, a blanket of matter such as fallen leaves, shredded or chunked bark, cocoa shells, grass clippings, peat moss or composted sawdust, usually only one type at a time, that is laid over the soil about 2 inches deep. Mulch helps discourage weeds, conserve water and insulate the soil from extremes of temperature. And, at the rate of an inch or two a year, mulch is gradually

converted into topsoil by the action of beneficial microbes in the soil surface. Rotate your mulch materials in the permanent landscape in the same way that vegetable crops are rotated in the garden so that various soil nutrients are involved. A combination of mulches, such as compost over chopped hay, may prove to be the best way to protect and improve the soil.

All the time and energy spent preparing compost and adding decomposed plant material to the soil may seem wasted when it would be so much easier to water in some chemical fertilizers. This would certainly be the case if the only consideration was the time spent on preparation and application, but the disadvantages of chemicals do outweigh their advantages.

Chemicals can destroy the bacteria that create humus, so the gardener is harming future soil quality with every application. With chemicals, plants receive jolts of nutrients rather than slow, steady supplies that can be taken up when needed. Chemical salts build up in the diminishing topsoil, creating a toxic environment for plant tissues and contributing to the pollution of the ground water. And chemical fertilizers are expensive, although they contribute none of the essential organic matter to the soil and make it gradually less able to recover from drought or flood and more susceptible to compacting. Even the occasional use of chemical fertilizers can damage the humus, a delicate balance of competing organisms.

In fact, compost or mulch will

Jennifer Bennett

improve any type of soil, while chemical fertilizers help only those low in nutrients. Soil is classified by type, size and texture of the rock particles that it contains, as well as by the acidity or alkalinity of the mixture. Sandy soil consists of large, coarse sand particles that do not stick together easily. If you squeeze a handful of damp, sandy soil in your hand, it will crumble as soon as you open your fingers. Sandy soil is light, allows roots to penetrate easily, drains quickly and warms up early in the spring. On the other hand, it does not retain nutrients well and can dry so quickly that frequent watering is necessary. Clay soil consists of very fine, sticky, tightly packed particles. If you squeeze a handful of damp, clay soil, it will hold together and display the imprint of your fingers when you open your hand. It is slow to drain, hard to penetrate, clumpy when dug, slow to warm and will harden and crack in dry weather. A balance of the two types is ideal: it will lightly hold its shape and will be crumbly, not sticky. When combined with organic matter, it is called loam.

ALTERING ACIDITY

The acidity or alkalinity of soil is known as its pH. A neutral reading is 7.0, and anything below that number denotes an acidic soil, anything above 7, an alkaline soil. Plant growth generally takes place between about 4.5 and 7.5, although some species will exist happily in the outer extremes. The optimum pH range for the majority of plant life is 5.7 to 6.7. The soil's pH can be checked with a home test kit available from most garden seed and nursery companies, but a full soil test is available more inexpensively from provincial departments of agriculture or state extension offices. These soil analyses

Agriculture Canada

also determine the nutrient content of the soil, and they will be returned to the gardener with a report indicating which fertilizers should be added. If the information is requested, usually for an additional fee, the tests can also indicate the presence of toxic elements such as cadmium or lead, which are especially prevalent in soil near a highway or by a wall finished with lead-base paint.

Alkaline soils can be made more acidic by the incorporation of peat moss or other acidic amendments, while an acid soil is usually corrected with limestone. Both types can be neutralized to some extent with compost. But to change the pH more than one point requires large amounts of often costly additives, and is traumatic for the soil unless the adjustment is made over several years. It is better, and cheaper, to work with what you have, growing rhododendrons or blueberries in acidic soil, prairie wildflowers in alkaline. Keep in mind that most popular plants will thrive in all the average garden soils, whatever their pH. If you do want to grow a specimen with a peculiar soil preference, plant it in a pot filled with custom-mixed soil.

Good drainage is another aspect of the soil that is vital to the success of the landscape design, both for the soft (plant) elements and the hard elements such as walks or patios, which will be far less useful if they are decorated with deep puddles after every rain. An open, light soil with plenty of humus is the best drainage protection for the plants, but a patio or walk needs a firm, compacted base upon which to sit if it is not to be subjected to frost heaving, chipping and breaking. The choice of base material, called granular, depends upon the surface material and its intended use. For instance, a brick path could do with just 2 inches of coarse sand, while a concrete walk will need 3

A wet spot is drained by a series of parallel, perforated pipes laid over coarse gravel, that drain into a dry well, pool or stream. The pipes will be buried under more gravel which will in turn be covered with topsoil and then planted.

or 4 inches of ¾-inch granular (such as gravel) in addition to the 2 inches of sand. All hard surfaces should be laid on a slight slope, generally 2 to 3 percent, that falls evenly away from the house.

Be careful that excess water does not drain onto a neighbouring property or municipal land, or cause naturally low-lying areas of the property to receive even more runoff. Should the latter occur, the gardener may choose to "go with the flow" and create a pool or bog garden on the wet spot, or one could add enough granular fill to the low spot to bring it up to level, then cover it with topsoil. Another possibility is a dry well. This can be expensive and laborious to create, but is effective if the water table is 2 to 4 feet below the surface. With this method, trenches are dug in a herringbone pattern across the area to be drained, pointing down toward the dry well. A layer of coarse gravel is laid in the bottom of the trench and either porous clay or perforated plastic pipe is laid on top of the granular. More granular is added around the pipe, and the trench is filled in with topsoil level with the surrounding ground. The pipe then drains the water to the dry well, a

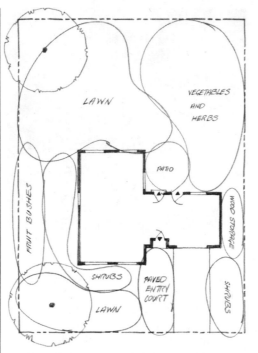

hole about 4 feet square and 4 to 6 feet deep that has layers of large stones and broken brick on the bottom, and progressively smaller granular material toward the top. The dry well is also covered with a few inches of topsoil.

The amount of sunlight a yard receives will vary with the season; what might be a sunny yard in winter could be quite shady in the summer when the deciduous trees are in leaf. On the other hand, the height of the house may restrict the amount of light that falls on the yard when the sun is lower in the sky in winter. Observe where and for how long the sun is in the yard, in all four seasons, and what path it takes across the yard. Note, too, whether the shade is dense or dappled. A high tree canopy that creates dappled shade can still provide enough light for many plants, but a low, close branch cover could seriously restrict one's choice of plant material. Could the careful removal of a few low-growing branches change dense shade to dappled? Gardeners in doubt about pruning large trees may choose to consult an arborist, listed in the Yellow Pages.

Wind exposure, another aspect of the microclimate, can also depend a great deal on the presence of trees, buildings and fences. Wind flowing over a more or less solid obstacle will create turbulence at the base of the object and an area of calm on its leeward side. A sitting area located in the path of local turbulence may be extremely uncomfortable, quite possibly unusable. If the wind can be diverted or lessened in intensity with properly placed plants or landscape features (see Chapter 3), the area can be made suitable for any number of uses.

As with all other features of the microclimate, temperature will be unique to the property. In the North, frost is the most important aspect of landscape temperature. A yard that is at the bottom of a hill will experience colder, frostier weather sooner in fall and later in spring than will one on a slope or the top of a hill. Plants selected for the frost pocket must be hardier than those in more protected or frost-free locations.

THE DESIGN PHASE

As soon as all the available information on the physical aspects of the land has been assembled and written on a base-map overlay, and as soon as the property owner has examined the desired uses for the outdoor space, it is time to develop a layout of the spatial elements within the yard. For this, an abundant supply of tracing paper, available in rolls from art supply stores, will help the gardener work out a number of different layouts without cluttering the base plan. These first "concept drawings" are most easily done in the form of bubbles, irregular circular shapes, each of which represents the relative size of an activity area — lawn, vegetable garden, patio, pool, service area and such. Make several concept drawings to get a really good idea of your own piece of property, your desires and possible designs. The bubbles will help you think about overall spatial designs without becoming bogged down in details. Think about the relationships between the spaces and how people will move about the yard. If one space receives all the traffic from every area, its intended use may be greatly reduced.

Once the best concept drawing has been chosen, impose some order upon the paper landscape. Place another piece of tracing paper over the original base plan, and make a grid by extending horizontal and vertical lines from

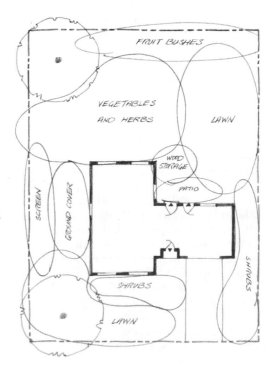

existing features such as the doors, windows and corners of the house, and from fence posts, the corners of a shed or garage and so on. This grid is somewhat like the latitude and longitude of geography, enabling the designer to place plants and objects in the landscape in known relationships to other landforms.

The next step is to decide whether you want a formal or informal, geometric or abstract, curved or angular landscape pattern. Whatever you decide, the same basic principles of spatial organization will apply. A design that is based upon one simple underlying pattern such as a circle or square, repeated and permuted, both boldly and subtly, becomes a cohesive, integrated whole. Too many different patterns break the space up into small, unrelated units, a jumble of areas with no central theme. Stick with something you like and that is compatible with the space and the structures within it. These patterns can produce feelings of motion or stasis. A flowing, dynamic pattern will make a small garden seem larger by allowing the eye to move easily around the space, while a static one can impart a sense of tranquillity. In either type of patterning, the eye should have something upon which to focus. A focal point can be a specimen plant, an arbour, a pond, a gazebo, or anything else you prefer. Without a focal point, the eye bounces about the space instead of being directed toward an object.

The final layout step is the combination of the two tracing paper overlays − the bubble diagram and the latitude and longitude grid − using the chosen pattern theme and integrating it with the elements you have selected. Begin to refine the drawings into one ''hard-line'' plan, accurately measured and drawn to scale. Use standard

The positions of the soft elements such as plants are chosen only after the overall shape and pattern theme of the landscape has been determined; a design based upon straight lines lends the property an air of tranquillity and formality, whereas curved lines suggest movement and seem to enlarge a small space.

Stephen Errington

drafting tools, such as a set square, circle templates, compass and such, to ensure that your work is as precise as possible. An accurate drawing will help enormously when it comes time to estimate costs.

Once you have formulated the two-dimensional landscape structure, the third dimension, the shapes and proportions of the elements within it, can be estimated. A useful way to visualize the shaping of the third dimension is to draw perspective sketches of various areas of the existing yard from a few different points of view. If you do not have experience in this type of drawing, an easy way to produce quite good substitutes is to take several photographs from various viewpoints in the yard. Have the prints enlarged to a size that will be easy to work with, say 5 by 7 inches or 8 by 10. Place tracing paper over the photos and sketch in the shapes and sizes that work well in relation to one another and to the negative space — the space between the forms. Try to think in terms of masses rather than individual plants.

STRATA STRATEGIES

Again, rhythm, through repetition and contrast, will be central to the unity and vitality of the design, whose main three-dimensional aspect is the planting. In nature, plants sort themselves out, according to their relative needs for light, into three general strata or levels — the upper or canopy storey, the middle storey and the understorey. These are usually thought of as the tree, shrub and ground-cover strata, but tall shrubs, low shrubs and ground covers have the same three-tiered relationship. A planting design that reflects the natural arrangement of tall through middle-sized to small will work to unify a design and will appear more pleasing

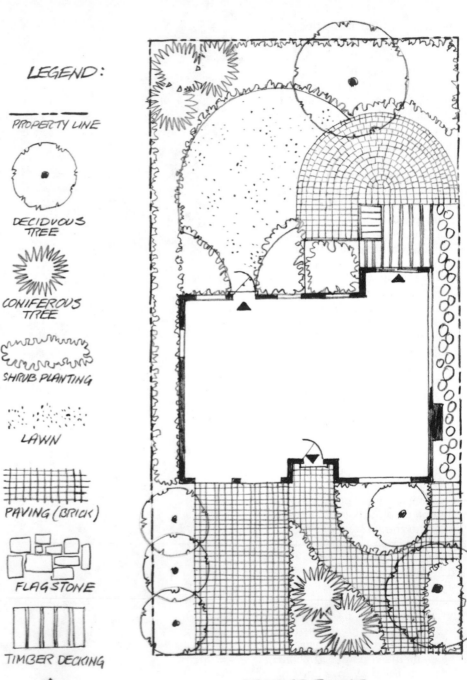

LEGEND:

PROPERTY LINE

DECIDUOUS TREE

CONIFEROUS TREE

SHRUB PLANTING

LAWN

PAVING (BRICK)

FLAGSTONE

TIMBER DECKING

DOOR

CIRCULAR THEME

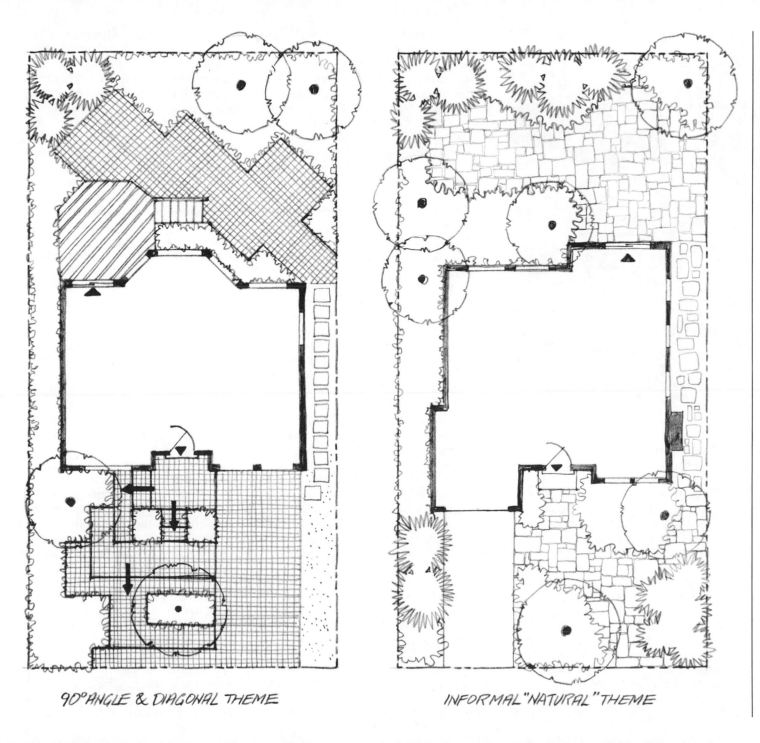

Three different types of finished designs, one based upon circles, one upon straight lines and one upon natural lines, create quite different moods and effects. Such themes can be echoed in garden structures, paving materials and even in plants, which can be global, formally clipped or irregular in shape. Elements of contrasting themes add interest to each design.

90° ANGLE & DIAGONAL THEME

INFORMAL "NATURAL" THEME

and more interesting than one that ignores this principle of proportion and scale. This is relevant not only to the sizes of plants within planting beds, but also to the relationship of beds to one another and to the hard elements of the design such as buildings and fences. Changes of scale between different elements should be smooth and flowing, not abrupt and awkward. Transitional links are useful for relating the varying sizes to one another, in the way that shrubs bridge the size difference between trees and flowers or ground covers. A 4-foot-high wall, for instance, will seem much more massive than it is if it is not related to the other elements of the scheme by an element of intermediate height between it and the ground-cover plants. A few groupings of low and intermediate shrubs at the base, a bench, or some other type of go-between, will reduce the tension between the two disparate heights. It is not necessary, however, to obscure all of the wall base to achieve this balance of proportions. Alternately concealing and revealing the wall will result in a flowing, proportional relationship, one with far more interest than if there were a continuous strip of plants of the same height. Perfect symmetry is fine in trial grounds and flower seed farms, but it does little to excite the imagination in a home landscape.

The creation of three-dimensional interest is achieved not only by consideration of the relationships between heights of various elements, but also by careful thought about the relationships of their shapes. Shrubs can be quite round or decidedly vase shaped, they can spread horizontally or vertically, tree branches can arch or zig-zag. Repetition will again help to unify the design, but the exclusive use of one shape will produce a very boring picture. The echoing of shapes between hard and soft elements, combined with accents of contrasting shape, will be much more visually exciting. If, for example, you have decided on the circle as the design element of your two-dimensional pattern, and have created round areas of paving, the theme can be echoed by the use of globe-shaped shrubs of varying heights. The addition of a few well-placed, contrasting shapes will accent the circular ones and intensify their relationship to the entire design. The placement of the accents establishes the rhythm and flow from element to element.

One interesting aspect of the three-dimensional landscape is texture, which has a visual as well as a tactile effect. Large, bold leaves, such as those of a hosta, have a very different quality and function than the lacy, finely textured leaves of a bleeding heart. The larger-leaved plant will appear closer than the one with the smaller leaves, an effect that can be useful if a space should appear larger or smaller than it actually is. Some leaves are shiny and thick and reflect quite a lot of light, while others are very thin, almost transparent looking, reflecting little light, and still others are thick but not at all shiny, or are covered with fine hairs that give the leaf a dull grey cast. The more light the leaf reflects, the closer it will appear to be. And the duller it is, the farther away it will seem, just as mountains in the distance appear to be a hazy, indistinct purple-grey.

THE GARDEN PALETTE

It is also important that the colour scheme have a central theme. The use of too many competing colours in a small area is disorienting and will detract from the unifying elements that have already been established. The predominant landscape colour will, of course, be green; there is not just one kind of green, however, but as many different greens as there are plants. How these sometimes complementary and sometimes competing hues are handled will affect all the other colours — the flower colours and hard element colours — of the landscape. The greens should contribute variety and contrast, but subtly, to function more as background than feature. They should enhance the relationships between the flower colours while at the same time providing some interest of their own. No plant is in flower for the entire growing season, most bloom for only a few weeks at a time, so the green framework has to be able to perform on its own during any season, including winter,

Stephen Errington

Alternately concealing and revealing a wall will result in a flowing, proportional view that is far more interesting than it would be were there a continuous strip of plants of the same height. Also, a wall seems less massive if it is related to the ground covers by elements of intermediate height.

when the evergreens become dominant.

In planning the remainder of the colour scheme, consider not only the flower colours but also their blooming times. There may be an entirely different colour scheme in spring than there is in late summer. Colours can be divided into two groups: the cool colours, blue, green and purple; and the warm colours, red, orange and yellow. Warm colours stand out and catch the eye first, while cool ones tend to recede. When white is added to a colour, the result is a pastel tint which is much softer than the pure colour, while a shade results from the addition of grey or black to the hue. It gives the colour solidity and substance, and at the same time eases the shade into the background in relation to its purer hue.

On a colour wheel, colours immediately adjacent to one another such as yellow and orange are harmonious and blend well together, while those opposite each other, the complementary colours, contrast. This is not to say that contrasts such as orange and blue, red and green or yellow and purple do not belong together, indeed they can promote interest through the tension they create.

Usually it is wise to restrict one's choice of colours to a narrow range. The predominant theme is carried by one colour and its adjacents and their tints and shades and is accented by the complement of the predominant colour. If, for example, yellow is the dominant hue, yellow-green and orange-yellow are the adjacents, and a bluish purple works

as an accent. White is a unifying and transitional colour, a valuable tool in any colour scheme. Consider carefully which colours you will feature and what mood you wish to create. A quiet, private area is more suited to cool colours, the tints and shades of warm colours rather than their hues, and white. Bright, warm hues are more in character with a busy, active area. Sunny areas show bright colours to best advantage, while white flowers and foliage glow forth from shady spots or in the half light of evening. Another consideration in the choice of a theme may be the colour scheme used in the house's interior. If there is a common range of colours, the connection between inside and out will be reinforced, making one seem the logical extension of the other. In a sense, the apparent size of the total space is increased by this device.

Just as a colour can link interior with exterior, so can the construction materials used for the hard surfaces of the landscape. These include the flooring material, the outdoor furniture and the details of other built features. A patio or deck seems much more a part of the house if the flooring material is the same as the siding of the house or the floor of the room that opens onto it. The same is true for the style of furniture. Mixing too many different styles results in a disconnected jumble, but the contrast that results, for example, from two different sizes or colours of paving material, one as the dominant and the other as the accent, can very effectively break up large expanses of a single material. Pathways that link different areas will reinforce the connection if the paving patterning is consistent throughout. The same applies to other structural elements of the design. If the house is wood and the deck is wood as well, use wood for edging the planting beds and for the retaining walls and fences. Patterning and the occasional contrast of another sympathetic material (such as brick with wood) will relieve the sameness of the wood. Again, the different parts of the spatial organization of the landscape will reinforce each other through consistency of detail.

Considered as a whole design composed of well-chosen, complementary parts, any landscape can become beautiful to look at and satisfying to be a part of, a place that fulfills "all the pleasures of the several senses."

Landscape designer Laura Berman was born in New York and studied fine art and landscape architecture in Toronto. She grew the Best Small Garden in the First Annual Harrowsmith Garden Contest of 1984.

PLANTING KEY:

TREES & SHRUBS –
A MOUNTAIN MAPLE
B SOFT MAPLE
C EASTERN REDBUD
D ASH
E RED PINE
F RED OAK
G CANADIAN HEMLOCK
H PINCUSHION KOREAN BOX
I ANNABELLE HYDRANGEA
J HOLLY
K HACKS RED HONEYSUCKLE
L JAPANESE PIERIS
M RHODODENDRON HYBRID
N NANNYBERRY
O UPRIGHT YEW

FERNS –
1 MARGINAL SHIELD FERN
2 OSTRICH FERN
3 CINNAMON FERN
4 CHRISTMAS FERN

PERENNIALS –
5 SNOWDROP ANEMONE
6 ROSE FALSE SPIREA (WHITE)
7 HEARTLEAF BERGENIA
8 PEACHLEAF BELLFLOWER (WHITE)
9 BLACK SNAKEROOT
10 BLEEDING HEART
11 HYBRID FOXGLOVES (CREAM-WHITE)
12 PLANTAIN LILY (WHITE)
13 SIBERIAN IRIS (WHITE)
14 VIRGINIA BLUEBELLS
15 SIBERIAN IRIS (VIOLET BLUE)
16 PRIMULA (MULTI-COLOURED)
17 FORGET-ME-NOT

GROUNDCOVERS –
18 LILY OF THE VALLEY
19 WINTERGREEN
20 BALTIC ENGLISH IVY
21 JAPANESE SPURGE
22 PERIWINKLE

ANNUALS –
23 BEGONIA (PINK)
24 BROWALLIA (BLUE)
25 COLEUS (PINK & GREEN)
26 CALADIUM HYBRIDS
27 IMPATIENS (PINK)
28 IMPATIENS (WHITE)
29 AGERATUM (LIGHT BLUE)
30 PULMONARIA
31 NICOTIANA (LIMEGREEN)
32 NICOTIANA (PINK)
33 NICOTIANA (DEEP ROSE)
34 SALVIA SPLENDENS (WHITE)

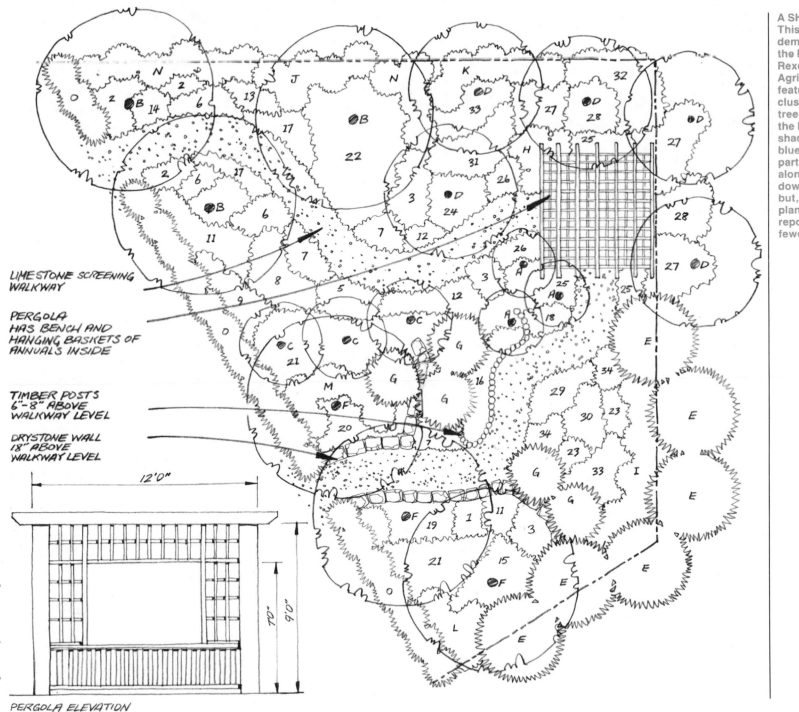

LIMESTONE SCREENING
WALKWAY

PERGOLA
HAS BENCH AND
HANGING BASKETS OF
ANNUALS INSIDE

TIMBER POSTS
6"-8" ABOVE
WALKWAY LEVEL

DRYSTONE WALL
18" ABOVE
WALKWAY LEVEL

12'0"

10"

9'0"

PERGOLA ELEVATION

A SHADY GARDEN
This design, based upon a demonstration landscape at the Humber Arborotum in Rexdale, Ontario, in Agriculture Canada zone 6, features a pergola and a cluster of shade-tolerant trees, shrubs and flowers, the latter in harmonious shades of white, pink, rose, blue and violet. This particular lot is 65 feet along the top boundary, 50 down the right-hand side, but, in a different yard, the plants could be repositioned and planted in fewer or greater numbers.

A TOWNHOUSE GARDEN
Here, an urban backyard, 24 feet wide and 67 feet long, has been made intimate with a perimeter board fence and a lattice screen that faces the house. There are seating areas under the gazebo and around the house. The design is based upon a demonstration landscape at the Humber Arboretum in Rexdale, Ontario.

PLANTING KEY :

TREES –
A SERVICEBERRY
B BRISTLECONE PINE
C DWARF CRAB — CULTIVAR 'A'
D DWARF CRAB — CULTIVAR 'B'

SHRUBS –
E BUGLEWEED
F HICKS YEW
G EUROPEAN CRANBERRY

PERENNIALS –
H WALL ROCKCRESS (8)
I IRIS "AMETHYST FLAME" (25)
J SIBERIAN IRIS (17)
K PLANTAIN LILY (18)
L OSTRICH FERN (23)

GROUND COVERS –
M PACHYSANDRA
N BUGLEWEED
O SILVEREDGE GOUTWEED

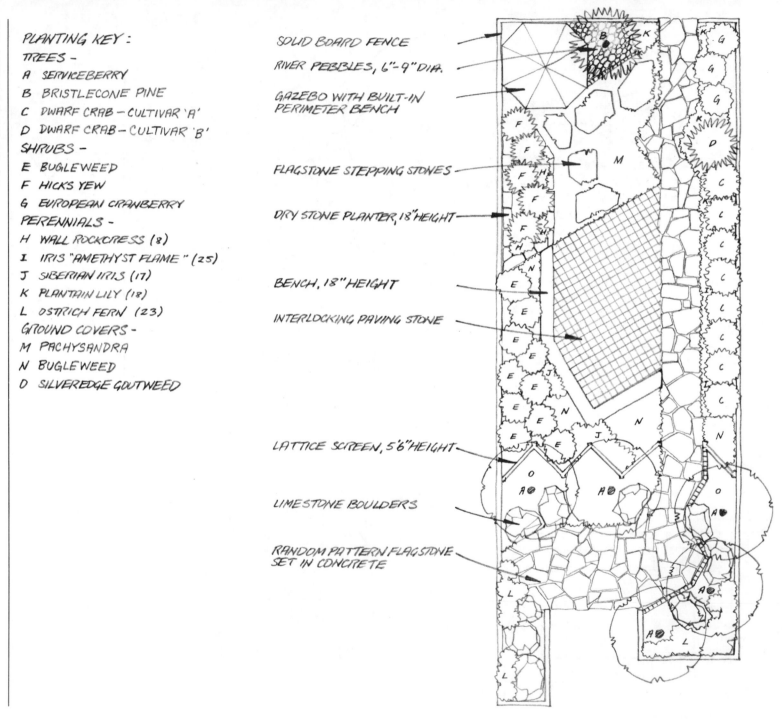

SOLID BOARD FENCE

RIVER PEBBLES, 6"-9" DIA.

GAZEBO WITH BUILT-IN PERIMETER BENCH

FLAGSTONE STEPPING STONES

DRY STONE PLANTER, 18" HEIGHT

BENCH, 18" HEIGHT

INTERLOCKING PAVING STONE

LATTICE SCREEN, 5'6" HEIGHT

LIMESTONE BOULDERS

RANDOM PATTERN FLAGSTONE SET IN CONCRETE

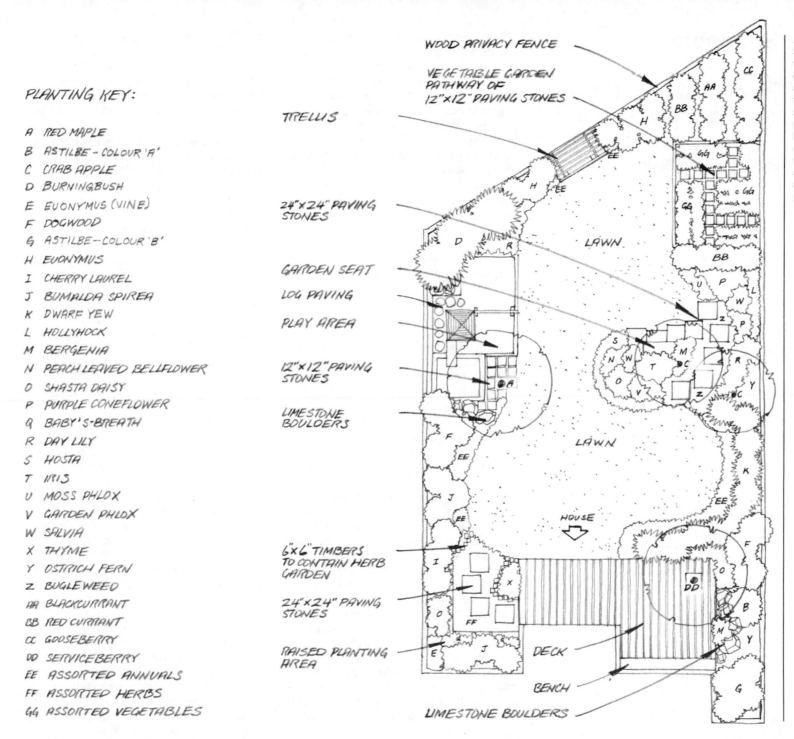

PLANTING KEY:

A RED MAPLE
B ASTILBE – COLOUR 'A'
C CRAB APPLE
D BURNINGBUSH
E EUONYMUS (VINE)
F DOGWOOD
G ASTILBE – COLOUR 'B'
H EUONYMUS
I CHERRY LAUREL
J BUMALDA SPIREA
K DWARF YEW
L HOLLYHOCK
M BERGENIA
N PEACH LEAVED BELLFLOWER
O SHASTA DAISY
P PURPLE CONEFLOWER
Q BABY'S-BREATH
R DAY LILY
S HOSTA
T IRIS
U MOSS PHLOX
V GARDEN PHLOX
W SALVIA
X THYME
Y OSTRICH FERN
Z BUGLEWEED
AA BLACKCURRANT
CB RED CURRANT
CC GOOSEBERRY
DD SERVICEBERRY
EE ASSORTED ANNUALS
FF ASSORTED HERBS
GG ASSORTED VEGETABLES

WOOD PRIVACY FENCE

VEGETABLE GARDEN
PATHWAY OF
12"×12" PAVING STONES

TRELLIS

24"×24" PAVING STONES

GARDEN SEAT

LOG PAVING

PLAY AREA

12"×12" PAVING STONES

LIMESTONE BOULDERS

6"×6" TIMBERS TO CONTAIN HERB GARDEN

24"×24" PAVING STONES

RAISED PLANTING AREA

LIMESTONE BOULDERS

BENCH

DECK

HOUSE

LAWN

A YOUNG FAMILY GARDEN Space for berry bushes, a vegetable garden, a herb garden and a children's play area are included in a 35-foot-wide suburban yard surrounded by a wooden privacy fence. This plan, based upon a demonstration landscape at the Humber Arboretum, also features a garden seat, a deck with a bench and a perennial flower border.

3

Sunspots

Planning for energy efficiency

By Charmaine Gaudet

The site: six acres of bare, wind-scoured turf that slopes steeply down to a rocky cliff overlooking the Atlantic Ocean. Completely bereft of mature trees, studded with scrawny brush and rounded boulders, it lies wide open to the unrelenting ocean winds and to heavy spring runoffs after the tumultuous Maritime snows. Not even sheep would graze on it.

The task: To turn this forbidding seascape into an integrated home-and-site plan that would fulfill the owner's dream of a 6,000-square-foot, passive-solar, near-zero-energy home surrounded by extensive gardens — including a late-Victorian formal garden — an orchard, two tennis courts, a swimming pool and a patio. In short, to create a microclimate that would provide the home with year-round comfort: privacy and shade in summer, shelter from the winds and salt sprays of winter. And to do it all in one year.

Peter Klynstra, a young Halifax landscape architect, accepted the challenge. His plan made use of a carefully calculated site layout and planting scheme that deflected the ocean winds and salt sprays and moderated the climate of the site by creating "fair-weather pockets," as he calls them. Thick plantings of spruce and pine to the north and northwest provide shelter for the house and future orchard. They also act as backdrops for the ocean view, which remains virtually unimpeded from the living room, while screening less desirable views to the north and northwest. Closer to the house, Klynstra has left openings in the belt through which prevailing winter winds keep the driveway clear of snow. A pine shelterbelt to the northeast also has a multiple purpose: it protects the house from northeast storms, creates a shelter pocket near the house for the gardens,

and it ensures privacy around the pool. A rose hedge along the south and southeast cliff edge is mainly for safety and beauty, but it, too, offers some protection from wind and creates a microshelter for more tender plantings in its lee.

"What we've done," says Klynstra, "is bump the whole site up one plant-hardiness zone." On a loftier level, what Klynstra has done is transform an arid, uninhabitable wasteland into a veritable earthly paradise.

Thirty-five hundred miles away in Saskatoon, Saskatchewan, landscape architect Doug Clark faced many of the same problems on a different site: five acres of flat, tinder-dry pastureland scoured by a merciless prairie wind. Owners Gustova and Lorraine Pocobelli wanted to preserve the wide-open feel and much of the natural vegetation of their prairie acreage, but they also wanted to introduce such urban trappings as a deck where they could entertain, a green lawn for the children to play on, some decorative shrubbery, an orchard and an extensive vegetable garden. Complicating the design was the position of the existing house, with the garage and front door facing north, the driveway approaching the west side of the house and the problem that, although the winter winds blew in from the northwest, the best view was to the north. "Our relationship with climate is basic here," says Clark. "The big problem is that there is too much wind. On the homestead, if you didn't plant trees and shelterbelts, you were a goner."

Unable to change the northern exposure of the doors, Clark took advantage of a bluff of aspens to the west and planted a three-row windbreak — Scotch pine to windward, mountain ash to leeward and willow in between — to the north of the driveway,

Stephen Errington

where it protects the house and keeps snow off the lane without interfering with the view from the house. For summer shade, he sprinkled fast-growing poplars among long-term plantings of slower-growing green ash to the south of the house. South-facing sun decks were kept low to avoid wind turbulence, and fruit trees were planted right up to the decks for maximum shading. The trees, in turn, provide wind shelter for the garden, which lies south and east of the house. A patch of lawn on the south side of the house, no bigger than any suburban backyard, and a few shrubs beside the house require watering, but the rest of the property has been left to native grasses and indigenous trees that can withstand the dry prairie conditions. The Pocobellis preserve moisture in the garden with a thick layer of straw mulch.

There is nothing new about the notion of landscaping for climate control. Before the balmy days of cheap energy, our pioneering ancestors knew the value of proper site selection, planting windbreaks to protect the house and leaving fencerows to shelter the fields — generally keeping themselves sheltered from the harsh extremes of our northern climate. These days, it seems, most homeowners are well versed in the benefits of insulation, vapour barriers, weatherstripping and multiple glazing, but are less inclined to give adequate thought to controlling the temperature outside the home. The role of insulation and air/vapour barriers is to slow down the rate of heat transfer between the inside and outside of the house, which is a function of the difference between the inside and outside temperatures. By moderating or even raising the outdoor temperature during the heating season, however, the temperature difference is reduced, and the rate of heat transfer is

slowed down. The same applies during the summer. By funnelling and concentrating cooling breezes through the site, the homeowner can reduce the home's reliance on electric fans and air conditioners. The results in energy savings inside the home can be as much as 40 percent — the result outside the home can be a more pleasant, more usable outdoor living environment throughout the year.

"We design and adapt outdoor spaces for people to use," says Cary Vollick, another Halifax landscape architect. "Site planning involves identifying and understanding the physical conditions on a site and the impact they are going to have on the way we use that site. One of the main physical conditions to consider on any site is climate, which can be responded to in one of two ways. The most obvious is to accept it as it is, to tightly seal and insulate our homes, to air-condition them in summer, heat them up in winter and, generally, to let the extremes of climate batter us around.

The solar skyspace is the area bounded by the sun's path on the summer and winter solstices and by its position at 9 a.m. and 3 p.m. Trees that infringe upon the lower part of the skyspace block valuable winter sunlight, but those planted closer to the house may provide welcome summer shade without obstructing solar gain in winter.

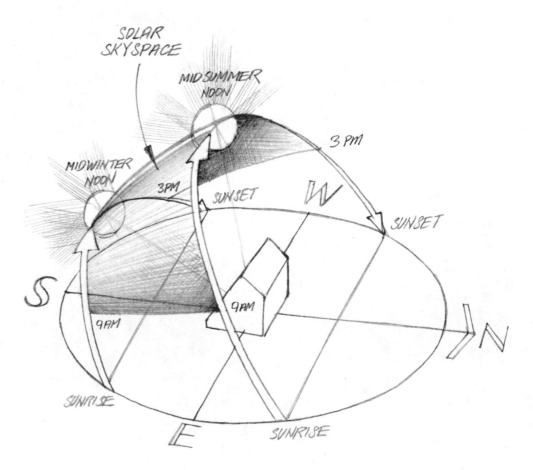

We make the assumption that the climate isn't something we can change. Actually, to varying degrees, we *can* change climate, depending on the site. An alternative way to look at climate is to attempt to moderate it, to warm up the site in order to make it easier to warm up your home."

The results of this approach can be spectacular. Consider, for example, that approximately one-third of a home's BTU demand for heating in winter is created by the wind. Even in an airtight home, windchill makes the outside walls colder and reduces the effectiveness of the insulation. Protecting a house from wind can reduce the windchill factor by 75 percent and cut the heating demand by 25 percent — the difference between a heating bill for $1,000 and one for $750 or between burning eight cords of wood and six. Similarly, every degree of summer heat requires an additional 5 to 7 percent of cooling energy, so a 10-degree (F) reduction in outside air temperature, achieved through a judicious arrangement of shade trees, can reduce energy consumption for air-conditioning by 50 to 70 percent. Clearly, for anyone planning an energy-efficient home, it makes as much sense to consider what is outside the walls as what is between them.

SITE ANALYSIS

The first step in site planning is taking a complete inventory of everything that exists on or affects the site and considering how it will affect the use of the area. Site analysis helps determine the site's feasibility for building, the possible activities it can accommodate and its potential for solar gain and energy conservation. The site-analysis process can be used in three ways: as the basis for site selection; as a guide to locating buildings, gardens, patios, walks

A grapevine shelters a south-facing porch during a Winnipeg summer, when it also provides edible fruit. In fall, it will lose its leaves, allowing the winter light to enter the porch and warm the adjoining rooms.

and drives, wood and mulch piles and other uses on the site; or as an aid in designing site improvements around an existing home. This process is identical to that described in Chapter 2, except that in this case, energy efficiency will always be one of the highest priorities.

Before beginning, obtain or draw an accurate plot plan of the property on which to record relevant information. Show as many of the existing features of the site as possible, including the exact position of true, or solar, south — because magnetic north is near Bathurst Island in the Northwest Territories, some 900 miles from the north pole, compasses point to a "south" that is as much as 25 degrees away from true south. Fortunately, solar south is easily plotted on the ground using the sun as a

guide. Contact the local weather office to determine the exact times for sunrise and sunset, then calculate the midpoint, known as "solar noon," the time when the sun is directly south. Drive a six-foot-high stake into the ground in a sunny spot, and at solar noon, set a second stake at the end of the first one's shadow. A line from the second stake to the first points to solar south.

The role of the sun in climate is the obvious starting point for a site analysis, and plotting the sun's relationship to the property is the key to sensible energy use. To do this, it is necessary to refer to two sources of information. The first, the annual meteorological summary, available for $2.25 from regional offices of the Atmospheric Environment Service, showing the average daily

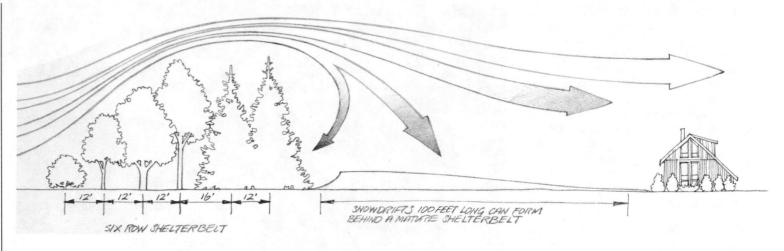

12' 12' 12' 16' 12'

SIX ROW SHELTERBELT

SNOWDRIFTS 100 FEET LONG CAN FORM BEHIND A MATURE SHELTERBELT

amount of sunshine, the number of cloudy days per month and the number of heating degree-days as well as temperature and precipitation data. The second source is a sun-path chart for the appropriate latitude, found in any of the solar-energy design books in most public libraries. From the chart, one can determine both the direction and the angle of the sun's rays at any time of any particular day of the year.

For example, on the shortest day of the year, usually December 21, the sun rises in the southeast and follows a short, low-angled path across the sky to set in the southwest. On this day, the sun rises and sets at its most southerly point, and the rays form their lowest angle with the ground for the year. Using the sun-path chart, one can plot the shadows that trees, landforms or buildings will cast on the ground at different times of the day. On December 21, these shadows will be at their longest for the year, the "worst-case" situation for shading. Plot the shadows for December 21 on a plan using the direction and angle information for a least three different times during the day: 9 a.m., noon and 3 p.m., thus bracketing the six-hour period

during which 85 percent of the day's sunlight falls. Sun-angle information can also be used to calculate sun penetration into existing or proposed building windows for various times of the day or year.

Repeat plotting the shadow paths, this time using the sun angle and direction information from the chart for the longest day of the year, on or near June 21. On this day, the sun rises in the northeast and follows a long, high-angled path across the sky to set in the northwest. This is the day in the year when the sun rises and sets at its most northerly point and when the rays form the steepest angle with the ground — the "best-case" benchmark, when shadows are at their shortest. No site will get any more sun exposure than it does on this day.

Every other day of the year, the sun is somewhere between these low and high points, and that area in which the sun shines throughout the year between 9 a.m. and 3 p.m. is the "solar skyspace." Make sure nothing protrudes into this space if you want maximum solar gain during the heating season. On the other hand, knowing the sun's angle and

position allows the deliberate introduction of obstructions to shade part of the site with trees, awnings, et cetera.

Now consider the site's topography, which can also affect the amount of sun that the site can use. A south-facing slope takes more advantage of the sun by increasing the angle of the sun's rays to the ground, creating shorter shadows (and therefore more sunlight) than on a flat site. Also remember that on a slope, the energy of the sun penetrates and warms the ground surface more efficiently, because less energy reflects off the surface. However, building on slopes is more difficult and costly than building on flat sites, so a good compromise between solar access and "buildability" is a slope of about 5 to 15 percent (5 to 15 feet of rise for every 100-foot distance).

By this point in the site analysis, the homeowner will have a pretty good idea of where the sunny and shady areas of the site are at various times of the day and year. This is an important consideration when locating gardens or sun decks, determining where overhangs, trees or fences should be placed for shading and for judging whether shadows cast by nearby buildings, trees and hills will obstruct solar access.

AIR APPARENT

A homestead's environmental comfort depends not only on solar accumulation but also on air movement, so the next step in the site-analysis process is to examine the effects of wind. Using the regional weather-data charts, plot the direction of prevailing winds and storm winds for various times of the year on the site plan. In Canada, wind is mainly a problem in winter, and a 20-mph wind on a 10-degree F day can make the air temperature feel like a bone-chilling minus 23, exaggerating the discomfort of draughty houses and making furnaces work overtime. By protecting the house from cold prevailing winds — that is, by building into a slope, by taking advantage of natural forest protection, by planting a shelterbelt or building a windbreak — homeowners can significantly cut down on windchill and thereby on fuel consumption.

The secret of wind control is understanding that when wind meets an obstruction, it flows in a graceful, arcing path around and over it and does not return to its former pattern for some distance to leeward. This effect, called "wind shadow," is relatively predictable and can be plotted on the site plan. Though wind shadows may extend for a distance equalling 20 times the height of the obstruction, they provide maximum protection only between 2 and 5 times its height to leeward. A study done by the Prairie Farm Rehabilitation Administration in the winters of 1981-1982 and 1982-1983 shows that heating costs for a house placed in the lee of such an obstruction are reduced by 5 percent for every 8 mph of average

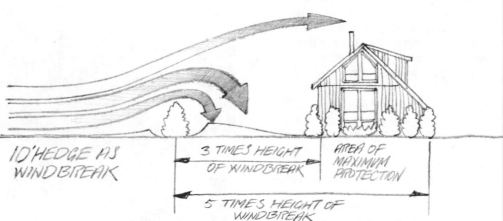

10' HEDGE AS WINDBREAK

3 TIMES HEIGHT OF WINDBREAK

AREA OF MAXIMUM PROTECTION

5 TIMES HEIGHT OF WINDBREAK

open-field wind speed. Thus a house with an $800 heating bill exposed to 24-mph average winds would have its oil bill reduced to $680 by the creation of a simple windbreak.

As wind flows over and around an obstruction, it increases speed, and by locating landscape elements in, or away from, accelerated wind paths, the imaginative homeowner can tailor sheltered or breezy areas to suit his or her purposes, whether they be sunbathing or windmill construction. By placing a driveway, say, in the accelerated wind area at the end of a windbreak, winter winds can be concentrated to blow away snow and keep the driveway clear. But care is needed in such plans — not all the effects of wind flow are desirable. For instance, because the sheltered area directly behind a windbreak has a lower air pressure than the surrounding wind flow, snow tends to accumulate there. This may be fine for an area where tender garden plants need a protective blanket, but it is far from welcome in a driveway or in front of the back door.

Air, like water, is dense when cold and settles in lower elevations, but cold air

pockets can also occur on slopes when the downflow of cold air is dammed by forests, hills or even large buildings. Unlike water, however, cold air also accumulates on level land next to a low area, and gardens planted next to a drop-off will suffer frost damage before neighbouring gardens farther from the edge. Warm air, on the other hand, is lighter and rises to higher elevations, causing noticeable variations in microclimate along hillsides. The coldest areas tend to be at the foot of the hill, on the side facing prevailing winds, and at the crest, where wind speeds can be 20 percent greater than on the flat land below. This is why, as a general rule, building sites, like orchards, are best placed at middle elevations. An opening in a forested area can also attract a cold air mass, which will skim the treetops until it finds an opening and then drop into it like a well-putted golf ball, a phenomenon that often comes as an unwelcome surprise to solar enthusiasts who have cut down trees to open up their solar skyspace.

Finally, look at the visual elements. Beauty may lie in the eye of the beholder, but it must also lie in the *view* of the beholder. Most of us, in fact, are as much inspired by sweeping vistas as by the prospect of saving a few energy dollars. Few homeowners are likely to plant a shelterbelt that obstructs the view — perhaps the very reason for choosing the site in the first place.

By this point in the site-analysis process, some of the pieces should be falling together. Areas will start to match up with outdoor uses, and relationships between various areas will begin to align themselves. But there is one important step left in this process: analyzing and defining the objectives and priorities for energy use, conservation and day-to-day enjoyment.

"Weighing all of the elements with all of your objectives is what site planning is about," says Reinhart Petersmann, a member of the Canadian Society of Landscape Architects. "In site planning, you cannot have only one purpose — for example, energy conservation. That would be like designing a wood stove to be only airtight. If you forget about airflow, the stove won't burn. Same thing with the site. In considering anything for energy conservation, you must also consider the impact it will have on other elements of the site and on all of your other objectives — in other words, on your general use and enjoyment of the site. So, the question you must always be asking is, 'What do I want to gain, and what am I willing to lose?' "

Vollick suggests compiling what he calls "a wish list: everything you want from the site — energy conservation, a more pleasant outdoors, a big garden, a place to sunbathe, a swimming pool, a bird sanctuary, whatever. In making the list, you should be as subjective, extensive and creative as possible."

Critically review the list. Is absolute maximum solar gain in winter really

desirable if it means frying in summer? The wish list should reflect a balance of use and energy conservation objectives. Now, compare it with the site-analysis information and strike off the items that are too expensive, too complicated or just plain impossible. That dream of an in-ground pool will have to go if the lot is sitting on bedrock, or perhaps the site is not sunny enough for active solar collectors. What remains will be a list of the things you *can* do — the site design.

A SHADE COOLER

Putting that design into practice, integrating what is on the site with what one wants to obtain from it, is the reward for careful site analysis and design. For new sites, it means locating buildings and other outdoor areas (gardens, patios, driveways, et cetera) with regard to solar gain and wind protection; for older homes, it may mean rearranging some of the outdoor areas to take better advantage of existing features. In either case, it involves the use of plants, fences or earth berms to enhance the microclimate for improved energy efficiency and comfort. Perhaps more than any other landscape feature, trees, shrubs and other plants play a determining role in creating the outdoor environment. Not only do they beautify the property and increase its value, they offer privacy and can reduce both heating and air-conditioning costs while making the home and yard more comfortable places to live.

The most obvious use of plants is to provide shade in the summer months. Air temperature above a lawn on a sunny day is 10 to 14 degrees F cooler than over bare soil or pavement, and a large tree shading the south or west wall of a building from the hot afternoon sun can lower the temperature inside the house by the same 10 to 14 degrees.

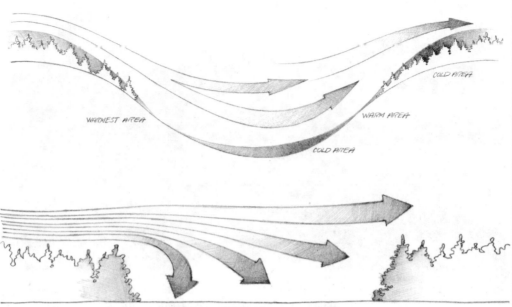

WARMEST AREA / COLD AREA / WARM AREA / COLD AREA

FORREST CLEARING COLD TRAP

Like water, cold air seeks the lowest level, but unlike water, it tends to puddle on the high side of a drop-off. The warmest building site, then, is halfway up the south face of a hill, but a house in any position can be protected by a row of trees or tall shrubs.

Deciduous trees are often planted on the south of a house because they provide shade in the summer yet let in the winter sun, but caution is advised if expecting substantial amounts of solar heat: the bare limbs of such densely branched trees as oaks and maples can eliminate as much as 70 percent of the solar radiation they block when fully leaved. Slow-growing hardwoods like oak, ash, maple and elm are the classic North American shade trees, but poplars and willows will also do the job and are much faster growing. Many landscapers interplant hardwoods with poplars to get the best of both worlds — the poplars provide relatively quick shade and can be removed as the more attractive trees mature.

Those landowners without a strategically placed shade tree can protect south-facing windows from the summer sun and still welcome the winter sun into their homes with a careful arrangement of overhangs or awnings. The size of the overhang, whether made of wood, metal or canvas, varies according to the latitude — the farther north one travels, the lower the sun and the longer the overhang. At 48 degrees north latitude (Victoria, Thunder Bay and St. John's), a two-foot overhang will prevent any sun from shining through a four-foot-high window at noon on the longest day of the year. On every other day, some sun will enter the window, and at noon on the shortest day, when the sun is at its lowest point in the sky, it will shine through all but the top 10 inches of the window.

Exposed walls can be protected from the summer sun by deciduous vines, whose leaves block incoming radiation but allow warm air to move away from the house. Virginia creeper, Boston or English ivy, honeysuckle and various wild and domestic grapes are readily available fast-growing vines that will

lower inside temperatures when allowed to grow on south or west walls as effectively as shade trees. Though vines should not be grown directly on wooden walls, they can be trained on detachable trellises, and even fast-growing annuals like runner beans, sweet peas, *Sugar Snap* peas or morning glories can provide substantial shade during the hot months.

Evergreens cast shade as well, but because their shading is year-round, they reduce solar access in winter. In cool climates, it is better to put them to use as insulators. A row of dense evergreens, like arborvitae, hemlock or spruce, planted close to an exposed north, east or west wall creates a dead airspace between plants and wall. Not only does such a planting block incoming wind but it traps escaping warm air, effectively "pre-insulating" the outside wall of the house and reducing the interior/exterior temperature differential. Because heat leakage from the foundation can kill the tree or shrub by preventing the root ball from freezing completely and because some roots seek out and enlarge cracks in the foundation,

evergreens should be planted at least 2 feet away from the house.

Although planting an insulating row of evergreens is a trick that can be used even on the smallest of city lots, those with more room may prefer to redirect the prevailing winter wind with a windbreak. Whether a single row of evergreens, a fence, a wall or even a well-situated building, a windbreak should be placed at a distance from the house equalling three to five times the height of the windbreak — any farther will not provide maximum protection, and any closer will put the house in the snowdrift that forms behind the windbreak. Generally speaking, tall, narrow and dense arrangements are the most effective: a gently sloping windbreak allows the wind to cling to its shape, while a vertical windward face causes the wind to "bounce" high and far. At the same time, however, the growth must extend to the ground, because a space under the branches can aggravate an existing problem by forcing wind under the windbreak at an even higher speed. Fences and walls provide

more immediate shelter than a row of plants, although a compromise may be reached by installing seedlings behind a fence and removing the fence when the hedge is grown. Once again, densely branched species like spruce, hemlock and cedar are more effective than pines and other widely branched plants.

If wind can be blocked, it can also be channelled. Indeed, winds travel 20 percent faster around the ends of a windbreak than across an open field, and they can be put to use clearing snow from a driveway or garnering a summer breeze to cool a shaded patio. Wind can even be funnelled, although because the wind is so erratic, this is the most difficult of techniques to master. The only reliable rule of thumb is to keep the open, windward end of the funnel at least twice as wide as the mouth. The funnel must be aligned with the prevailing wind, since trying to bend the wind flow can result in unpredictable turbulence that can cause unwanted breezes or severe snow deposits.

Although solid windbreaks effectively break the wind flow, they leave a strong low-pressure area directly behind them that is filled by swirling eddies of air movement. In contrast, partially porous windbreaks, such as louvred fences, allow the space to be filled with low-speed air filtered through the windbreak, making a calmer, less turbulent area behind the fence that is better for sheltering livestock in winter or barbecuing in summer. According to Agriculture Canada tests, a fence with 20 percent porosity (four-inch boards nailed on five-inch centres) leaves the least turbulent air pocket in its wake.

Fence porosity is also the key to controlling snowdrifts. In general terms, the more porous the fence is, the more snow it will catch and the longer the drift will be. Solid fences collect little

Prairie Farm Rehabilitation Association

building, enclose a homestead on at least three sides and can capture snowdrifts over 100 feet long. Shelterbelt designs vary with climate and site but are ideally six rows deep: an outer (windward) row of fast-growing shrubs such as caragana, lilacs, saskatoons or *Rosa rugosa*; a second row of short, ornamental trees like cherry, crab apple, mountain ash or tulip; an intermediate row of long-lived deciduous trees like ash, oak, maple or hickory; a central row of fast-growing deciduous trees like poplar, willow or alder; and two inside rows of spruce or some other long-lived, dense conifer. The shrubs should be planted 1 to 3 feet apart in their rows, the trees 6 to 8 feet apart and staggered. Space the rows 12 feet apart, except between the deciduous trees and the conifers, which should be at least 16 feet apart, making a shelterbelt that is 80 to 100 feet wide.

FIELD SHELTERBELTS

On the farmland of the Prairies, where the flat landscape, cold winters and howling winds make the expense and cumbersomeness of shelterbelts practical, if not essential, a series of field shelterbelts is also recommended. These are three-row plantings, typically caragana, *Northwest* poplar and either white spruce or lodgepole pine, spaced 750 to 1,000 feet apart, or seven to a section of land. Although these field belts use 40 acres of land per section, they cut wind speed, reduce erosion from wind and spring runoff, conserve moisture and reduce grain lodging, so overall crop yields are increased as much as 25 percent despite the loss of tillable land. In addition, there is the incalculable bonus of the increase in birds and wildlife because of improved shelter and food conditions.

Though shade trees, windbreaks, shelterbelts and hedgerows have an

The direction of the prevailing winds changes from summer to winter, but a knowledgeable planner can take advantage of both seasons. In summer, south-westerly winds send cool breezes across the patio but are barred from the vegetable garden by deciduous trees and shrubs. Northerly winter winds (overleaf) require a different pattern of shelterbelts.

snow in their wake and, because of a swirling high-pressure area to the windward, have little snow between the fence and a characteristically tall, clifflike drift. For this reason, a sidewalk that hugs the windward side of a solid windbreak rarely needs to be shovelled, and a solid fence around a barnyard will keep most of the snow on the outside. A 20 percent porous fence will create leeward snowdrifts equal to four times

the height of the fence; a 50 percent porous fence will leave snowdrifts the same depth that are 10 fence-heights long. Obviously, although a more dense fence can catch a good deal of snow in close quarters without filling in the driveway, snow fences need lots of room to be most effective.

So do shelterbelts, widely spaced rows of trees that, unlike single-row windbreaks planted on one side of a

A windbreak deflects winter winds from the house and funnels them along the driveway to keep it clear of snow. Heating costs for such protected houses are reduced approximately 5 percent for every 8 miles per hour of average, open-field windspeed in the area.

Most provincial governments have a programme to assist residents wishing to plant trees, offering some combination of free seedlings, a subsidy on tree purchases, technical advice or low-cost planting crews. The Prairie Farm Rehabilitation Administration, for example, gives tree and shrub seedlings for shelterbelt plantings to eligible farmers and municipalities in Alberta, Saskatchewan and Manitoba, but there and in other provinces, those who are buying trees by the handful instead of the gross may have to bear the cost themselves. They would do well to heed the advice of a nearby nurseryman about species that are adapted to local conditions and their own particular soil.

Despite the expense and the delay, however, homeowners who invest in an energy-efficient landscape will be richly rewarded, not only by increased property values and the gratitude of their grandchildren but by an improved microclimate. Yet, for all their impact, these energy improvements are not as readily measurable as, say, the R value of insulation. Site conditions are simply too changeable, too individual and too complex. "I used to preach energy efficiency," comments Doug Clark, "but most homeowners and developers weren't responsive because you can't always attach a dollar benefit to these kinds of improvements. Now I approach it in a slightly different way. I say, if you're going to plan a site, if you're going to do some landscaping, if you're going to put in some plants — for whatever reasons — then consider the energy impact. It usually costs no more to do any of these things in a way that makes them energy conserving."

Charmaine Gaudet, a professional writer who specializes in energy issues and travel, lives with her husband, a landscape architect, in Halifax, Nova Scotia.

unquestioned value for comfort and energy efficiency, they are not obtained without heavy applications of that inseparable duo, time and money. The length of time hardwoods require to become useful shade trees is measured in decades, and even a windbreak can take 15 to 20 years or more before it is tall enough and branched densely enough to be effective. Truly, as 19th-century writer Alexander Smith pointed out, "a man does not plant a tree for himself; he plants it for posterity." Those trees that are fast-growing tend to be more short-lived — poplars have a life span of about 60 years — and are less attractive than the massive oaks and maples. Still, though these trees cannot be rushed, interplanting them with fast-growing species or building fences to supplement young windbreaks can produce results much more quickly.

A well-planned prairie farmstead uses a series of shelterbelts, both shrubs and trees, to protect the house and driveway from winter snow and wind and to protect the vegetable garden from early frosts and dry, desiccating summer winds.

4 | Return of the Natives

Work on the wild side with indigenous trees, shrubs and flowers

By Robert S. Dorney
with Douglas H. Allen

"Mr. Dorney, what are you doing?"
"Finding the sun angle in June."
My 8-year-old next-door neighbour was vocally skeptical. "It isn't June and the sun isn't out."

Yet there I was, months out of date and miles out of place, preparing to plant a prairie garden in Waterloo, Ontario. "Well, yes, but it's a make-believe thing, sort of. I can pretend it's June and the sun is out and it's noon, and by walking back and forth I can tell if I'll be in the sun or not." I tried to explain the importance of the angle-calculating inclinometer that would tell me where my lot would be sunny enough for the prairie natives. Not entirely satisfied, the child went off muttering something about funny ways to get a suntan.

If my unconventional suburban landscape, part prairie, part woodland, all undomesticated, has sometimes been a neighbourhood conversation piece, it nevertheless has an impeccable heritage, in the concept of natural gardening that was born in the bleak, war-blighted urban landscape of postwar Holland. From that crucible arose my own impulse toward the natural gardening movement: a desire to guide nature, not regiment it; a desire for a *pax naturalis*; a wish for the tranquillity of green leaf and brilliant flower free from the whine of the lawn mower and the noxious scents of gasoline and herbicide. The inclinometer may be the only piece of 20th-century technology really useful in my garden.

With the purchase of a bulldozed piece of hard-packed Waterloo clay in the winter of 1968, our family had bought into the North American postwar trend: conventional tract housing with foundation junipers and shiny, new-cut keys. The lot was sun-baked in summer and wind-whipped in winter. And there is nothing like standing in an icy wind admiring a large drift across the driveway to remind a new homeowner that nature is fickle and not always forgiving.

The wheels began to turn. How would a snow fence look propped up on the front lawn? Ugly and out of place. So there was more drifting, more shovelling, more cursing. Another thought. Would a prairie windbreak be incongruous in the front yard of a 65-by-130-foot lot? A good idea, but there wasn't enough space. Any other ideas? The next blizzard started a flurry of ideas, and in 1969 I began to imagine a living, miniaturized windbreak in my front yard. Could it be done simply and inexpensively, with hand tools? Where would the plant stock be obtained? How would it be designed? Would the neighbours accept it or would they torch it in the dark of night?

First, I decided to grow only native species, for a number of reasons: they can grow tightly together to form a thicket, whereas ornamentals require more room; maintenance costs with natives are low because of their natural resistance to insects, thus eliminating the need for harsh chemical insecticides. Armed with permission from a local developer and with shovel and bushel basket, the expeditions to salvage native plants from other, as yet undeveloped lots began.

Call it what you will: natural landscaping, mini-ecosystem gardening, wildflower gardening, natural gardening, low-maintenance landscaping or natural heritage gardening (my preferred title). The terms are less important than the changes they encompass—a movement away from the manicured look, from the fussy, high-maintenance and expensive flowerbeds toward a more unfettered, dynamic natural plant system. And why native plants? Hardiness, disease

Stephen Errington

resistance, robustness, ability to reproduce — the very characteristics of the native plants become desirable in this new gardening ethic. The expensive and fastidious hybrids and domesticated cultivars are not only unnecessary but anachronistic: they become representatives of another era when man had to dominate nature, to bend it to his will. This new era's hallmark is enjoyment of the subtle beauty of nature, prized now because it lacks the human egotism implicit in the highly bred flower or shrub.

TURF CITY RECONSIDERED

Essentially, new landscaping traditions are the preserve of the few, and so far only two groups have arisen and converged into a natural gardening movement. One group consists primarily of a few professional landscape architects in Canada, the United States and Europe who are interested in avant-garde design and who have explored this new "medium," building upon more traditional forms. The other, somewhat larger group is more diverse in its membership, comprising home and cottage owners with green thumbs and strong backs and a willingness to experiment. This group might be called the rugged individualists — youthful naturalists, factory workers, retired folk. What they all share is an interest in nature and wild plants, as well as, generally, a desire to avoid the tedious and expensive management a formal garden requires. Not lazy, just cagey. (They may inhabit turf city but they don't worship it).

The professional landscape architect usually serves only the wealthy upper and upper-middle classes. Those who can afford gardeners and expensive plants normally have little desire to design and build inexpensive, informal

gardens. Their gardens are elaborate, artificial — even ostentatious. On the other hand, the middle-class suburbanite interested in native plants has been left to his or her own devices. So far this has led, I believe, to more innovation and less conformity, doubtless a blessing in disguise for a new and emerging practical art form. There will be time enough later for professionals and philistines to play with it.

But why, one asks, should a small, grass-roots movement have started among homeowners of more modest means? Haven't all the great garden traditions come from the monied palaces such as Versailles and the manor houses of southern England? I believe natural gardening is done less to impress the neighbours than to provide a means for

personal enjoyment, an enjoyment which can take many forms: a child discovering a spider's web, a hummingbird feeding on a trumpet creeper flower, a rabbit nesting under a stump or the pleasure of growing native plants now rare in the wild. All natives may not be colourful bloomers, but they do exhibit a wide variety of forms and shapes. As our perception of humanity's destruction of nature expands and focuses, some concerned environmentalists can be expected to value more the small, wild pieces of green and, where these are absent, to try to recreate them.

The area dedicated to a natural heritage garden need not be large. The setting can be a corner of the yard, front or back, a small or medium-sized industrial lot or a cottage property; I myself have developed small-scale natural woodland gardens in all three settings.

GOING NATIVE

Although special requirements for natural garden design are few, nature can be unforgiving if one makes mistakes. A very domineering species, for instance, could quickly overwhelm all other plantings in a small area. The reason is straightforward enough: natural dynamics will be given a more-or-less free rein; once planted, the landscape will take care of itself. In fact, this hands-off approach is the essence of natural gardening, and thus any designer must recognize natural dynamics and accommodate them: in a conventional garden, on the other hand, the owner puts nature "in its place," at a considerable cost in labour and technology.

The first factor to be recognized and integrated into any design is the element of shade. Prairie-native plants require

Another perennial border features delphiniums, Shasta daisies, peach-leaved bellflowers, foxgloves, woolly lamb's ears and sweet William.

Left, Sheridan Nurseries Ltd.; right, Jennifer Bennett   Overleaf, John Scanlan

Baltic ivy (left) is a relatively cold-tolerant cultivar of the perennial climber English ivy that will survive winter in Agriculture Canada climatic zone 6. Variegated large-leaved hosta and the smaller periwinkle (right) provide an interesting contrast as neighbouring ground covers.

Perennial flowers (overleaf), ground covers, shrubs and trees are placed so that the eye of the beholder can move easily from shape to shape and so that each plant is shown to its best advantage. In an Ontario garden, a Northstar sour cherry grows in the colourful company of irises, Canterbury bells, sedum, coral bells, spiked Veronica, gayfeather and wild musk mallow.

Pink *Pastorale* phlox (above) complements blue *Superba* salvia in such a way that each colour is made to seem more intense than it would without the contrast nearby. English ivy (below), used as a ground cover under a mature beech tree, replaces turf to produce a carpet that is easy to tend, durable, inexpensive and beautiful to look upon.

Royal Botanical Gardens

Freek Vrugtman

Intertwining knot gardens were once the height of fashion. Now less common because they are labour-intensive and best viewed from on high, they are still outstanding as settings for compact perennials such as box and small-leaved herbs like rosemary.

Derek Fell

plenty of sun, while the forest interior conditions necessary for most woodland herbaceous species can only be provided by the shade of taller shrubs, trees, buildings, or a combination of these elements. The delineation of these shade zones, if shadows are cast by a building or by trees on adjacent property, can be easily done in either of two ways. On the longest day of the year, stake the boundary of the sun-shadow areas at 10:00 a.m., noon, 2:00 p.m. and 4:00 p.m. Within the shaded area, woodland conditions will be approximated for the entire growing season. Alternatively, the gardener can use a compass, an inclinometer and sun angle tables; hand-held varieties of these instruments are sufficiently accurate and are usually available in universities and colleges which offer programmes in engineering, forestry and geography.

Shade being the first dynamic to consider, moisture is the second. The moisture regime of some plants is more demanding than that of others, and moisture is dependent upon the soil texture and, of course, the depth of the water table. Well-drained soils (which are dry except after heavy rains) or imperfectly drained soils (those that hold standing water after spring melt-off or heavy rains) define one's possibilities. Species for well-drained soil include: aspen, birch, choke cherry, highbush-cranberry, dogwood and some wild roses, while those that can tolerate imperfectly drained soils include green ash, white cedar, common elderberry, Virginia creeper, Jack-in-the-pulpit and Maidenhair fern. A sunny bog might support pitcher plants, bog rosemary, Labrador tea or dwarf birch.

A third factor, of slightly less consequence than the others, is the wind. It is important to recognize that some taller species (5 feet and higher) may require protection from the wind's force and desiccating effects. These three dynamics, then, lead to the necessity for designing natural gardens which conform to certain configurations and which make use of particular species. The effect of the soil's acidity or alkalinity is usually not severe enough to warrant consideration as a factor in selecting many species.

Although garden design must conform to certain aesthetic specifications, there is a variety of configurations to choose from for any given site and its conditions. For dry, upland sites only occasionally wet in spring and summer,

Facing page: Royal Botanical Gardens

FOREST   FOREST-PRAIRIE EDGE   PRAIRIE

CROSS SECTIONAL SIDE VIEWS

OVERHEAD VIEWS

UPLAND SITE

N

TREES   SHRUBS   PRAIRIE (MEADOW)

Five possibilities for a native garden in a fairly dry, upland site. Each plan is designated by a cross-sectional side view (top) and its corresponding overhead view (below). The gardens themselves need not be circular, but the same general pattern of shrubs, prairies and trees should be observed, whatever the final overall shape.

Mother-of-thyme (facing page) is one of the most graceful and accommodating of ground covers for a rock garden or for filling spaces between paving stones wherever foot traffic is not overly heavy. Although it is not the best of thymes for the kitchen, it spreads fairly quickly and blooms white, mauve or purple in summer.

for example, there are five possibilities illustrated here, any of which would serve the natural gardener well. These circular designs (which can be adapted to oval or rectangular shapes as well) include three structural components: shrubs, trees and prairie (meadow) species. The placement of shrubs in a band 3 to 9 feet deep on the western, northern and southern sides of the area forms a "skin" protecting the interior woodland from direct exposure to sun and wind. (White or red cedars or white pines can be substituted for the shrubs to form part of the edge.) An east or north side of a house or wall provides equivalent shade and wind protection, trees making up the centre of such plantings. A prairie garden, on the other hand, does not require such an edge, although it is not harmed by one; similarly, a shrub "skin" is unnecessary on the eastern edge of a forest planting. The designer can choose an open or closed space. A more open configuration — opening eastward, preferably — will invite children and

adults to enter, whereas a closed configuration with a tight shrub or cedar edge can provide little else than a pathway for access. Suitable tree, shrub and herbaceous species for these habitats can be obtained from some

nurseries, or they can be carefully dug from certain wild locations.

A wetland garden, on the other hand, can be either natural, dug into the existing water table, or created by an impermeable liner laid over a depression in the soil, and then filled with peat and soil or floored with sand and filled with water. A permeable divider, such as a screen, within the pool liner, will allow a pond and bog garden in the same site. Rainwater from roof leaders and surface drainage swales between properties can sometimes be tapped into a man-made pond, or the pond area can be filled by hose and topped up occasionally.

Setbacks for legal easements (water, gas, hydro, phone, TV cable, drainage between lots) should be permanently marked before planting, as the utilities' maintenance people must have access to them at any time. Similarly, drainage easements cannot be blocked, as such blockages affect other property owners. Snow from driveways and sidewalks must also be taken into account; heavy snow piles flatten trees and shrubs, and

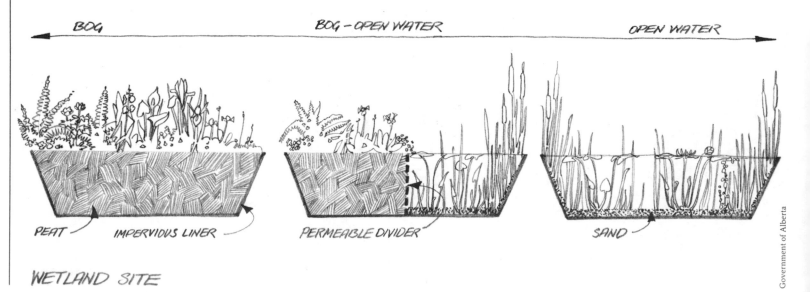

BOG   BOG – OPEN WATER   OPEN WATER

PEAT   IMPERVIOUS LINER   PERMEABLE DIVIDER   SAND

WETLAND SITE

any salt in the snow will damage woody vegetation. Prairie vegetation or meadowland, however, is not damaged by heavy snowdrifts, and it will also tolerate drought, heat from nearby asphalt parking lots or the dry, shady north side of buildings. A particular word of warning: if your natural garden is designed to trap snow, be sure it is trapped where you want it.

If stones, stumps, walkways, outdoor lighting, pools, berms or timber construction are to be incorporated into your natural heritage garden, they should be in place before the plants are put in. Often, large boulders pulled up by foundation excavation are an expensive nuisance in new subdivisions, and developers are more than happy to push them over onto your lot. Otherwise, heavy stones need a crane for placement, and this can tear up other landscaping and driveways. Sand or earth for mounds or berms generally require heavy equipment access, and so there is the same risk of damaging both driveways and other landscaping.

On street corners or at the openings to driveways, visibility can be blocked by tall shrubs and trees. The driver's line of vision is only 3 to 6 feet off the roadway surface, so even short shrubs planted in clusters can block one's view, which can be especially hazardous where children play or ride bicycles. In most situations, plantings are never close to the roadway, but in corner lots where traffic is relatively heavy and plants are designed to cut out noise and dirt, it is a matter for some concern.

Seasonality creates special opportunities for natural gardening. Prairies are visually lacklustre until June when they begin to grow: then, in late summer and fall, they "meet their maker" in a blaze of colourful flowers and grass stems. Natural woodlands start

out gloriously in April, May and June, and then go flat and dull until autumn colours herald the end of the season. Massed leaf shapes provided by woodland-loving plants such as may apple, ostrich fern or large-leaved aster can alleviate the lack of summer colour, displaying a "cool" visual impression. A careful combination of shrub, woodland and prairie vegetation can provide a better-balanced and longer-term display of colour and flower, offering cuttings and enjoyment throughout much of the growing season.

BACKYARD FORESTS AND PRAIRIES

The quickest and least expensive way to begin a backyard forest is to plant on a ploughed or rototilled, clean, grass- and weed-free surface some rooted cuttings of balsam poplars or hybrid poplars; these fast-growing trees will serve as a nurse crop. The cuttings, usually made from dormant stems in April, are about 12-18 inches long and ¼ to ½ inch thick.

These cuttings are first soaked in at least 9 inches of water for 5 to 10 days at a cool, basement-like temperature until small roots begin to sprout in the form of white protuberances. Then the cuttings are planted at least 8 inches deep with only a few buds showing at the top. The cuttings should be spaced out in centres 4 to 6 feet apart — so that each plant has 4 to 6 feet of clear space all around. Lining them up in rows lengthwise and crosswise facilitates rototilling weeds that appear during the first two summers.

By late summer they will have sprung shoots up to 3 feet in height, and by late summer of the second year they may attain heights of 6 to 10 feet. (Standing over these ambitious shoots could be hazardous without safety glasses and steel-toed boots!) At this point the stand will have achieved "closure" — the state reached when plants have filled in space as fully as can be expected for those species — and henceforth any weed growth will be low to negligible.

59

Trembling aspen (*Populus tremuloides*) will substitute nicely for balsam, but there must be at least 3 feet of root and a shoot of 1½ to 3 feet before it is planted. Because of the horizontal root, this species is generally more time-consuming to plant. Of course, weed control is mandatory until the cuttings take hold and the ground is colonized by native woodland herbaceous species.

To obtain a forest-like herbaceous ground cover quickly and effectively, plant close to the base of each poplar, balsam or aspen cutting one herbaceous plant, selecting randomly from the following five choices: Virginia creeper (*Parthenocissus* spp), blue violet (*Viola* spp), wild strawberry (*Fragaria* spp), loosestrife (*Lysimachia ciliata*), and Canada anemone (*Anemone canadensis*). At the base of the tree cuttings, these sun-loving herbs are out of the way of the rototiller and will thus spread outward from the cuttings, reducing grass and weed competition by the end of the second growing season. These herbaceous plants work well in clumps and clusters as well. After the stand closes, usually at the end of Year Two or Year Three, shade-demanding herbs such as hepatica (*Hepatica acutiloba*), trilliums and bloodroot (*Sanguinaria canadensis*) can be planted.

To plant a prairie meadow, the natural gardener once more requires a weed-free seed bed, although in this case it should be quite sunny. If soil needs to be brought in, a layer of deep pit-dug coarse sand should be spread *at least* 2 inches deep and preferably a foot deep over the bed. The sand serves to reduce grass and weed competition, as it is too dry for quick germination and growth, and the few exotic weeds that do establish themselves can be easily removed by hand or hoe. Next, spread the prairie grass and flowering plant seed, plus a nurse crop of annual rye grass or oats. A good source of cultural information for the prairie garden is the Wehr Nature Center, 5879 South 92nd Street, Hales

60

Corners, Wisconsin 53130, which publishes a 74-page softcover *Prairie Propagation Handbook* ($2.80 U.S. in 1985). By the second growing season many prairie species will be blooming, and by Year Four the prairie will be 4 to 7 feet tall, thick and colourful. It will produce enough seed by the fourth year to double its size from then on, should you so desire. Once it is self-sustaining, the annual appearance of such species as prairie smoke (*Geum triflorum*) becomes a wild calendar of delight.

The boundary separating the natives from the lawn or other plantings should be clean, a division best attained by burying a plastic border 6 to 12 inches deep to form a barrier to encroachment from either side. Wood, stone or crushed rock can be placed over the buried border, concealing the (usually) lurid green plastic from view.

Unfortunately, prairie seed is not available from most Canadian seed houses, so the would-be Canadian prairie gardener must usually gather his or her own — probably only a few hours' collection — or purchase it from United States sources, for more-or-less the same amount of money that would be spent on more conventional plants such as tulips.

The preferred sources for herbaceous plants, shrubs and trees are the commercial and government nurseries, whose stock is well grown and free from disease. The government nurseries usually sell only to homeowners with large acreage, but government stock is of high quality and inexpensive, albeit rather small and immature, mainly two-year seedlings or two-year-plus transplants. Some commercial nurseries sell small seedlings called "liners" for very low cost. Trees larger than 6 or 7 feet dug in the wild generally do poorly for four years, if they survive at all. Only

smaller trees should be tried; they are best moved in April and May or October to December, when they are dormant. If root-pruned by shovel one growing season in advance they move more easily (see illustration on page 136). For some trees and shrubs such as black walnut, oak, dogwood and viburnum, it is best if tops are removed and only their root systems are transplanted. Herbaceous plants move well, as a rule, particularly if moved before they are full grown and blooming. Sufficient soil should be moved with them to "acclimatize" them to their new bed.

I have suggested that the natural gardener obtain the landowner's permission before lifting native plant stock, but there is one additional caveat: some provinces and states have given rare plant species legal protection and thus transplanting is not possible. Furthermore, parks and nature preserves are off limits to salvage operations. However, on the edges of cities many public and private lands, both woodland and prairie meadow, are slated to become housing subdivisions and industrial parks, and usually permission to salvage plants from these sites is given quickly and free of charge. With friends or youth groups recruited to help dig, hundreds of wildflowers, shrubs and small trees can be saved in the space of an afternoon.

Since many wildflowers are prolific seeders or spreaders via root or stem, once a small woodland garden has been established the plants themselves can provide considerable stock to start new areas. Swapping with neighbours (those who can figure out what you're doing) quickly builds a diversity of species in many gardens. Virginia creepers and strawberries spread by runner, and Canada anemone and loosestrife both move via underground root extension.

These four ground-level species not only rapidly reduce weeds and exotic grass, as already mentioned, but also produce enormous numbers of seedlings and seeds each year; their high reproductivity makes them very desirable colonizing species. As the woodland matures, these species lose vigour, thereby allowing the more fastidious woodland species such as trilliums and yellow lady's slippers (*Cypripedium calceolus*) to succeed.

The woodland planting, if started on a clean seedbed otherwise untreated, will quickly degenerate into weeds, since the soil normally contains many residual weed seeds. It was previously suggested that if poplars were planted as a nurse crop — a temporary crop designed to facilitate the growth of other, more

Shade-demanding wildflowers such as trilliums should be planted in the woodland garden only after the fast-growing trees achieve closure in two or three years, forming an umbrella of dappled shade that is the preferred habitat of these and some other spring-blooming species.

Ontario Ministry of Agriculture and Food

permanent vegetation — a stand should attain closure relatively quickly, and the sooner the better since this closure reduces problems with weeds and unwanted grasses. By the eighth year or so the poplars will be ready to be harvested selectively to allow the underplanted, permanent hardwoods and conifers, such as pine and hemlock to progress rapidly. Although not a particularly dense wood, poplar burns well in any fireplace on a frigid January afternoon. Actually, a 40- by 20-foot woodland plot could yield more than one face cord — 4 by 8 by 1½ feet, 48 cubic feet — by the eighth year, surely an added bonus for the natural gardener.

AU NATUREL WEEDING

The control of grass and weeds, as has already been pointed out, is critical in the first two springs. If bluegrass or quack grass sod does take hold it will choke out the poplars, slowing their growth substantially. Furthermore, if the sod is heavy enough, field mice will invade, debarking the more edible hardwood seedlings and saplings. Rototilling between the poplars is best where room and incline of the slope permit. Otherwise, hoeing and hand weeding are the gardener's best defenses against insidious weeds and grasses. Besides, weeding by hand is in keeping with the *au naturel* approach to gardening I am describing.

While weeding is time consuming and less than exciting, the garden, even in the first year or two, demands less maintenance work than does a conventional vegetable or flower garden. Returning to our 40-by-20-foot model plot, the annual total of weeding hours would, typically, be as follows: 10 hours in the first year, 8 hours in the second, 1 or 2 hours in the third and fourth and an incredible 1 hour a year thereafter. If the garden's design allows for rototilling, the time could probably be halved for the first two years. The maximum effort required is from May through July, when the bluegrass and dandelions spring into action before the woodland begins growing. A similarly sized area of grass requires about two hours (or about 14 cuttings) a year for life, plus approximately $8.50 in gasoline, fertilizer and herbicides. While the natural garden will not produce savings substantial enough to pay for a trip to Rio for Carnival, the natural heritage approach to gardening nevertheless benefits the homeowner in that it decreases his or her dependence upon the noisy, smelly lawn mower and those equally obnoxious fertilizers and herbicides. And it gives a quiet boost to backyard wildlife.

In fact, the choice of fruit-producing plants may attract more small animals and birds than the gardener had in mind. If one plants wild shrubs or herbs with edible berries, there is the extra advantage of having — in their less refined form — preserves and fruit cocktails at the back doorstep. Strawberry, raspberry, choke cherry, highbush-cranberry and elderberry all produce berries suitable for jelly, pies and homemade brew — if, of course, you can beat the neighbourhood children to them; robins and cedar waxwings also offer the natural gardener stiff competition. One can even brew palatable teas from purple or wild bergamot leaves and New Jersey tea (*Ceanothus americanus*) leaves. The rose hips on *Rosa carolina* or *R. blanda* make a fine cup in addition to being high in vitamin C. And, in purely aesthetic terms, the red berries of the highbush-cranberry (*Viburnum trilobum*) remain over the winter and serve as natural magnets for hungry birds and animals eager to partake of this "emergency"

Anemones and ferns carpet the ground of the well-established natural woodland garden. Like any landscape, the wild garden requires work at the outset, but its more subtle beauty is thenceforth less demanding.

Agriculture Canada

Stephen Errington

food supply in late winter storms.

A few large, well-established natural heritage gardens provide examples of what can be achieved with native plants in the landscape. The most memorable of all is the Botanical Garden in Chapel Hill, North Carolina. Started by the University of North Carolina at Chapel Hill in 1952, it is a magnificent combination of miniature landscape zones. If you don't lose a leg to the carnivorous plants, you may also view a herb garden, a sand hill collection, a coastal plain zone and a mountain zone. In the herb garden alone there are 64 species on display. Wild plants grown in beds and in greenhouses are sold to the public.

Interest in cultivating natives, I am pleased to say, is growing. Gardeners and conservationists are at the forefront of this movement to study, preserve and propagate many rare species of North American plant life. Out of this interest and enthusiasm may emerge an appreciation of the natural landscape of North America as a vital component of the larger cultural landscape. Given this new insight, we must learn to adapt our gardening traditions, with their emphasis on artifice, regimentation and chemicals, to the rhythms and dynamics of the natural world. And we can begin with one or more uncommon or rare native plants, integrated into a miniaturized natural community, nurtured and enjoyed for posterity.

Robert S. Dorney is a doctor of biology who teaches land use planning in the Planning School at the University of Waterloo. He is a consultant in landscape analysis, assessment and rehabilitation, which includes revegetation of pipelines and ravines. During the last 15 years, he has designed and created several natural gardens in Ontario and the United States. Douglas H. Allen is a graduate in English from the University of Waterloo.

5 | The Epicureans

Merging herbs and vegetables into the ornamental garden

By Patrick Lima

The most memory inducing of all the senses, it is said, is smell. Certainly, my first whiff of the rue bushes we grew to fill out the lines of a flower border instantly transported me to the treeless city street of my childhood, where I discovered for the first time, having taken no notice then, that old Mrs. Rice next door planted rue beneath the craning lilacs and snowberries in a cramped corner of earth she had wrested from the encroaching concrete.

Years later, Mrs. Rice and I have something in common. My rue, too, is a flower garden inhabitant, where it is valued chiefly for its elegant, lustrous, blue-grey, lobed foliage that persists in good condition until winter arrives in earnest. Gardeners who love pomp and riotous colour in the landscape — the non-stop scarlet glare of salvia, or the self-important floor-mop dahlias — will not find the quiet-natured rue (*Ruta graveolens*) thrilling. But anyone who likes a garden to be a soft-toned, soothing haven might plant two or three rue plants. Just ask Mrs. Rice.

Like rue, many herbs and vegetables are suited to playing the dual role of contributing both beauty and utility to the home landscape. Indeed, gardeners with limited space — especially urban growers, ground-level or high-rise — may find all the ornamentation they need among these plants. Many, like rhubarb, lettuce and chard, are striking foliage plants, while bee balm and chives have attractive flowers, and others, including peppers and bush tomatoes, produce edible fruit as well.

The usual way to include these useful plants in the landscape is to confine them to their own plots, a tradition that has its uses. Most vegetables are sun-loving annuals, so the kitchen garden can be located in the sunniest available site and the entire plot tilled or spaded in spring or fall; herbs tend to be fairly small and subtle, so a knot garden or a small enclosure of raised beds shows them off well. The herbs John Scanlan and I most use for cooking in our Bruce Peninsula, Ontario, home — lovage, spearmint, chives, savory, oregano, thyme — we have planted in raised beds by the kitchen door, around a stone-paved patio where little colonies of fragrant seedlings have taken possession of the chinks between the warm, flat rocks. What was begun as an exercise in convenience has become one of the garden's friendliest landscaping features.

On the other hand, the relegation of herbs to herb gardens and vegetables to vegetable gardens can result in a prospect lacking imagination and interest. Many herbs and vegetables fit beautifully into nooks, crannies and borders among other plants considered strictly ornamental, or in positions usually reserved for ornamentals only. If Gertrude Jekyll, turn-of-the-century English landscape gardener *extraordinaire*, could plant sweet corn in the back of her famous flower borders, then surely we can follow suit. And city dwellers, first candidates for an edible landscape, could do no better for on-site instruction than to wander through the neighbourhoods housing large Chinese or Italian populations. See how that useless adjunct to most city houses, the front lawn, has vanished entirely, and in its place are neat, narrow raised beds crammed, cheek to jowl, with pac-choy, mustard greens, garlic chives, paste tomatoes, bush beans, and kohlrabi, with perhaps a fat dahlia or two nodding benignly over all — the whole as lovely as it is productive.

THE PERENNIAL HERBS

Herbs are especially accommodating in the landscape. Seldom showy or

Stephen Errington

Drawn to a scale of 1 inch to 6 feet, a yard with a central lawn and a patio (at bottom) facing the house, is planted with hardy herbs, berries, vegetables, annual and perennial flowers and a fruit tree. Shade-tolerant species have been relegated to the upper right hand corner. The numeral after the plant name indicates the approximate number of specimens that will fill the indicated space. Where two plants bloom in succession in the same space, they are divided by an oblique line (/). This garden is hardy at least as far north as climatic zone 5.

PLANTING KEY

1 LOVAGE (1) UNDERPLANTED WITH NARCISSUS
2 TARRAGON (1)
3 LAVENDER (5) UNDERPLANTED WITH CROCUS
4 PURPLE CONEFLOWER (5) / TULIPS
5 RUE (3) / NARCISSUS CHEERFULNESS
6 SWEET BASIL (8)
7 ROSA RUGOSA (2)
8 DAYLILY (3)
9 ARTEMISIA "SILVER MOUND (5) / CROCUS
10 LILIES (8)
11 PARSLEY (8-12)
12 TOMATOES, POLE BEANS, CUKES, FENCE TRAINED
12a TOMATOES (2) UNSTAKED
13 CHIVES (3)
14 LEMON THYME (5)
15 CURRANT BUSHES (2)
16 CREEPING OR WINTER SAVORY (5)
17 SWEET WOODRUFF GROUNDCOVER / NARCISSUS
18 CHERRY MONTMORENCY
19 CLEMATIS JACKMANII
20 ROSE LOOSESTRIFE (4)
21 SEDUM SPECTABILE (5) / DAFFODILS
22 GARLIC CHIVES (3)
23 SWISS CHARD
24 ARTEMISIA ABSINTHIUM / NARCISSUS
25 HIGHBUSH CRANBERRY (1)
26 HOSTA (5) / DWARF SPRING BULBS
27 DAYLILY "HYPERION" (6) NARCISSUS
28 SERVICEBERRY OR SASKATOON (2)
29 TALL FERNS (5)
30 VIRGINIA BLUEBELLS
31 RED AND GREEN LEAF LETTUCE (12)
32 SIBERIAN IRIS (2)
33 SWEET CICELY (2)
34 COLUMBINE (3) / NARCISSUS
35 ROSA RUGOSA
36 BUSH BEANS
37 SIBERIAN IRIS (2)
38 CLEMATIS JACKMANII
39 ROSE LOOSESTRIFE (3)
40 ORIENTAL POPPY (1)
41 STACHYS LANATA (3)
42 LILIES (6)
43 VARIAGATED APPLE-MINT
44 BLUE VIOLA (12)
A POTTED ROSEMARY (SUNK INTO ½ BARREL) / NASTURTIUMS (SEED)
B DWARF CALENDULA OR MARIGOLDS FROM SEED
C SMALL-FRUITED TOMATOES / BUSH BASIL
D PEPPERS (3) AND ANNUALS OR ZUCCHINI (1)

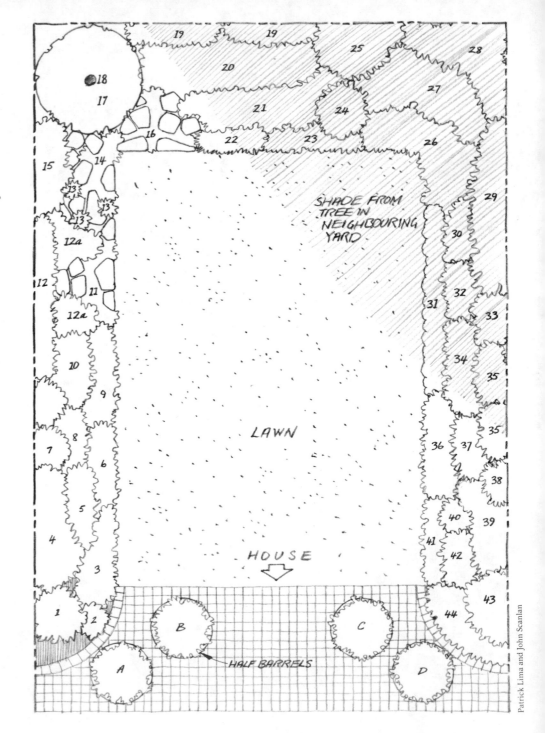

Patrick Lima and John Scanlan

flamboyant, most possess a quiet beauty of leaf — grey, velvety sage; metallic, blue-green rue; the silver artemisias; small-leafed thymes. A garden landscaped largely with herbs must always be a calming place, a fragrant refuge. In Larkwhistle Garden, John and I have no herb garden per se, but manage still to include close to a hundred species and varieties of herbs in different places about the landscape.

Herbs there are, tall and short, ground-hugging or broadly spreading, that will fill many a niche in the landscape. For example, the gardener who is not a keen collector of alpine plants might consider herbs — especially those native to the stony, sun-baked slopes of Mediterranean regions — to furnish the little plains and valleys of a rock garden with fragrant greenery. Of best value here are several species and varieties of thyme which encompass a wide area, both botanically and spatially. The lowliest member of the clan, *Thymus serpyllum*, called mother-of-thyme, creeping thyme or wild thyme, aspires to the great height of an inch or so, but extends laterally into a dense green rug that, once a year, is lost under a galaxy of minute white, mauve or purple flowers. Classically used between paving stones, the gentle creeping thyme is nevertheless no match for shoving weeds or heavy traffic, and is happier to clothe a sunny place in a rockery, where it may be underplanted with the smallest of spring bulbs. We are able to keep a sharp eye out for weeds, so have planted this thyme on either side of a flight of stone steps leading up to a porch of flat stones laid over sand. After several seasons, small patches of low green have appeared between the porch stones, nourished somehow by rock and sand. A variety of creeping thyme, woolly thyme (*T. lanuginosus*), has been aptly

A good selection of common vegetables, herbs and annual flowers can be purchased from garden shops, plant nurseries and rural grocery stores in spring and early summer, affording the beginning gardener the easiest, most dependable way to obtain healthy specimens for a first foray into epicurean landscaping.

christened "mousy thyme" by a neighbour; this species blossoms sparsely, but as one old-time garden writer observed, "its silvery soft foliage is somehow flowerlike in appearance, and its wide mats are always effective flowing among stones or spreading down a sunny rock wall." These two thymes are not the best for the kitchen.

Of definite culinary value, however, is lemon thyme (*T. citrodorus*). Few plants are as sweet — the scent is citrus and spice — few as decorative among rocks. We plant lemon thyme between and just behind the large limestone rocks that edge the flower borders; the plants soon tumble and sprawl into a small cascade of deep green or gold-flecked round leaves and a shower of pale lavender blooms. Generous picking for kitchen use, or a summer shearing when flowering is past, will keep lemon thyme (and most others) compact and bushy.

Useful as a ground cover or edging in dry, sunny places is golden creeping thyme, which forms dense, wiry, expanding mats of fragrant yellow-green,

while the thyme of spice racks, *T. officinalis*, English thyme, is a small (10-inch), eventually woody-stemmed shrublet of tiny, arrow-shaped leaves and sparse, pale blooms. This thyme is neither as decorative nor as enduring in the garden as forms of creeping thyme, but worth a place in the sun for its pungent foliage. It is one of the few thymes that comes true from seed. Far prettier is silver thyme, with grey-green, white-edged leaves, a sparkling plant for a rock garden or edging. Caraway thyme (*T. herba-barona*) is low and spreading, forming a loosely-woven tangle of branches clothed with small, caraway-scented leaves. All the thymes are excellent low plants for warm, sunny places; all resent the encroachment of stronger plants, all appreciate a summer shearing and a covering of springy evergreen boughs during the winter if snow is sparse; all are friendly and fragrant dwellers in any garden, however small.

Also ideal for planting among rocks are winter savory (*Satureja montana*) and creeping savory (*S. repandra*), the first an upright, small shrub growing to 10 inches in height, the latter a low-growing, mat-forming plant with small spikes of white flowers. Both are useful for seasoning. A gardening neighbour who started with a rooted slip of creeping savory from our garden has multiplied her original plant over several years so that its soft mats now festoon the edges of a 40-foot-long bed outlined by railway ties. Creeping and winter savory are easily grown from cuttings — see the diagrams on pages 82 and 83.

Mints are distinctly pushy plants, about 2 feet tall, that move quickly into any and all available space with little consideration for their neighbours. I would not be without a patch of head-clearing peppermint (*Mentha piperita vulgaris*) for tea, or the lighter green, pebbled spearmint (*M. spicata*) that is so good in green, grain or potato salads. But for sheer beauty of leaf, the variegated form of apple mint (*M. rotundifolia variegata*) is best by far. Apple-green, slightly woolly leaves are flecked and bordered with creamy white, and the plant is not as aggressive a spreader as others of its kin. I have seen this mint used to good effect as a foliage accent among perennials, and I can think of few plants — herbs or otherwise — that would better brighten a shaded corner in a city garden. Mints, for all their wandering ways, are easily checked with spade, trowel, or knife, and you will no doubt have willing recipients of the fragrant excess. Gardeners really concerned about keeping it within bounds can grow mint in a container, where it will appreciate frequent waterings.

Although they are seldom used today, several members of the genus *Artemisia* will mingle their silver foliage to good effect with the green, golden or glaucous

colours of other plants in the landscape. My own favourite, *A. schmidtiana* — quite a mouthful of Latin — is, thankfully, encountered in nurseries simply as *Silver Mound*, an apt name for the low-spreading hummocks of feathery silver.

The debilitating effects of the infamous liqueur, absinthe, are portrayed in the Toulouse-Lautrec painting, The Absinthe Drinker — a numbed, glum figure sits, head propped on hands, in a Paris café, behind a glass of milky liquid. Absinthe is made no more, but the namesake of the bitter brew, *Artemisia absinthium*, wormwood, is still a garden herb in good standing. Its woody shrubs stand about 2 feet tall. The cultivar *Lambrook Silver* has whiter leaves, a shorter stature and is a fine-leaved filler for sunny, dry places. One plant is a "drift" and ought to be trimmed back, especially in spring, to keep it shapely.

Southernwood, old man, smelling-wood, lad's-love, maiden's-ruin, kiss-me-quick-and-go, sloven-wood: if a proliferation of common names indicates that a plant has found a garden place for many years, *A. abrotanum* is clearly a fragrant favourite. Thread-leaved, hoary bushes (to 4 feet) smell of lemon and bitterness; the French name, *garde-robe*, underscores its moth-repellent qualities. Branches of several artemisias, including this and *Silver King*, are used dried as a foundation for herbal wreaths, but the dowdy, delicious tarragon, *A. dracunculus*, is the only culinary artemisia.

A handsome herb for any place in the landscape, sun or shade, where there is room for its considerable girth (about 2 feet around) is lovage (*Levisticum officinales*), a green giant (to 6 feet) in daily demand for flavouring virtually every dish save dessert. Locate this heavyweight carefully in the garden; it is not easily moved once established. Lovage is handsome enough — deep green, broad-leafed — to mingle with the posies toward the back of a mixed border, or to stand sentry by the side door, easily accessible from the kitchen. It is also well-placed in a corner of the vegetable garden with rhubarb, asparagus, horseradish and other perennial food plants. Celery-flavoured lovage branches dry very easily if hung in an airy, shaded place.

In her book *Home and Garden*, Gertrude Jekyll commented that "as much as I love the flower garden and woodland, I am by no means indifferent to the interest and charm of the kitchen garden," and admitted that when she had a free moment for "a quiet stroll for pure pleasure of the garden, I often take it among the vegetables." It was Jekyll who first drew our attention to sweet cicely, an umbelliferous plant whose early ferny foliage she liked among spring bulbs. "*Myrrhis odorata*," she said, "for its beauty, deserves to be in every garden . . . it is charming, with its finely-cut pale green leaves and really handsome flowers." We have a grouping of sweet cicely, interplanted with narcissus in front of some clumps of common white cedar and edged with an exuberant mass of white-flowered dead-nettle (*Lamium maculatum*). This is a no-care corner of the landscape, perennially cool green and white. Sweet cicely is a favourite nibbling herb with garden visitors, and neighbouring children keep coming back for more "licorice" — the

stems and especially the unripe seeds are intensely anise-flavoured. For neatness' sake and to prevent too-free seeding, we cut back the flowering stalks of sweet cicely just before the seed ripens black and scatters. This feathery, fragrant herb grows well in shade; one plant will be enough for a small garden.

Best known of the herbal onions and often planted in beds or borders of flowers and herbs are the easy chives (*Allium cepa*), anyone's plant in perpetuity, for the mere setting out of a few seeds in early spring either indoors or directly where they will grow. Chives have spiky foliage and fluffy mauve flower heads, pretty enough to consort with any "ornamentals," but the gardener should set them somewhere accessible, for they have 101 uses in the kitchen. Pink vinegar tasting of onion is easily concocted by steeping chive blossoms in white vinegar with or without a few sprigs of tarragon or lovage for extra flavour. Besides regular snipping for flavouring, we give the chive clumps an annual close haircut after the flowers are past to encourage the growth of a new crop of leaves.

Very decorative in a mass, in sun or light shade, are garlic chives (*Allium tuberosum*). Their leaves are flat, narrow, arching and distinctly garlicky in scent and flavour, and the plant hoists countless loose, white umbels on swaying, foot-high stalks in late summer. I have a note in my garden book to set clumps of garlic chives in front of a drift of *Sedum spectabile*, the showy stonecrop; the two always bloom together and both are very attractive to nectar-hungry butterflies, perhaps fuelling up for a trip south. Garlic chives are every bit as useful in the kitchen as regular chives, and as easily grown from divisions, starter plants or seeds. We snip off faded flower heads before the

In British Columbia one may take advantage of the enormous selection of vegetable cultivars and varieties that are available to a gardener with a bright, warm place suitable for growing plants from seed. If any plant is to be grown in quantity, starting it from seed represents the least expensive option.

seed ripens to avoid forever rooting out stripling garlics.

Unlike the onions, rue (*Ruta graveolens*) is an acquired taste, certainly an acquired smell, and probably an acquired appreciation as a garden plant. It is one of the herbs that is not useful in the kitchen, nor do the small, greenish yellow flowers make any show at all. But there is an aura of mystery hanging about the plant. Perhaps it is the wealth of lore lauding the plant's healing virtues, specifically against the plague, or its mythical ability to ward off the evil eye, or simply the bitter pungency of the crushed leaves — the evocative fragrance that took me back to Mrs. Rice's long-ago garden.

For me, lavender (*Lavandula angustifolia*), too, carries the scent of

Jennifer Bennett

69

City gardeners, first candidates for an edible landscape, can do no better for on-site instruction than to wander by Chinese or Italian neighbourhoods. In his small Montreal backyard, Italian-Canadian gardener Raphael Cristofaro grows a lush vegetable and herb garden, complete with flowers and a grapevine.

nostalgia. I was always slightly sickened at fall fairs by the heavy smell hanging in the air like smog around vendors of lavender-filled wicker baubles for tossing into drawers or hanging in cars. I can only guess that someone had been far too free with the lavender oil or, more likely, that the fragrance had nothing at all to do with herbs and flowers, and everything to do with chemical concocting. Only the fake strawberry essence was more cloying. But now that I have grown lavender in the garden, I can understand why, with its clean, invigorating odour, it has long been considered the best of the "nose-herbs" (a "nosegay" was, incidentally, a bouquet chosen for its pleasant scents, capable of making the nose gay). I like to mark the pages of favourite books with slender spikes of lavender, and be surprised some late winter by a sudden sweet breath of summer.

In most Northern gardens, except those on the west coast, lavender does not attain the great height and purple profusion that it does in England or its native Mediterranean home. Here, it usually grows only 1 to 2 feet high. But I know one central Ontario garden, as cold and clay-bound as any, where the hardy dwarf *Munstead* lavender, child of Gertrude Jekyll's Munstead Wood garden in England, edges a bed of roses and lilies, and sends up countless scented spikes over a long season, the 40 or 50 plants all raised from a single pack of seed. And in a small-town nursery near us, there grows an enormous bush of lavender; the tireless woman who tends to the job of plant propagation calls it "my mother-plant" and each year roots hundreds of cuttings to sell.

All this may give a clue to the secrets of growing lavender in the North. Choose a hardy cultivar started from seeds or locally grown plants. Seeds take

Harold Rosenberg

about a month to germinate, and the seedlings will require winter protection the first year. Trim all lavender plants back at least halfway after the flowers are faded, or as spikes are forming, if you want them for drying. Compact plants winter well with a loose covering of straw or evergreen boughs laid down in early December. Sun and good drainage are other essentials. When the old-fashioned roses bloom above the modest grey-leaved lavender, I inhale deeply and know that the bit of extra work involved in growing healthy, bushy lavender is rewarded many times over.

Leaving almost the best till last, one herb we must include is *Monarda didyma*, known as bergamot, Oswego tea, monarda or bee balm and familiar to many as the flowery aroma that pervades Earl Grey tea. A well-grown, 3-foot-tall clump of red bergamot or the softer *Croftway Pink* alive with hummingbirds is a lovely sight all on its own, but add a cloud of baby's breath in front, a few creamy or wine-dark lilies nearby and the reaching sky-coloured spires of delphiniums behind, and you have a picture to satisfy a garden's soul, a glimpse to be stored in your memory for the snow-bound season.

Bergamot is amiable enough, quite willing to produce its crowns of glowing flowers, but it has a few very specific requests: organically rich ground that will not dry out (or the plant will lose its lower leaves); elbow room, and a free circulation of air (otherwise it will become lanky and mildewed); division first thing in spring, every three years or so (otherwise it spreads, mint-like, into a choked mat of weak shoots). Division is exceedingly easy — all the roots are close to the surface — but one must ruthlessly toss the spent and woody centre of the clump, and retain three- or

five-shoot divisions from the outside as new plants, a rule that applies to all spreading perennials. One plant is a fine specimen where the sun catches it for at least six hours and where there is room for its dominating height; three or four make a fine drift in a mixed border. Thus considered, bergamot will be the jewel of the July garden, and its leaves will make many a cup of fragrant tea.

Of the hardy perennial herbs that I know and grow, the foregoing are among the best for consideration as permanent fixtures in the landscape; all are able to hold their own beautifully, and provide quiet contrast among more showy things. There are other herbs, of course, that clamour for inclusion: tarragon, for instance, is indispensable in the kitchen, but one of the dullest plants I have ever laid eyes on — stringy, muted green, with no beauty of form, flower or colour. It has a corner to itself in the vegetable garden.

ANNUAL & BIENNIAL HERBS

Among the ranks of annual herbs are two of the best tastes of summer — basil (*Ocimum* spp) first and summer savory (*Satureja hortensis*) a close second. Several seasons ago, we began to grow annual herbs, these two as well as marjoram and a few scented geraniums, in wooden half-barrels or very large (18-inch) clay pots of light loam, as a simple expedient to outwit voracious earwigs at ground level. The result was so aesthetically pleasing that the "herb barrels" have become permanent and prominent features in the landscape. If an apartment balcony or a sunny city patio and several earth-filled half-barrels were my total lot of land, I would grow all the herbs I needed for summer seasoning, with plenty to spare to dry or freeze for winter use. One barrel would

hold annuals, the other a plant of lovage and perhaps tarragon, chives, tumbling winter savory or lemon thyme.

Among the basils, there are lettuce-leaved types, some with tiny leaves, and the regular bush-type, foot-tall plants, either green or purple. There are also species with different scents, such as camphor basil, lemon basil and cinnamon basil. All can be attractively nestled amongst flowers or other herbs, lend themselves to all kinds of culinary uses, and can be easily dried for winter use. Grow them from seed planted indoors or directly in the garden, or buy transplants. Summer savory, which grows as high as 18 inches and has narrower, darker green foliage than winter savory, can also be grown from seeds or transplants, and is easily situated in a sunny location among annual flowers or along a border.

VEGETABLES

When is a vegetable more than just a vegetable? When it supplies the table with goodness *and* fills out the lines of a landscape with sparkling greenery. Almost all vegetables are good to look at,

but not all are suitable landscape subjects. Leeks, for instance, grow wide, arching grey foliage that would be the envy of many an ornamental, but their culture involves digging trenches and hilling soil around the growing plants, earthworks that are far too disruptive and just plain messy in an orderly piece of ground. In the food garden, of course, they may be placed to good aesthetic advantage – perhaps as a grey edge to a row of raspberries. On the other hand, regular cooking or Spanish onions – sets or seedlings – can be planted among annual flowers for attractive tall green spears of foliage that will remain until late summer, when they flop over and the bulbs are ready to harvest. Just be sure to give them enough space – about 3 inches around each onion – so that their bulbs can expand fully.

What we need for landscaping are vegetables that:
• stay put all season – this rules out peas that are mildewed and shrivelled by midsummer, however ornamental they may be in early stages
• do not sprawl and swallow up everything in sight – winter squash and pumpkins are *verboten* unless you want

to train the vines to cover a sturdy trellis
• are relatively disease- and insect-free – members of the cabbage family, save kale, are far too buggy for dependable use in landscaping
• have interesting and enduring foliage

Most will be annuals; they will have to be replanted every spring. Only rhubarb, whose huge, dark green leaves can soften the conversion from shrubs or trees to ground covers during spring and fall, and which needs about 2 feet of space all around each plant, and asparagus, whose 4- to 6-foot-tall ferny foliage is prized by florists, are dependable landscape perennial vegetables. Plant asparagus crowns at the back of a bed or against a wall, and fertilize them well. Remember, after harvesting shoots in spring, to leave several shoots on each plant to grow into graceful ferns, the plant's method of storing food for another year.

Green peppers display their true perennial nature when grown in pots taken indoors before the first fall frost. Pots, the bigger the better, filled with rich, light soil and kept diligently watered, can be used for almost all relatively small vegetables, making it possible to move them from sunny space to sunny space throughout the day or from porch to patio to take advantage of a summer rain. Pot-grown herbs and ornamentals, too, have a long landscaping tradition.

ANNUAL VEGETABLES

The first of the annual vegetables that suits the landscaping criteria is Swiss chard (*Beta vulgaris*), a foot-tall, leafy form of beet that may be sown very early outdoors and soon grows to presentable size. Its glossy leaves and striking white or red ribs and veins are very decorative and remain in good shape until well past the first fall frost.

The harvest may last up to four months without diminishing the crop, if a leaf or two are removed from the outside of each plant and the centres are left to grow. And – a prime consideration – simple, steamed chard, buttered and salted, is the most delicate and delicious of greens. Swiss chard grows in sun or part shade and likes a rich, loamy soil of neutral pH for best development.

Red-veined *Ruby* chard is highly touted as an ornamental vegetable, but I would rather see the shorter, red-veined beet foliage and be able to harvest both roots and tops. For landscaping, *Winter Keeper* beets are a good choice; the roots stay in place until late fall, so there are no gaps left in the bed or border until the very last. The large beetroots store for months and are sweet winter eating. *Burpee's Golden* beet, whose foliage is veined yellow rather than red, is an interesting colour alternative.

Carrots (*Daucus carota*) will fringe a flowerbed with feathery greens about a foot tall. Again, look for long-season or storage types, rather than baby carrots to get maximum food and landscaping value. The related parsley (*Petroselinum crispum*) is often grown as a moss-green edging for flowers, herbs or vegetables. The standard curly parsley, which produces a bush of greenery about a foot tall is the most attractive, while the plain-leaved or Italian parsley, which has celery-like stems and foliage about the same height as curly parsley, is more tender and tasty. The dual-purpose *Hamburg* parsley has flat, flavourful leaves above, and parsnip-shaped roots below that are good in soup.

The leaves of lettuce (*Lactuca sativa*) may be wavy, fringed or crimped (leaf lettuces), softly folded (butterheads or Bibbs), or crisply upright (cos or romaine), from all shades of green to coppery-red. Each year we plant several

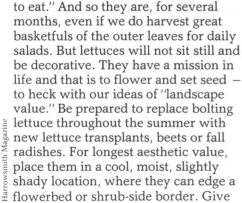

rows of alternating green and red lettuces in the vegetable garden; each year we secretly think, and visitors declare, that lettuce rows are "too pretty to eat." And so they are, for several months, even if we do harvest great basketfuls of the outer leaves for daily salads. But lettuces will not sit still and be decorative. They have a mission in life and that is to flower and set seed — to heck with our ideas of "landscape value." Be prepared to replace bolting lettuce throughout the summer with new lettuce transplants, beets or fall radishes. For longest aesthetic value, place them in a cool, moist, slightly shady location, where they can edge a flowerbed or shrub-side border. Give

each a full foot of space to fill out and show its true colours. And skip the head lettuce, neither as attractive nor as tasty as its leafier kin.

If you are intent on growing as much food as possible while maintaining a landscaped look, consider replacing the more usual petunias and geraniums (yawn) in that sunny strip of ground between front porch and front lawn with peppers, eggplants and bush beans. All are surprisingly pretty, bushy plants. The occasional potato, too, will produce an attractive bushy plant about 2 feet tall — but leave it enough space so that you can dig down and harvest the potatoes in fall without uprooting ground covers or flowers. Widen the

strip to 3 or 4 feet, send *Scarlet Runner* pole beans, climbing (not bush) cucumbers and *Sweet 100* cherry tomatoes, pruned to three lanky stems each, up netting, wire mesh or sturdy strings attached to the porch, and you may sit like a sultan in the privacy of your screened and shaded verandah, plucking a glistening red globe or cool cuke on a sultry summer evening. While cucumbers and beans will hang onto the supports by themselves, the tomatoes will need to be tied at intervals.

The sweet corn Gertrude Jekyll grew at the back of a flowerbed may have been arresting to contemplate, but gardeners who wish to follow her example should realize that corn is wind pollinated and thus must be planted in patches of several plants, each of which has about 6 inches of free space all around. Fewer plants than about 10 and you risk picking no cobs at all. Corn needs rich soil, but, in rich or poor soil, it will attract raccoons and squirrels intent on harvesting the cobs before the gardener.

Zucchini and summer squashes are also demanding of space, growing about 4 feet tall and at least as wide. If there is enough room, zucchini bushes are handsome enough to stand on either side of the front steps where their large, scalloped leaves can be impressive. Edge the strip with lettuce, parsley and basil, and you have all the makings of delicious salads as good to look at as the bed in which they grew.

Along with his colleague John Scanlan, Patrick Lima has worked for 12 years to create ''a thriving organic garden of fruits and vegetables, flowers and herbs, shrubs and trees'' on Ontario's Bruce Peninsula. This garden, which supports its owners, is, they say, ''a balance of beauty and utility that reflects our deep love of earth, and our commitment to peace.''

Potatoes produce attractive, bushy, occasionally flowering plants about 2 feet tall. The gardener should allow enough space, about a foot around each plant, so that he or she can dig down and harvest the tubers in fall without uprooting surrounding ground covers or flowers.

6 | Leaves of Grass

Cooling the ground and cushioning the feet are the lowliest of landscape plants, the ground covers

By Eva Hoepfner

Another time, another place . . . and another way of looking at landscapes. A photograph taken 70 years ago in Bavaria shows my grandmother lounging on a lawn sprinkled with thousands of tiny, white daisies. The enchanting image transports me to my childhood in Germany, where I spent many hours weaving daisy garlands. That type of flowery lawn is still acceptable in Europe, and yet most North American landowners diligently avoid it. When I allowed violets to brighten a lawn in Toronto some years ago, friends expressed admiration for the purple profusion, but my neighbour did not share the pleasure. For a couple of years he cast anxious glances over the fence until he finally sank root-enclosing metal strips along his property line, literally defining both his space and his taste in ground covers.

"Ground cover" is such a comforting term, sounding like "round" and "lover" and prompting visions of a green blanket hugging the earth. Indeed, nature's living carpet knows little restraint. Wherever soil and water meet sun, diverse plants creep into rocky nooks, push against arctic ice and venture to the edge of the sea. Ferns, vines and leafy herbs feed and shelter wildlife; grass and velvety mosses cool the ground and cushion the feet; shrubs bind soil and capture water. In nature, ground covers scent the air and mark the seasons with a gorgeous array of twig, leaf, flower and fruit. Nature must truly love filling a vacuum to create such profusion.

With a little selective taming, the bounty of the wild is easily transferred to the home landscape. Any plant, native or exotic, deciduous or evergreen, moss or shrub or even tree can serve as ground cover if its leaves are dense enough to suppress weeds throughout the growing season. Shrubs will stabilize a crumbling bank, vines embrace a gentle slope. Ferns can add lacy coolness to a stand of trees or alongside the house, and the cracks between paving stones can be softened by mosses. Perennials will brighten the garden and invite the bees, birds and butterflies. And lawn grasses comfort feet and give rest to tired eyes.

If carefully chosen for the site, all ground covers should be able to look after themselves with little help from the gardener. All, that is, except one. The lawn is an artificial creation unable to survive without man's constant attention. Before you decide to devote large parts of your landscape to turf, consider what is involved in its establishment and maintenance. Observing the landscape development in a new subdivision can be enlightening.

First the land is stripped of all vegetation. If the topsoil has been stripped as well, new soil — often of inferior quality to what was removed and sold — is trucked in and levelled. Peat moss and chemical fertilizers are applied, and the soil is densely seeded. When the grass sprouts, it is mowed to an even inch. Because grass grows from a point just above the roots, it can take a good deal of punishment by having its tops lopped off time and again. However, this does weaken the plants, allowing tough weed seeds to elbow in: short, weak grasses pose little competition in pleasant growing conditions that include plenty of sun, fertile soil and water. Potent herbicides are applied. And the pale, weakened grasses need more fertilizer, which makes them grow vigorously, so they need to be cut down to size, weakening them once more. And so the lawn maintenance cycle begins, a season-by-season fight against nature. A recent press release from the Lawn Institute of

Grass is the best ground cover for areas subject to a lot of foot traffic, but overused, it is time-consuming and expensive to maintain. The spring routine alone may include raking, liming, reseeding, fertilizing, mowing, dethatching and aerification.

Tennessee includes in its recommended spring routine raking, liming, reseeding, fertilizing, mowing, dethatching and aerification.

Although lawn care keeps almost everybody busy, it also keeps many people grumbling. Yet the slavish routine is continued because lawns have less to do with practicality than with keeping up appearances. From its humble beginnings as grazed pasture to its present standard of imitation Astroturf, the lawn has emerged as the single most important status symbol in the landscape. It was imported from class-conscious Britain, where every lord and lady apparently whiled away the hours by tapping wooden balls across lawn-lined estates. Spurred by the desire for prestige, or simply lacking other examples, middle class landowners in North America quickly followed the lead of the wealthy, and lawns proliferated on mini-estates across the continent. Today, suburbia boasts the neat sterility of a green and black sea of turf and tarmac.

Ground covers entered the domestic landscape only about 50 years ago as understudies to the star of the garden, the lawn. (Although the lawn is technically a ground cover, it is still considered by many gardeners as a separate entity.) Where deep shade discouraged grass growth, lawns were replaced with ivy, periwinkle or pachysandra, ground covers that thrived in shade and formed sheets of foliage resembling lawns.

But these lawn look-alikes were soon found to be hardworking, versatile performers that needed no mowing weeding or dethatching. Over the years their self-sufficient, ecologically sound talents became more appreciated. Functionally, they compete with grass. Visually, they unify, wrapping disparate landscape elements like a shawl. They set off flowering plants and define space; they soften architectural elements and provide dramatic effect. Their leaves and flowers add colour, texture, fragrance and movement to the garden. Of interest to the Northern gardener is their value in the winter landscape, where low-growing shrubs can add a tracery of twigs, a sprinkling of red berries or mounds of evergreen boughs to a bleak expanse.

GRASS ROOTS

If you feel you must now follow your conscience and give up grass for pachysandra, wait. There is a middle ground, a compromise which lets you have the advantages of the lawn without investing in the high-cost, high-energy, high-maintenance cycle of contemporary lawn care. For there is no denying it: healthy turf is still the best ground cover for areas subject to a lot of foot traffic. It is resilient, soft and cool. It is unbeatable for roughhousing and picnicking. Even routine lawn maintenance has advantages if a rotary mower is used: the soothing purr of oiled blades, the smell of cut grass. This has become the stuff of

Stephen Errington

nostalgia in the power age, yet it is not something to be quickly dismissed as Luddite stick-your-head-in-the-sand ignorance. First, if you do want an area of lawn, become familiar with the types of grasses available and what they will offer:

Kentucky bluegrass (*Poa pratensis*) is one of the most popular turf selections. It forms a long-lasting lawn and grows rapidly in cool, moist weather. But it also needs irrigation during hot, dry periods and will lose quality unless it receives nitrogen fertilizer. It spreads by rhizome and is somewhat slow to establish. Many cultivars are available, some from as far north as Sweden (*Birka*) and Alaska (*Nugget*), differing greatly in appearance and price.

Perennial rye grass (*Lolium perenne*) sprouts quickly but does not spread and is generally not as hardy or as demanding of nutrients. Improved types, most developed at Rutgers University in New Jersey, are less coarse looking and respond better to mowing than do the earlier types. They are especially valuable on a slope where erosion is likely, or where there will be a great deal of wear and tear.

Fine fescue (*Festuca rubra*) is well adapted to shady, dry, infertile soil. It requires less water and fertilizer than bluegrass, but can suffer in wet, poorly drained soils. Some cultivars do not spread; others such as *Ruby* and *Ensylva* do. Bent grass (*Agrostis* spp) is extremely demanding of care and fertilization and tolerates very low mowing, so that its primary use is on golf courses. It can become weedy in home lawns, crowding out other species.

Tall fescue (*Festuca arundinacea*) is a very coarse-textured, short-lived perennial turfgrass with good tolerance to wear, heat and drought but little cold hardiness.

One of the main problems with lawns is that most are too big to be maintained without the use of power. Trade a big lawn and power mower for a small lawn and rotary mower and you save on fuel, fumes and noise. Unless your lawn serves the local minor baseball league, you probably don't *use* most of the lawn. And if status is unimportant to you, take pleasure in the fine points of a small lawn. Decide where you want to sunbathe and stroll or play and restrict the lawn to those areas. Then raise the cutting level of the mower to at least 2 inches. This will let the grass muster strength to combat weed competition, and it will reduce the amount of water and chemical aids it needs to flourish.

If you are not intimidated by the Joneses, try an old-fashioned lawn-seed mixture that includes clover. Then add some bugle (*Ajuga reptans*), violets, low-creeping Veronica and even wild strawberries for real variation of texture and colour. All these plants will tolerate occasional mowings. You can go even further and try naturalizing spring bulbs in the lawn. In the fall, lift sections of turf, keeping one part attached like a hinge, dig soil pockets underneath the

If carefully chosen for the site, all ground covers should be able to look after themselves with little help from the gardener. Most are not only less demanding than lawn but can fill spaces that would otherwise be difficult to mow.

With their fragrant foliage and variously coloured flowers, many varieties of statice are airy, clump-forming perennials that can fill spaces in a rock garden or flower border.

turf flap, add some organic matter and plant very early bulbs such as crocus, scilla or snowdrops. After they bloom, delay mowing for about two weeks, so that the bulb leaves will have a chance to store some food for next year.

If you have reduced your present lawn to a manageable patch and have a large amount of space left over, consider letting it grow out into a meadow of wildflowers and grasses. When Freek and Ina Vrugtman bought a small abandoned apple orchard near Burlington, Ontario, they decided against the look of closely-cropped turf. Instead, they let the grass grow long, scything it only once a year. Ina introduced drifts of narcissi and snowdrops under some of the trees; in April, the white blossoms beam like pale lights in the taupe landscape. Later in the season, the meadow is painted with violets and wild strawberries, then asters, goldenrod and black-eyed Susans spring up spontaneously. During the summer, a curved path is mowed through the meadow, adding a delightful contrast of cut grass against tall stalks. In fall the entire meadow is cut down to about 6 inches, to prevent large areas of dead, matted thatch in spring. The gardener who is impatient for colour can speed up the process of wildflower growth by using one of the seed mixtures now available in many garden centres. Several mixtures on the market are adapted especially to regional climates. But do check the seed contents: some mixes may contain only annuals unsuited for reseeding in one's climate. The result can be a gloriously colourful display the first year, followed by a drab palette if there are few or no perennials to renew the colour. As well, check the seed mixture with regional noxious weed lists. Sometimes seeds of flowers such as Queen Anne's lace and chicory,

which are considered weeds in some areas, are in the mix. Although these flowers are attractive and one's little plot will probably not greatly increase their pervasiveness, there is no sense in arming a petulant neighbour against you and your beautiful meadow.

If you like, gather your own wildflower seeds from local meadows. You will probably have less colour and more surprises, but the flowers will be more representative of your geographical area — though again, watch for weeds.

One technique for adding wildflowers to a lawn is to rent a dethatcher and run it over the grass several times to lift plugs of turf; then mix the seed with damp sand, scatter it and rake it in hard. In a couple of years the yard should consist of waving grasses along with a gay profusion of such flowers as orange butterfly weeds, black-eyed Susans, asters and goldenrod. Accompanying them will be bees, birds and butterflies.

To plant a wildflower meadow from scratch, proceed as for a new lawn, removing all existing turf and weeds, raking a smooth layer of fertile topsoil over it, avoiding herbicides and adding

organic fertilizer such as manure or compost. Then seed according to the package directions, or use about an ounce of mixed seeds for 250 square feet of soil. Once the meadow is established, you will have to weed out woody seedlings by hand, perhaps leaving some native shrub groups for added interest. Cut the meadow once or twice a year with a portable heavy-duty string trimmer.

SCULPTING WITH GROUND COVERS

Wildflower meadows are not always appropriate: if small, they are ineffectual, and in suburban havens you risk scorn and sometimes even a lawsuit. Ground covers, on the other hand, can enhance any area normally occupied by lawns.

It used to be that only low-growing evergreen carpeters were considered ground covers, but today any plant that provides a weed-proof cover is a candidate for the title. A ground cover is not a particular breed of plant, but rather a general job description: on the moist banks of a large property, a mass of red osier dogwoods several feet tall would be a ground cover; in a small garden, one dogwood would be a specimen shrub. This opens up vast possibilities for designing with ground covers: one can borrow dwarf conifers and creepers from the rockery, herbs and berries from the kitchen garden, shrubs, herbaceous plants, ornamental grasses, ferns, even mosses from the wild. As long as it produces a mass effect that discourages or smothers competing plants, any species can be a ground cover.

Scale, then, is the overriding factor in designing with ground covers and requires that one take a critical look at all the elements in the garden, from the size of the property and house to the size

of the area to be covered. The height of ground covers should be in proportion to adjacent trees, shrubs, or walls. Small gardens appear most restful when planted with low-growing plants of fine texture, yet they are not restricted to these. Taller plants and those with coarse texture can be used sparingly for accent or at a distance from the house. To draw the eye down, graduate the plants from taller at the back to shorter in front, but not slavishly. More natural effects are achieved by planting in casual drifts and letting a taller plant occasionally spill to the front. Neatness and straight edges might spell

respectability, but they are not necessarily synonymous with beauty. Combining plants of various sizes can produce different effects. The tranquillity of a forest floor can be approximated by underplanting a stand of trees with an even mat of periwinkle (*Vinca minor*); yet those same trees can be given a lively forest-edge effect if planted with a front of mixed shrubs and herbaceous plants.

Mixing ground covers in one area is contrary to conventional planting schemes, which stress segregation — a

Bugle, Veronica, wild strawberries or violets (left) will add colour to a lawn while tolerating occasional mowings. Most ground covers, such as starry campanulas (right), are best allowed to flourish without competition.

common example is the kidney-shaped island of Japanese spurge or pachysandra (*Pachysandra terminalis*) floating on a sea of turf, an effect both static and two-dimensional. By combining different species of plants, however, one can turn a plain sheet of greenery into a dynamic sculpture.

Combining ground covers for happy coexistence is a challenge to be met with daring, imagination and experimentation. Ground covers exist in an almost infinite variety of form, texture and colour of leaf and flower, and all characteristics should be considered for best effect. If this challenge intimidates, a gardener should start with a couple of species and add more as his or her knowledge of plants and property increases. For drama, contrast large-leaved plants such as

rhododendrons, where they are hardy, with small-leaved pachistima (*Pachistima canbyi*). If plants of similar leaf size are used, subtle shadings of leaf colour can add interest; for instance, dark green yews (*Taxus* spp) can be planted alongside blue junipers (*Juniperus* spp). Or juxtapose plants with contrasting form, like billowing lady's mantle (*Alchemilla mollis*) with upward thrusting ferns. Contrasting textures can be particularly interesting if plants of similar colours are mixed — for a sunny slope, nestle downy lamb's ears (*Stachys olympica*), silver pussytoes (*Antennaria* spp) and dusty catmint (*Nepeta* × *faassenni*) among pincushions of blue fescue (*Festuca glauca*).

Because ground covers are often vigorous multipliers, one should pay attention to the growth habits of the

plants. If two strong carpeters of similar height are pitted against each other, ajuga and periwinkle, for example, one plant will probably squeeze out the other. The gardener can make a sport of watching the fight, or can combine plants of different habits: carpeters, plants which increase via rooting stems, will usually defer to broad shrubs or to clump formers, which grow in spring from winter buds or rosettes that have overwintered. To be on the safe side, separate creepers by a buffer zone of taller, dense shrubs. There are few pat rules for designing with such a wealth of material. Books can help, but observing what grows in gardens, in the woods or along a country road is still the best inspiration for any gardener.

MATTER OVER MIND

Once a gardener has chosen the ground cover effect for a certain landscape, it is time to select plants whose needs match the site conditions — the soil, sun and wind exposure and moisture content. A list of ground covers, which outlines their requirements, heights and hardiness, appears in Appendix B. The ground covers must thrive if they are to prevent weed invasion: *Sedum* species will cover beautifully in areas of full sun but will languish in shade. Steep slopes demand plants with extensive root systems if they are to stabilize the soil. Shrubs such as broom (*Cytisus* spp), dogwoods (*Cornus* spp), junipers and cotoneasters have roots that will descend farther into the ground than herbaceous perennials or surface-rooting plants like ivy or Virginia creeper (*Parthenocissus* spp). Save those for gentle banks or flat areas.

Be selective, too, about the growth habit of the plants. In a sense, scale applies not only to the size of the plant and garden, but also to the area the plant will cover within a period of time. Rapid spreaders will quickly cover a small area and then devour the rest of the garden with gusto. Such invasiveness can be an advantage if plenty of ground must be covered, but maintain a long-range view if the plants are to stay within limits. Many rapid growers such as ajuga and lady's mantle can be easily removed if they overreach their bounds; others, particularly those with tough underground runners or suckers, are more tenacious — use goutweed (*Aegopodium podagraria*), crown vetch (*Coronilla varia*), Chinese lantern (*Physalis alkekengi*) and Hall's honeysuckle (*Lonicera japonica halliana*) with care.

On the other hand, many choice ground covers such as dwarf conifers are slow growers and thus often expensive. One can space them closely together for faster cover, or, in the interest of economy, interplant them with rapid growers, which will smother weeds until the desired ground covers mature. Self-seeding annuals and biennials such as sweet alyssum (*Alyssum* spp), portulaca and forget-me-nots (*Myosotis alpestris*) work well in a sunny spot and disappear when the desired ground cover shades them out. In shade, where few annuals thrive, rapidly growing but easily removed perennials such as cranesbill (*Geranium* spp) can serve as living mulch. A little homework matching temporary with permanent ground covers can save the gardener a bundle when planting larger areas.

THE BIG CHILL

Sometimes, however, doing one's homework can have drawbacks. I am often seduced by photographs of picture-perfect gardens, and if the plants fall barely within (or barely outside of) my climatic zone, I sometimes ignore

common sense and send my money off to distant suppliers who ask no questions. Occasionally I believe I have succeeded in introducing a new plant to the neighbourhood for all to see and covet: my flowering dogwood put on a magnificent show — for one year. The next three winters were harsh, so the tree leafed out but did not produce blossoms. Don't set your heart too firmly on a plant that sits on the warmer side of your climatic borderline. On the other hand, don't be afraid to experiment. But start small — prepare a trial for a year or two before investing in an acre of plants. Serious climatic zone experiments are not conducted everywhere, and you just might be heir to a miniclimate that can support the object of your infatuation.

Gardeners in difficult climates can always look to nature for help if nurseries offer a limited choice. Native plants have evolved genetically to withstand the rigours of the climate, and they self-perpetuate freely, unlike many imported plants that reproduce only vegetatively. For cold, dry areas, a tried-and-true native commercially available is pussytoes (*Antennaria*) — a diminutive grey-leaved plant topped with stalks of rosy or white flowers. Also very hardy is evergreen bearberry (*Arctostaphylos uva-ursi*), a native plant that thrives on a starvation diet of sand if exposed to full sun. It is prized for its even mat of shiny evergreen leaves, pink flowers and red berries loved by wildlife. The main problem seems to be availability, since the plant is difficult to propagate and must be dug while the ground is frozen. In less severe zones, choice ground covers native to woodlands are ferns, violets, foam flower (*Tiarella cordifolia*), wild ginger (*Asarum canadense*), partridgeberry (*Mitchella repens*), Solomon's seal (*Polygonatum* spp) and false lily of the valley (*Maianthemum canadense*). If balmy Pacific mists spray your garden, allow Oregon grape (*Mahonia aquifolium*) or salal (*Gaultheria shallon*) to cover the ground for you. You can even stop liming the lawn and encourage an undulating carpet of mosses or accent it with dwarf conifers, azaleas and ferns for a stunning, low-maintenance garden.

Less frequently considered, but not unimportant, are utilitarian and edible qualities of ground covers. Many native (and indeed non-native) ground covers perform such dual functions — among the natives fiddleheads (*Matteuccia struthiopteris*), strawberries, salal, bayberry (*Myrica* spp), may apple (*Podophyllum peltatum*), Oregon (or wild) grape and wild roses can be more than pretty additions to the garden. Add to them thyme, chamomile, oregano,

Ontario Ministry of Agriculture and Food

Crown vetch is a rapid spreader that must be situated with care and then kept under control, but such invasiveness can be an advantage if plenty of ground must be covered in a relatively short time.

everbearing alpine strawberries and even day lilies for a delectable stew.

For some reason, plants which are praised to heaven in certain areas, and which are listed as very hardy are seldom seen in Canada and the northern United States. *Epimedium*, for example, is one of the few plant species that tolerates dry shade. Its tissue-paper leaves unfurl pink, then green up for summer and blush crimson in fall. In the the spring it sends up dainty blossoms of pink, yellow and lavender. Less hardy, but closely related is the exquisitely delicate *Vancouveria*, a North American native. Lady's mantle (*Alchemilla mollis*) is greatly valued overseas and in parts of the United States, and although it is supposed to be hardy to zone 4, it rarely appears in the North. Its velvety grey-green leaves catch silver raindrops, and the sprays of sulphur-yellow blossoms last well as cut flowers. They grow quickly, cover well, yet are easily contained and removed if desired.

Hardy geraniums puff up in no time into fluffy pillows of pink, mauve or magenta bloom. They tolerate sun and shade and are easily contained. Similarly, cinquefoil (*Potentilla* spp) will bloom in hues from cream through yellow to red for an extended season while producing small, neat shrubs. Many bamboos and ornamental grasses add exotic notes to a garden. They make very effective ground covers requiring almost no maintenance. Used alone or in conjunction with broad-leaved plants, grasses add an unmatched grace with their fine texture. Some species are highly invasive, spreading by rhizomes, but many reproduce only by clumping, gradually spreading over a larger area.

PLANT PROPAGATION

There seems no limit to the number of fine plants useful as ground covers. Match the diversity of plants with imagination and daring, and the possibilities for covering the ground become infinite. The ubiquitous ivy, periwinkle and pachysandra may suit your site, but overuse can detract from their abundant virtues. Don't hesitate to experiment. A chic Toronto restaurant is landscaped with a ground cover of neatly contained horsetails (*Equisetum hyemale*). When such a smorgasbord of plants can be obtained, it seems a shame to stick to porridge.

Ground covers may be expensive to install at one fell swoop, but gardeners who don't want to spend a lot of money to cover the ground don't have to. Most of the plants are easily propagated vegetatively or started from seed. The easiest methods are division and layering. Clump formers like *Bergenia*, day lilies and lamb's ears are easily divided. Fork up a clump and gently pull the plants apart. Plants such as ivy, ajuga and wild strawberry, which spread by runners, can be propagated in much the same way. Some surface runners need a little help — euonymus and broom, for example: scrape the underside of a low branch, secure it to the ground with a forked stick, and cover with soil. When the low branch has rooted, snip it so that the roots are retained with the cutting, and replant it where needed. Keep it watered until it begins to grow.

Stem cuttings are often the best way to propagate woody plants such as heather and cotoneaster. Immediately below a leaf node, take a section of tip growth 1 to 3 inches long, remove the lower leaves, dip the base of each cutting in rooting hormone powder and start it in a mixture of sharp sand and peat moss. Keep it evenly moist and, if possible, warm, encased in a plastic bag until it roots.

Starting some ground covers from seed can be simple, too. Pinks (*Dianthus* spp), primulas, perennial candytuft (*Iberis sempervirens*), coral bells (*Heuchera* spp) and even day lilies (*Hemerocallis* spp) will germinate without much fuss. Most will not bloom the first year, but a year's wait is often worth the money saved.

STEM CUTTING WOODY PLANTS

IMMEDIATELY BELOW A LEAF NODE TAKE A 1"-3" SECTION OF TIP GROWTH

Start these seeds indoors or in a nursery bed, and transplant them to the permanent site after the first season. (See Appendix E for seed sources.)

Although ground covers are often shallow-rooted and hence easily moved,

CUTTINGS SHOULD BE KEPT MOIST AND WARM ENCASED IN A PLASTIC BAG

planting beds should be regarded as permanent features in the landscape. The ground should be well prepared to maintain a thriving plant population for some time. The gardener who decides to replace lawn with ground covers faces the back-breaking task of sod lifting. For large areas, or for a speedy job, rent a sod-cutter to lift most of the lawn. Unfortunately, this method still leaves behind many pieces of underground stems or rhizomes, which must be removed by hand. Twitch grass rhizomes left in place can quickly regenerate an entire plant. Sod cutting also removes much of the topsoil nutrient content, which will have to be replaced by other means.

An easier method, but one which might try the gardener's patience, is to cover the grass with newspaper about ten sheets thick, weighted down with wood chips, soil or stones. Three to six months later, the grass should have suffocated — dig down to make sure before replanting — and enterprising earthworms and microorganisms will have added newsprint nutrients and lawn humus to the soil.

Once the soil is free of weeds — rake through it several times and pick out all perennial weeds — prepare it as you would for any shrub or perennial. In average soil conditions, dig down a spade's depth, incorporating plenty of organic matter — compost, rotted manure, peat moss and bone meal. Most ground covers require good drainage, so if the subsoil is heavy or compacted, loosen it by forking in sand and peat moss. Dig generous holes and plant the ground cover in staggered rows, spacing the individual plants according to their eventual spread. Vigorous herbaceous plants should be allowed 4 inches to a foot of space all around, while shrubs should have 2 feet. Water well and then apply an organic mulch of wood chips, straw, leaves or compost. Keep the area well watered for the first couple of years, or until the plants are established. Hand weed as required.

Slopes should be disturbed as little as possible in planting. Dig pockets into the slope, add organic matter, and then centre the plant in a slight depression that will act as a catch basin for water. Stabilize steep banks by building miniature terraces with rocks or planks set on edge and secured with spikes.

MAINTENANCE

Once the plants become established, little maintenance should be required. Pulling the odd weed and watering during dry spells is usually all that is necessary. It is wise to install barriers to keep spreaders within bounds — paving or wood or metal edging that extends about 6 inches into the soil is effective. Clip the plants for a neat edge, or let the stems spill wantonly over paths. An occasional shearing and pruning will plump up many plants by encouraging side shoots — some such as ivy and ajuga can even be topped by a rotary mower. In the autumn, let leaves lie where they fall, unless there is an excessive build-up; in this case remove the bulk of the litter, leaving some to enrich the soil. Fertilizing is generally unnecessary, although a spring dressing of compost or manure does no harm (except for plants on lean diets, such as bearberry, which need nothing).

Before long, you may find yourself stripping away more and more turf to bring the understudies out of the wings. There is no need to segregate them — let them dance in mixed company, blurring artificial borders between grass and ground cover, shrubbery and flowerbed. Allow the house to rest comfortably on a

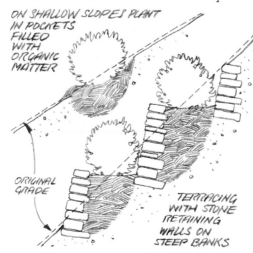

ON SHALLOW SLOPES PLANT IN POCKETS FILLED WITH ORGANIC MATTER

ORIGINAL GRADE

TERRACING WITH STONE RETAINING WALLS ON STEEP BANKS

verdant cushion. You will be amazed how luxuriant your garden can be.

An extensive list of ground covers suitable for Northern gardens can be found in Appendix B, page 153.

Disturb a slope as little as possible in planting it. Dig pockets into a gentle slope, add organic matter, and then centre the plants in a slight depression. Steeper slopes should be terraced with rocks or secured planks before the ground covers are planted in the newly created beds.

With a background of studies in Art History, Eva Hoepfner, who was raised in Vancouver and "transplanted to Toronto," now describes herself as "not a lawn worshipper. I risked altering the suburban streetscape by killing all the turf in the front yard and substituting an organic mix of fruit, vegetables, native and exotic ornamentals. The challenge to make it visually coherent continues . . ."

7 | Flora and Fondness

Flowers bring fleeting colour and fragrance to the landscape

By Patrick Lima

I know a gardener, impatient soul, who is not willing to wait for winter's final surrender and removes the old malingerer bodily from the garden. Muttering, "Enough, enough, and it's April," he attacks the soggy snowdrifts clogging the garden paths and heaves snow by the spadeful over the garden fence. Mothlike, he makes a few holes in the cloth of winter. I suspect that he is lusting after a glimpse of dark earth; and indeed, around the edges of his snow burrows, where sun strikes bare ground, there is an encouraging drip, drip, a steady receding and, miraculously, a spark of colour.

But the simultaneous appearance of colour in our own Ontario garden is even more miraculous, because here, there is still snow. In many gardens, the familiar fat Dutch crocus heralds spring, but there are other flowers that will greet the new season weeks earlier. From spring thaw until snowfall, as nature moves through her tantalizing dance, two steps forward, one step back, our Bruce Peninsula landscape presents John Scanlan and me with a changing pattern of perennial and annual flowers. The schedule of their appearance will vary in other gardens — in warmer areas, they will bloom sooner, in cooler ones, later or perhaps not at all — but the order of their appearance remains constant across the reasonably temperate zones of the continent.

MARCH, APRIL, MAY

First to bloom in our garden, often through the last veil of snow, are wild relatives of the Dutch crocus, dauntless species native to the flanks of the world's mountain ranges. *Crocus ancyrensis* is a tiny, orange star, always earliest of all, opening impatiently just as soon as "winter's icy grip" is relaxed; several dozen bulbs will, in a few years, form a small, brilliant patch of colour warm enough to thaw our own winter-bound senses. Following soon after are such cultivars of *C. chrysanthus* as *Cream Beauty*, *Ladykiller*, *Snow Bunting*, *Blue Pearl*, *Zwanenburg Bronze* and others.

We have come to expect the crocus in earliest spring, but an iris at this season is a distinct and welcome surprise. Two small, jewel-like species colour the cold landscape of March and April. Always first is *Iris danfordiae*, a diminutive Turkish mountaineer, cool yellow flecked with green, sweetly scented and all of 5 inches tall. Shortly, *I. reticulata* and its few hybrid forms appear.

Most first-blooming garden flowers hail from the world's high places — snowy, windswept slopes in winter, sparkling briefly under a short-lived summer sun. The "wild" tulips are no exception. Of extraordinary beauty in sunny places in the landscape, where they will not be swamped or hacked by hoe and trowel, are several species of the genus *Tulipa*, wildflowers from Central Asia that are very much at home in our Northern gardens. Although they are true tulips, they may not be recognized as kin to the stately flowers we know so well. The earliest, and my own favourite, is *Tulipa kaufmanniana*, whose red-flashed, pale yellow petals open nearly flat to catch the sun, giving rise to its common name, the waterlily tulip. If this tulip is interplanted with *Chionodoxa luciliae*, glory-of-the-snow, on a rock garden plane or along a border edge, the result will be a beautiful early picture: the two invariably bloom together, the cream tulip cups above a sea of blue. *Chionodoxa* is a flowering bulb that seeds freely to create ever-widening pools of spring colour.

On the heels of the waterlily tulip comes the subtly coloured and

multiflowered *Tulipa turkestanica*. Above slender leaves rise stems carrying 6 to 12 olive and ivory flowers, enlivened by bronzy stamens. Another small sun lover is *T. tarda*, never happier than when snuggled at the base of a south-facing rock; here, the white-tipped, yellow flowers expand into great starry sheets. The tiny "onions" that spring up around the parent bulbs indicate that this highland dweller has settled down to seeding, a sure sign of contentment. Nor would I want to be without *T. pulchella*, whose pink stars on 3-inch stems shine above a mat of creeping thyme; or *T. clusiana*, the lady tulip with its slender, pointed white-and-crimson dark-centred blossoms. We grow the latter near a bush of *Daphne cneorum*, which is a dwarf evergreen crowded with brilliant pink, intensely fragrant blooms. If you chance upon the *Daphne* in a nursery, do not begrudge the rather steep price that will be attached to the bushling. *D. cneorum*, the garland flower, is sweet, friendly, enduring and without peer for a sunny place among rocks or fronting evergreens in a foundation planting beneath a window, where you will catch the keen spring scent.

As the earliest flowers fade, Dutch crocuses — purple, lavender, gold and white — begin to expand in the warming sun. These adaptable corms are content to grow in any well-drained, sunny or lightly shaded place — rock garden, border edge, thin grass (though they will not multiply as freely here) or beneath shrubs that the sun penetrates.

These early flowers deserve to be more generally known and grown, especially in city gardens where space is limited. There are simple ways to provide these first visitors with comfortable garden quarters: large rocks — limestone is a nourishing "soft rock" — sunk halfway into the ground

John Scanlan

and arranged in natural-looking outcroppings and ledges afford both protection from chilly spring winds and a perfect setting for the mountain natives. Even three or four rocks grouped together in a sheltered place, perhaps on a sunny side of the house or on the lee side of shrubs or evergreens, and planted around with small early bulbs, will create a sparkling, vernal picture.

Now the tulips and daffodils begin to bloom. And while I cannot imagine the garden without a few clumps of flaring tulips, for most garden purposes, I think daffodils or narcissi are more satisfying to grow. They are not just yellow, nor do they all bloom at once. I have planted a glowing bouquet for an extended season of bloom along with diversity of type and colour.

A striking but seldom seen plant to accompany the narcissus is the crown imperial, grandly named *Fritillaria imperialis maxima*. Looking every bit the Persian native it is, the crown imperial pushes an impressive "nose" through the cool earth, accomplishes 3½ feet of leafy growth in a month and displays large, burnished orange bells topped with a crown of foliage. Deep in the flowers are five conspicuous pearls of glistening nectar.

Every garden grows a few tulips, generally the May-flowering *Darwin* and cottage types familiar as the bold and regimented decorations in public parks. In the home garden, tulips may be allowed to break rank and gather in casual drifts of nine or a dozen in the company of such plants as the old-fashioned and very graceful bleeding heart (*Dicentra spectabilis*). This genteel relative of the woodland wildflower, Dutchman's breeches, sends up arching wands hung with intricately fashioned pink hearts; it blooms for an extended

period and is as happy in flickering shadows as sun — one of late spring's choicest gifts. If a flowering crab is somewhere in the picture, so much the better.

The placement of daffodils and tulips in the landscape is often problematic. While we welcome the exuberant first growth and flowering, we may not be willing to give garden space to what soon becomes a patch of flopping, yellowing foliage. A workable solution is to plant the larger spring bulbs in the neighbourhood of some late-rising but ultimately spready perennials. All our peonies, for instance, have attendant groups of daffodils nearby (but not pressing close to the peony crown). When the bulbs are in full bloom, peony shoots are showing as brilliant crimson and beginning to unfurl; then, as the bulb foliage starts to wither, nourishing next year's flowering, the leaves of the peonies grow up and out like a concealing umbrella. Other plants of later-flowering, persistent foliage and

spreading habit suited to masking departing spring bulbs include cultivars of *Hosta*, which are broad-leaved plants suited to flickering shade and moist soils; day lilies (*Hemerocallis* spp) in wide variety; baby's-breath (*Gypsophila* spp); phlox; loosestrife (*Lysimachia* spp); Siberian iris (*I. sibirica*); yarrow (*Achillea* spp); rue (*Ruta graveolens*); wormwood (*Artemisia absinthium*); and hyssop (*Hyssopus officinalis*).

I cannot bid the early season farewell without mention of the primroses. When we first moved to rural Ontario, we were heartened to see masses of tall white lilacs enduring by the crumbling stone foundation of the former farmhouse. The easterly side of these shrubs is one of the few shady places in the garden. "Perfect for primroses," we thought, and filed the idea under things-to-do when the vegetable garden was well established and the house had progressed to the livable stage. Some years later, a 4-foot border, heavily enriched with old manure — the delicate

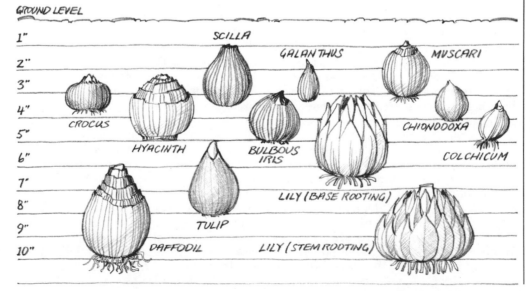

GROUND LEVEL

1"
2"
3"
4"
5"
6"
7"
8"
9"
10"

CROCUS HYACINTH DAFFODIL TULIP SCILLA GALANTHUS BULBOUS IRIS LILY (STEM ROOTING) LILY (BASE ROOTING) MUSCARI CHIONODOXA COLCHICUM

Tulips, daffodils or narcissus, lilies, crocuses and many other flowering bulbs are planted in fall. Although this diagram indicates depth rather than spacing, many species can indeed accompany one another in fairly close company to create a colourful spring of constantly changing bloom such as that described by the author.

87

An instructive approach to landscaping with perennials is to think in terms of seasons of bloom and pictorial associations. In summer, a perennial border in Summerland, British Columbia, presents a picture that includes scores of different plants such as carnations, pinks, chrysanthemums and Shasta daisies.

primrose has a big appetite — follows the broadly curving outline of the lilacs and sparkles in May, a many-hued ribbon of polyanthus, mostly raised from specks of seed. The polyanthus is the most amiable primrose for general garden use and should be high on the lists of gardeners searching for shade-loving plants for small spaces. West Coast gardeners especially should investigate primrose possibilities; cool and moist conditions are very much to their liking, and the flowers will bloom all winter there. But I'm not sure I want to think about that as I look upon 4-foot snowdrifts at the end of March.

An easy way to create or add to a primrose path is to search out potted, blooming plants available in late winter at many city green grocers or florists.

You can pick from a range of brilliant colours. Enjoy the flowers indoors as winter rages its last, and then set the plant in the garden after spring has settled in — not *too* early for these coddled ones. Primroses will reappear every year thereafter if you remember that these natives of damp woods and meadows do not like to go thirsty and that they appreciate a covering of evergreen boughs over winter if the snow cover is not dependable. The true primrose, *Primula vulgaris*, parent of the polyanthus, is a simple, single-stemmed flower available in many colours, but traditionally — what else — primrose yellow. As the last of the tulips fade and the primroses prepare to retire into green obscurity for the summer, the first of the main crop of herbaceous perennials begins to bloom.

The subject of perennials is vast and complex — we began a casual cataloguing of the different sorts in our garden three years ago and are finally up to "L" for *Lythrum*. But for those who wish to fill out the lines of landscaping with undemanding, hardy plants that will endure in their place from year to year without need for laborious lifting, dividing and resetting, I have walked around the garden paths with an eye to listing just those perennials that fit the bill. To qualify, plants must be exceptionally beautiful in both leaf and flower and be able to look after themselves through all seasons, including a Northern winter.

An instructive approach to landscaping with perennials is to think in terms of seasons of bloom and pictorial associations, seasonal themes and accompaniments. When we began to grow perennials, we had no precedents to use for information, no gardens actual or in memory to give us clues about how best to use the plants

now interesting us; only a few well-thumbed old gardening books, friendly, personal and instructive, written by gardeners in a less hurried age. We hauled fallen fence rails from a back field, two at a time over our shoulders, to enclose the garden. We pried grey posts and boards, hard as stone, from a tumbling barn to build an entrance arbour and garden gate. After a past fashion, we dug and enriched long 10-foot-wide beds and mapped and planted for successive waves of flowers from the first crocus to final fall aster. We arranged and rearranged a growing number of perennials raised from seed, received in the mail or borrowed from ancient gardens long left to their own wild ways. We begged bits from any garden we happened to visit.

For several seasons, we kept a weekly record of "What's in Bloom" and still jot down changes and improvements to our flowery prospect — "Mass day lily *Hyperion* in front of tall white phlox in top border . . . . Split, enrich, and reset red bergamot in front of pale blue delphinium in entrance bed." And lest all our planning and work should detract from the enjoyment of the garden — as someone once said, "He misses much who has no aptitude for idleness" — sometimes we just sit here, still, in a place that is lovelier than we could ever have hoped at the start. "You turn the corner," my sister said, "and there is a little oasis of colour." Honeybees forage incessantly, fat, sated bumblebees drone, hummingbirds buzz through their aerial acrobatics, a deep peace pervades.

That said, I must confess that our garden is full-time work for two. And while I love to be down on hands and knees, lost in the back of the borders, grubbing bindweed from among thickets of phlox and sprawling delphiniums, my bare skin scratched and tickled by

Public Archives Canada PA 136941

prickly anchusa or twiggy honeysuckle, I can certainly appreciate that others would rather not. Nor is so much work necessary to enjoy perennial flowers. Even two or three species sharing a season will create a picture of contrasting forms of foliage and flowers and present colours singing a close harmony.

JUNE

For years, we could not resist the temptation to fill the garden with spring flowers, but we have learned to give thought to making the months that follow as lush and lovely. Conspicuous in June are Oriental poppies (*Papaver* spp). Bold groups of these flowers dazzle in their season but leave great gaps when the foliage disappears, soon after flowering, to emerge anew during cooler days of late summer (which, by the way, is precisely the time to move, divide or plant poppies).

A good plan is to plant three roots in a close triangular group or narrow drift, and set in front of them a plant or two of baby's-breath (*Gypsophila paniculata*) to provide a later screen of misty grey-green and white. If you know only the Chinese red poppies, the pink cultivars will delight you, especially planted behind an edging of silvery lamb's ears (*Stachys olympica*), airy coral bells (*Heuchera sanguinea*) and blue or lavender irises.

Scaled-down versions of their corpulent cousins, Iceland poppies (*P. nudicaule*) hoist mast and set sail weeks

Conspicuous in June are the large-flowered red, pink or orange Oriental poppies, best planted in groups that look spectacular in bloom and can later be hidden behind a screen of baby's-breath. Pleasing companions for poppies include woolly lamb's ears, coral bells and blue or lavender irises.

John Scanlan

earlier and then produce frail-looking crepe flowers, pink, yellow, orange and apricot, over a long season. This species has the advantage of being easily raised from seeds sown from early spring until midsummer. Sow several seeds in a small pot, and thin later to the huskiest single seedling. Set the young plants carefully — they will not stand much root disturbance — in the garden after six or eight weeks. If some plants disappear after a season or two, there will be small colonies of seedlings left to carry on. Not a major plant for landscaping purposes, the Iceland poppy is nevertheless a graceful, generous resident.

The iris, flower of the rainbow, displays a wide spectrum of colour to accompany and follow the poppy. Classically formed *fleurs-de-lis* emerge from a sheaf of either lance-shaped or reed-like foliage, depending on the species. Our garden grows 11 species and numerous cultivars of iris, but the two best suited to permanent, low-maintenance plantings are the bearded iris, descendents of *Iris pallida, I. florentine* and other faithful old garden "flags" and cultivars of the Siberian iris, *I. sibirica*, which is finer of foliage and opens light, butterfly blossoms less opulent than their showy, bearded kin.

The bearded iris, one of the few perennials that *must* be set in the garden in midsummer, shortly after flowering ends, is a plant for sun-filled places in well-drained soil moderately enriched with bone meal, wood ashes and a little very old manure or compost. To plant an iris rhizome, which is an enlarged, horizontal segment of the rootstock, trowel out *two* small holes, 5 or 6 inches deep, side by side, then snug the rhizome down on the ridge of earth between, and spread roots, as they naturally grow, into the two holes, backfilling and tamping the soil firmly and watering moderately to settle the soil. The rhizome will be just barely covered with earth, which rain will eventually wash away to expose the brown backs to the sun, a condition suited to the health of the plant. Set individual rhizomes at least 8 inches apart.

We have a long, 2-by-60-foot border of light soil, edged with alternating groups of thyme species and different sedums, and planted with what is literally a rainbow of iris, the plants grouped to follow the colours of the spectrum. This is a truly low-maintenance planting: no watering is necessary to sustain these drought resisters. Flower stalks of the iris are cut at ground level when blooms are past, and the most tattered outside leaves are removed occasionally to allow fresh growth from the centre.

Siberian irises have been unaccountably ignored by gardeners, although their landscaping value is high. If their blossoms are not as showy as the bearded beauties, they have an airy grace all their own, and the arching foliage remains in good condition through the season — an important

consideration. Extremely hardy plants, virtually free of disease or insect damage, Siberian irises may remain in place for many years. If you have a soggy spot to landscape, you could do no better than to arrange clumps of blue Siberian iris with feathery Astilbe, loosestrife, ferns, primulas and native red- or yellow-stemmed dogwoods.

Ordinary garden soil ought to be enriched with quantities of leaf mould, manure and/or damp peat moss for these moisture lovers, and a thick, constant mulch of leaves or grass clippings around the crowns will obviate the need for any further attention. Plant Siberian irises in September. I like to plant them in front of *rugosa* roses, with an edging of pinks and accompanied by painted daisies (*Pyrethrum roseum*) and a few foxgloves (*Digitalis* spp) for a picture of pink, blue, crimson and lavender.

Peonies, too, are hardy, dependable and lovely. We grow them underplanted with primroses in a 3-foot border on the east side of some lilacs, but not so close to the shrubs that the shoots will stretch for light and topple. Healthy foliage persists into fall and gives a last glow of autumnal colour. Peonies last: they last

for decades untended in a thatch of field grasses, if that be their fate.

Peonies are planted in October or November. Generous initial soil preparation will be repaid: we like to prepare "rose holes" for peonies,

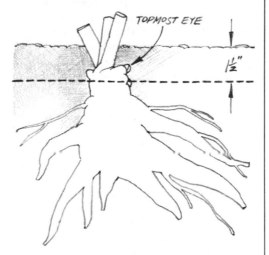

TOPMOST EYE

1½"

trowelling out a hole large enough to hold the brittle root without bending it. It is better to start with a three- to five-eye division from a good nursery (see Appendix D) than to disturb an established peony clump for divisions — old plants seldom move well. When planting make sure that the topmost "eye" — a red bud — is not more than 1½ inches below the soil surface; deeper planting will inevitably delay or prevent flowering. Mulch during the first winter with evergreen boughs, straw or peat to prevent roots heaving. In subsequent years, mulch with old manure, fine compost or leaf mould. Staking is easily done by hammering three sturdy 4-foot lengths of 1-by-2 lumber in a triangle about a foot from the peony crown and tying soft, strong string or strips of cloth around it as the plants grow; the stakes can stay in place year-round. In late fall, cut the

Bearded irises (left), here growing in company with giant alliums, are planted in summer, after they bloom, sufficiently shallowly to allow the surfaces of the rhizomes to be exposed to the light. Peonies (right), however, must be planted more deeply in fertile, weedless soil in the fall. The topmost "eye," a red bud, must not be more than 1½ inches below the soil surface.

Stephen Errington

peony foliage to ground level, and remove to the compost heap. Not a lot to ask for such beauty.

Peony season spans more than a month if early and late varieties are selected. If I could grow only one flower, it would probably be the peony. I am always startled that anything so tough and hardy can be at the same time so fragile and lovely. If June gave us only irises, poppies and peonies, this flower gardener would be gratified. But there are also columbines, most elegant of flowers, spritely coral bells, clove-scented pinks and the ethereal flax flowers.

Graceful, soaring columbines (*Aquilegia* spp) are at home in a mixed border but are perhaps even more beautiful grown by themselves or in the select company of ferns and Siberian irises against a backdrop of green. Columbines adapt to sun but seem to prefer light shade, and they will reward you with lusher growth and better bloom if the soil is organically rich and fairly constantly moist. Rock gardeners may want to scout out seeds or plants of some of the dwarf treasures, especially *A. flabellata*, *A. caerulea*, *A. alpina* and particularly *A. akitensis*, 8 inches tall with blue-and-cream pendant flowers.

An edging plant or ground cover without rival is coral bells (*Heuchera sanguinea*). Even if the plants never flowered, they would be prized for their green-and-bronze marbled foliage. But flower they do, with extraordinary exuberance, slender wands hung with small, red, crimson or pink bells materializing over several months. There is always a buzz of hummingbirds by the coral bells. Any moderately rich soil will grow them; groups of 8 or 12 plants set 8 inches apart in sun or light shade create a sparkling effect. Nor is it difficult to work up a stock of plants: older clumps

of coral bells are easily pried apart by hand into numerous two- or three-crown divisions. Discard the woody centre every three or four years or when flowering diminishes. At that time, enrich the soil with old manure or peat moss.

Once seeded, the airy flax flower (*Linum perenne*) — perennial cousin of the useful flax of flaxseed, linseed oil and linen fame — will see to its own continuation in the garden. Knee-high, many-stemmed fountains of fine, grey-green foliage break into sprays of round, sky-blue flowers that remain open until early afternoon, then sprinkle the ground with flakes of blue as the plants prepare for the next day's early flowers.

Pinks (*Dianthus* spp) provide useful ground covers for small and early bulbs. Also an excellent summer-blooming edging for rock garden plants, pinks are among the easiest perennials to raise from seed. From a 90-cent packet of *D. allwoodii* — a strain of single- or double-flowered pinks that may be uniformly pink, zoned with crimson or white edged with red — sown in May, the low, green or grey mounds set in place in September or April following, we have furnished the entire edge of a 60-foot bed of perennials and herbs with spice-scented flowers.

Especially fine plants may be propagated by taking 3-inch cuttings of new growth in early summer. Dip cutting ends in rooting hormone powder, and set them in a pot of moist, sandy soil — a dozen cuttings will fit a 4-inch pot. Slip the pot into a loose-fitting clear plastic bag to maintain humidity, and keep it in a shaded place, indoors or out, for nicely rooted new plants in a month or so. Pinks are plants for full sun and well-drained soil.

JULY

Time was when our flower-filled June garden gave way to a subdued July. So, garden visiting being a favourite summer pastime, we kept our eyes open for flowering plants that kept other gardens colourful and discovered the enduring day lily, rose loosestrife and especially lilies in all colours and forms.

Day lilies (*Hemerocallis* — beautiful for a day) provide drifts of persistent, arching foliage and many stems of flaring flowers — yellow, red, wine, apricot, peach, melon or zoned dark on light — in mixed borders or mass plantings. Organically enriched soil will feed the widening clumps for the many years they may be left in place, and a constant mulch will likely be all the attention they need. Plant them several feet apart, and the intervening space will be ideal for narcissi and tulips. A no-maintenance narrow border may be filled with just spring bulbs and day lilies — well, perhaps a few peonies to bridge the gap and maybe an edge of sedum. (Once your interest is stirred,

new species have a way of slipping by the garden gate, perhaps recognizing a congenial home.)

The bright magenta wands of loosestrife (*Lythrum salicaria*) could well spire behind the day lilies. This denizen of marsh and streamside is of outstanding garden value if planted in enriched, moisture-holding ground; it is happy, too, in clay soil. Even one plant creates a striking vertical accent, and clumps of hosta can provide foreground foliage; the two enjoy identical soil conditions. Seemingly immune to insects or disease, the long-blooming lythrum is a plant for permanence. Place it carefully in the landscape, and let it be.

For years, we grew no lilies (*Lilium* spp). The old gardening books that had us digging wide borders and exploring the world of perennials were rather discouraging on the subject of lilies, hinting at lack of hardiness, susceptibility to disease and general fussiness. But we were seeing lilies in many gardens nearby, and inquiries

revealed that, yes, they came up year after year, were healthy and, all in all, not excessively demanding of a gardener's time and skills.

Lilies grow from many-layered, scaly bulbs that are best planted in fall but may be tucked into place very early in spring. The slender lily clumps take up little space — city gardeners take note: five or seven bulbs will, after several seasons, create ever-increasing sheafs of stems crowded with pendant, out-facing or upturned flowers. Many of the showy trumpet lilies are not as persistent in cold gardens but do well on the gentler West Coast. But the splendid regal lily, *Lilium regale*, a trumpet type discovered growing by the thousands on the rocky hillsides of Szechuan province in China by plant explorer E.H. Wilson — a tale of landslides, broken limbs and perseverance — is an exception. Garden lilies are tough — almost all of the bulbs prospering in our garden came from a Saskatchewan grower. If you are richer in patience than cash, regal lilies can be

Stephen Errington

Irises represent the tallest plant element in an urban garden planted with a pleasing combination of evergreen shrubs, ground covers, perennial and annual flowers. Pinks, easily grown from seed, are well suited to such a sunny, low-growing landscape.

As perennial flowers require weedless, fertile soil, a good plan for the beginner who has a vegetable garden is to allocate one edge of that plot to flowers. This diagram, which features taller flowers toward the back (the top), has an attractive, curving front edge and could colour the border of a lawn or vegetable garden.

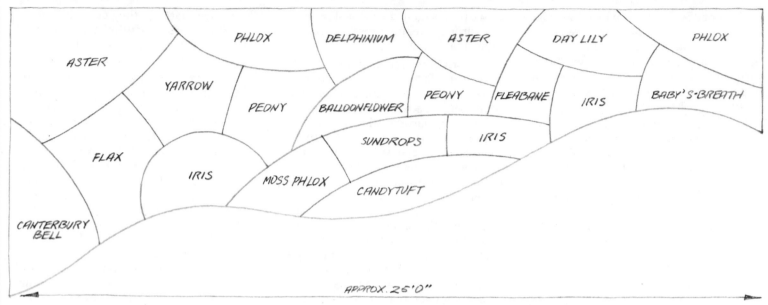

grown, in the manner of leeks or onions, from seed to flowering in two seasons: leave the adolescent lily bulbs in the earth over the first winter, and move them to permanent quarters the second fall. Few garden experiments are as satisfying or, with lily bulbs at three dollars apiece, as rewarding.

In the landscape, lilies may tower behind *Gypsophila* in a mixed border or be grouped between well-spaced clumps of day lilies if no spring bulbs grow there and the soil is nourishing. Lilies may also be planted among the peonies as their July successors, or groups may come up through primroses in a slightly shaded border between shrubs and lawn. Conventional wisdom has it that lilies like their roots in shade and their heads in the sun, so they appreciate a ground cover of shallow-rooted, low plants.

AUGUST

If July is the month of the day lily, then the old-fashioned tiger lily (*L. tigrinum*) is a dependable standby for August. Some gardeners turn their noses

up at this willing plant, preferring to fuss with tender gladioli or dahlias for late-summer colour, but give me a bulb that can quietly hibernate underground all winter and brighten its corner without attention. Let me pass on a suggestion from an old gardening book, tried to good effect in our garden: Plant tiger lily bulbs between clumps of monkshood (*Aconitum napellus Bicolor*), a tall-growing (to 6 feet) but slender plant that has spikes of hooded blue-and-white flowers. This is a good grouping for the back of a border or the centre of an island bed. You are probably not in the habit of grazing indiscriminately in your flowerbeds, but if you are, give monkshood a wide miss, for as one herbalist noted, "it is very hurtful and killeth out of hand."

Our garden is becoming beautifully overrun with another August bloomer, the hollyhock (*Alcea* spp). We leave only a fraction of the thousand seedlings and move some of these in September or April to the very backs of borders where the spires of many-hued, funnelled

blossoms may shine, while the sometimes tattered lower leaves are concealed by the bushy growth of peonies, false indigo (*Baptisia australis*), gas plants (*Dictamnus albus*), phlox or yarrow. Hollyhocks — in city laneways, vacant lots or any garden they can invade — seem to have an affinity for fences.

Yarrow (*Achillea filipendulina*) has silvery, fernlike foliage and abundant flat umbels of deep yellow bloom and is a no-work, drought-, insect- and disease-free perennial that may bloom longer than any other plant of late summer. There is a shorter cultivar, *Moonshine*, with silver leaves verging on white and pale yellow flowers that I have seen in the Royal Botanical Gardens in Hamilton, Ontario, but never in nurseries. I keep searching. Yarrow is well-placed in front of aconite (*Aconitum* spp) or hollyhocks, with a cloud of baby's-breath nearby.

Few plants are as lovely and useful in late July and August as baby's-breath (*Gypsophila paniculata*) and its cultivars

Perfecta, *Bristol Snowflake* and *Pink Fairy*. Drought-resistant in the extreme, this lime-loving perennial progresses from cool grey-green to an earthborne milky way, lightening its neighbours with stems of countless tiny white or pink blooms. *Gysophila* is taprooted and not happy to be moved around, so pot-grown plants should be set in well-drained soil, in a permanent, sunny spot. As the plants form drifts, give each 18 inches of space all around so that the webbed bushes may assume a nicely rounded form. A few twiggy branches pushed in around the clumps will support the brittle stems.

PERENNIAL CARE

It has been said that any ground that grows good vegetables will grow perennials. This is not to minimize the importance of good soil but to emphasize that these husky plants require at least the fertility necessary for a good crop of cabbages or potatoes. Preparing a new site for flowers is not an easy task, I know. But many sites have established vegetable gardens, often in a stretch of lawn, that have benefited from seasons of organic enrichment. A good plan, if you want to grow a collection of perennials, is to create a 4-to-8-foot-wide border at one end or side of the vegetable garden and arrange your plants from dwarf to tall, perhaps in company with some of the useful and decorative perennial herbs, so that the "living picture," as Gertrude Jekyll called it, is viewed from the lawn, from within the vegetable garden itself or from both sides, if the bed is planted from the middle and grades down to lower plants on either side. I would think this by far the easiest way to start with perennials or expand your repertoire — land is there ready, enriched.

When we turn lawn into flowerbed, we first mark the area with stakes and string or slice an approximate undulating line in the turf for a curving edge. Then, with a sharp spade, we cut the sod into liftable chunks. Over the next few days or weeks — an hour a day of this work is plenty — we do a thorough removal of sod and roots by beating and shaking the chunks of sod with a garden fork to retain topsoil. (We have a small mountain of twitch grass behind the barn — the stuff does *not* compost.)

After a good raking to catch stray bits of root, we either spot-enrich the bed for large perennials or turn old manure and such into the top 10 inches or so of the soil for dwarf, shallow-rooted plants such as coral bells, dwarf *Veronica*, most herbs and all annuals. Sometimes we build a fat, smothering compost heap of manure and succulent green stuff directly on the cleared patch and let this lie, unturned, for a season. Next season, we may plant a crop of potatoes or blanketing winter squash to discourage

weeds, all the while planning and dreaming of what permanent things will be planted that fall or next spring. Meantime we raise a crop of pinks or columbines from seed, scouring old gardens for treasures and exploring local nurseries. With schematic drawings and some impromptu "playing it by ear" in the garden, the bed takes shape.

ANNUAL ADDITIONS

Like all plants, annual flowers have advantages and disadvantages. On the plus side, few plants are as floriferous — annuals bloom nonstop, colouring their corner with little attention, from late June until frost catches them. They are quick: even if you start from seed sown outdoors, a good approach in many cases, you may expect flowers in as little as six weeks, certainly in eight. Instant floral gratification. Compare this with a full flowerless season from most seed-raised perennials.

But the garden landscaped afresh every year with purchased annuals is increasingly expensive. And if annuals are all you grow, the garden is sadly bereft in April and May, just when the eyes are most hungry for colour. Nor are annuals as friendly, somehow; we do not come to know and appreciate them in quite the same way as the permanent plants whose progress we observe from their first emergence in spring to flowering and fading.

Annuals do not a garden make. But they are just the thing for patio or balcony pots or window boxes — what could be better than tumbling nasturtiums, a plant or two of sweet-scented mignonette (*Reseda odorata*) or trailing ivy-leaved geraniums that are so much more graceful than their ubiquitous upright kin. Annuals are ideal to brighten a temporary garden or rented quarters. They will also do willing service for a season or two in beds or borders where perennial plants are fattening up. Permanent gaps may be left here and there in the landscape for favourite annuals — you may like snapdragons or be partial to tall, yellow marigolds. Truth be told, I would happily fill the shady border under the lilacs with pink and white impatiens if primroses didn't prosper so well there.

Indeed, I cannot imagine our own garden without plenty of annuals. But of a rather special kind. Over the years, we have come to rely on certain of them to sow their hardy seed and reappear faithfully, if not always in the same places. California poppies (*Eschscholzia californica*) are a case in point. Other hardy annuals we count on to look to their own continuance are sweet alyssum (*Alyssum maritimum*), which laps the border edges and flows into the paths until late fall and is sometimes capped, still blooming, with the first snows; cornflowers (*Centaurea cyanus*), bright blue bachelor's buttons that regularly reappear among the Siberian irises and *Rugosa* roses; rosy Shirley poppies (*Papaver rhoeas*, Shirley strain) that come back again and again from seed, as do the outlawed opium poppies (*P. somniferum*); and we can always count on calendulas to brighten the ends of the vegetable beds of their own accord. Violas, pansies and the pert Johnny-jump-ups find their own way around the garden. For years, the tall white tobacco flower (*Nicotiana affinis*) has returned, unbidden but welcome, to scent a corner near the garden seat. Just in case, we always sow a patch of the dowdy but exceedingly sweet evening-scented stock (*Matthiola incana*) — not much to look at even when the wizened buds open at dusk into small purple flowers, yet it floods the night air with a scent that one old book called "ecclesiastical" and a friend swears is exactly like coconut macaroons.

There may be circumstances where a new bed needs colour right away, or you would prefer to have the ground tidy and bare at the end of each season. I

Sheridan Nurseries Ltd.

suggest that five or six packets of seeds will do the job at considerably less cost than purchased plants. Many annuals are very easily raised from seed sown outdoors in their blooming position. Save for cosmos, zinnias, marigolds and nasturtiums, many are hardy enough that we can seed them the first of May here in central Ontario, a full month before frosts are over. Wait several weeks longer before sowing the frost-tender sorts. For most annuals, 8 to 12 inches is a good spacing. I find the necessary job of thinning much easier if three or four seeds are sown in close groups the required distance apart. As they grow, all but the huskiest seedling is removed.

The busy gardener can only be grateful for all this gratuitous colour and fragrance. Of course, if you are intent on filling a certain place with uniform colour and height all at once, you must avail yourself of bedding plants. But I would just as soon leave that for parks and formal beds in front of public buildings and let the garden mirror nature more closely. Think of a favourite stretch of undisturbed meadow, wetland or woodland. You will recall that the majority of plants come back each spring in the same places. In nature, perennials, be they woody or herbaceous, predominate, and a handful of annuals and biennials fling their hardy seed about and appear here and there among the more settled inhabitants. Can we be too far amiss in our gardening efforts if we take our clues from nature?

Patrick Lima is a frequent Harrowsmith *magazine contributor and is co-owner of Larkwhistle Garden in Ontario. He notes, ''Gardening is both science and art. One learns patience and perseverance (especially in a Northern frost pocket), and one's health is enhanced by the necessary physical work and the fine food.''*

W. Atlee Burpee Co.

Annual flowers have the advantage of blooming almost non-stop throughout the summer, and many can be grown easily and quickly from seed. However, any that do not self-sow must be replaced every year, a tedious and often expensive procedure. Here, annuals such as marigolds and celosia have been used exclusively to produce a brilliantly colourful, unusual border.

8 The Modern Shrubbery

Leafy and flowering bushes fill small spaces with colour and greenery

By Lawrence Sherk

In a forest or by a field, they are scarcely noticed except by foraging berry pickers. Grasses, flowers and trees are everywhere, but shrubs, quietly filling in the small spaces where shafts of sunlight penetrate, are usually too small to be spectacular, too stalwart to be coveted in the manner of wildflowers. In the landscape, too, shrubs are often afterthoughts, and indeed they have a relatively recent history of use in landscaping. It was only after the European discovery of China and Japan that these middle-sized plants came into vogue, especially in collections called "shrubries" or "shrubberies." By 1770, Thomas Wateley wrote in his *Observations on Modern Gardening* that a gardener should "range the shrubs and small trees so that they may mutually set off the beauties, and conceal the blemishes, of each other . . . . "

Shrubs are now known to make four main contributions to the landscape. First, they provide a gradation of height between tall landscape elements such as trees or buildings and low ones such as flowers, lawn or ground covers, mimicking the aesthetically pleasing canopies that exist in nature and allowing the eye to move easily about the landscaped space. Foundation plantings, simply plants grown in front of a building, are frequently composed of various shrubs either alone or in combination with other plants. Second, shrubs, which may range in height from only a foot or so to as tall as 20 feet, can take the place of trees as the tallest plant elements. Third, they are often used as hedges (see Chapter 9). Fourth, shrubs can be used like ground covers for such roles as stabilizing a landscape slope susceptible to erosion, which might be difficult to mow even if the gardener could establish a lawn there. Many such areas can be effectively planted with one or more of the shrubs that spread by underground roots or have branches that spread across the ground, such as the red osier dogwood, weeping forsythia, creeping juniper, fragrant sumach, Japanese rose, memorial rose and snowberries. These four landscape values are in addition to what attributes the plants themselves possess: beauty of leaf or bloom, winter interest, edible fruit and such.

Selecting a limited number of shrubs for my own landscape in central Toronto, an area only 18 by 35 feet, provided me with a real challenge. I had to limit myself to a maximum of seven fairly small shrubs, yet I wanted plants that would provide interest either in successive seasons or year-round. The selection would include some newer varieties that I wished to evaluate firsthand over a period of time. For winter interest I planted a bristlecone pine and a corkscrew hazel, which I have had to prune every year to keep it from overpowering such a small garden. A pair of new hardy evergreen hollies, *Blue Princess*, which bears red fruit, and *Blue Prince*, a male for pollination, are among the plants I wished to try. A hardy rhododendron provides evergreen interest year-round as well as a beautiful display of lavender flowers in late May, while a dwarf lilac is another compact example of one of my favourite flowering shrubs. It has a potential spread of 4 feet, however, so must be pruned to keep it within its allotted 30-inch space. An upright *Wichita* blue juniper has bright blue foliage which provides an excellent contrast with the green leaves of the rest of the garden.

The gardeners of larger landscapes need not be so restricted. The largest sites, in fact, allow for mass plantings of certain shrubs, which can then be enjoyed from a distance as well as close

up. However, regardless of the size of the site, hardiness — a plant's ability to survive winter — is the most important restriction upon plant choice in the Northern landscape. Only in the "banana belt" of the Pacific Northwest and southwest British Columbia can gardeners choose from a wide selection of plants that includes such flowering exotica as rhododendrons and camellias. In the temperate areas of zones 6 and 7, there is a good range of shrubs that can be expected to grow well, provided other essentials such as light, good soil and wind exposure are taken into consideration. However, prairie and Far Northern gardeners can choose from only a limited selection of shrubs. Fortunately for these gardeners, government research stations, nurseries and interested individuals have evaluated and selected many shrubs that are extremely hardy.

The best guide to plants that will survive and flourish, rather than succumb in the first harsh winter, is the experience of neighbours and local nurseries. Established nurseries that list national hardiness ratings (see the maps on pages 20 and 21) can also increase the gardener's chances of success. As long as they can be successfully transplanted, native shrubs from the gardener's own area will be sure to survive in the Northern garden. A natural native garden may be the easiest to establish and the most trouble-free to maintain (see Chapter 4).

After hardiness, one should consider one's own plant preferences. Do you look forward to cutting a bouquet of your favourite lilacs every spring? Do you like to have a garden that will attract different and unusual birds? Conversely, if the fragrance of the mock-orange does not appeal to you, do not plant it just because it has been recommended as

Agriculture Canada

Ontario Ministry of Agriculture and Food

one of the most floriferous of shrubs. Other dependable flowering shrubs include azaleas, flowering dogwoods, heaths and heathers, forsythias, hydrangeas, crab apples, ornamental cherries, roses, sorbaria, spireas, viburnums and yuccas. And do not forget that many flowering shrubs such as lilacs, mock-orange, forsythia, and beauty-bush stand out when in full flower but provide no interest except for ordinary green foliage or plain twigs for the rest of the year. Only the shrubby potentillas are noted for impressive shows of flowers that last more than a week or two. On the other hand, the serviceberry is always a welcome sight, with its early white flowers followed by bird-attracting summer fruit and later, by brilliant fall colour.

SHADE TOLERANCE

The amount of sunlight the plant will receive is another important consideration. Many shrubs, both evergreen and deciduous, will not grow well in shaded areas under trees, or along the north or east sides of buildings. For instance, lilacs will not grow well or flower well if planted in a place that receives fewer than six hours of sun a day. However, many evergreens such as yews, and deciduous shrubs such as alpine currants and several viburnums will do quite well in a shaded area, provided they were properly planted in the first place. There are other plants that will grow well in a shaded area but will not tolerate a soil clogged with the surface roots of plants such as willows or Norway maples. These include acanthopanax, mountain maples, aucubas, boxwoods, camellias, many dogwoods, evergreen euonymus, witchhazels, hollies, kalmias, mahonia, pieris, firethorns, rhododendrons, ornamental currants, sorbaria,

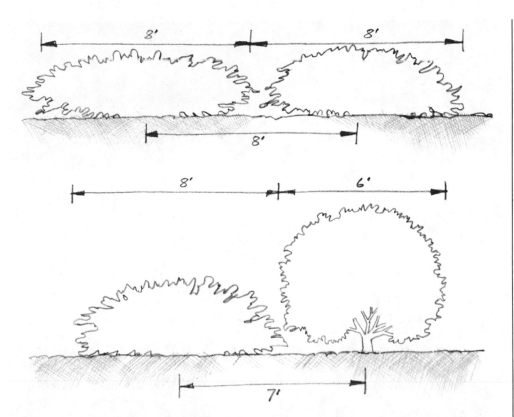

The ultimate height and spread of a shrub must be known so that it can be planted in proper relationship to other plants and to buildings. Leave sufficient space around each plant so that it fills the designated area only when mature.

snowberries, cedars and blueberries.

How high will it grow? What will be the ultimate spread? These questions must always be answered before the gardener selects shrubs for almost any situation. The only exception is a specimen plant, a tree or shrub that is set apart on its own in an open area so that there are no restrictions on its ultimate size. But around a home or in a shrub border, especially where different shrubs are planted together, ultimate size is important. For instance, the popular spreading evergreens Pfitzer junipers (*Juniperus chinensis*) are often planted 3 to 6 feet apart for immediate effect, although they can attain an ultimate spread of 20 to 25 feet. Unless a regular pruning schedule is started as soon as they are planted, overcrowded

plants must be hacked back to such an extent that they will lose all of their natural, informal shape. Where closely spaced plants are desired immediately, consider a slow-growing selection such as the *Compact Pfitzer* juniper or the similar *Ramlosa* juniper, both of which have an ultimate spread of 5 to 6 feet, well in keeping with most landscape plans. Conversely, be careful to keep shorter plants in front of taller ones; do not plant the low-growing, shrubby potentilla behind the much taller-growing lilac or mock-orange in a shrub border. Select shrubs carefully for ultimate size as well for hardiness and light requirements.

Consider colour as well, not only of blooms, but also of leaves and twigs, which can provide visual interest much

longer than flowers. Many of the most popular shrubs have green foliage, but others have contrasting silver, blue-green, red, purple, yellow or variegated green and white foliage, which can be striking if the plants are used in the landscape to complement and offset other colour elements. Once such shrubs are established, a few branches can also be cut for bouquets of cut flowers. The sea buckthorn, Russian olive and silver buffaloberry have silver leaves; the silverleaf dogwood, *Emerald Gaiety* euonymus and variegated English holly have white variegated foliage; several Japanese maples, the purple smoke tree, *Royalty* crab apple, purpleleaf sand cherry, *Shubert* choke cherry and purpleleaf weigela have purple leaves; and Spaeth's dogwood and the golden-leaved forms of juniper, false-cypress, privet, mock-orange, ninebark and elderberry have golden foliage.

The twigs of most shrubs are an unassuming grey colour, but the burning bush has interesting corky twigs, and several others have new growth that is bright green or even red or yellow. Such twigs add winter colour to the garden, and most will not suffer if the gardener cuts a few small branches to add to indoor arrangements. The gardener who wishes to plant a colourful twig plant should be sure to place it in a location where it can be seen throughout the winter; near a door, sidewalk or window, not at the far end of the garden. Broom (*Cytisus* spp) and kerria produce green twigs, Siberian dogwood and red osier dogwood, red twigs, and the yellowtwig dogwood has, of course, yellow twigs.

Coloured fruit, too, can often last well into winter, sometimes until the new growth appears in spring. Popular flowering shrubs such as lilacs, forsythia and mock-orange have very plain green fruit that does not stand out in the garden, but other species may have white, yellow, blue, black, orange or red fruit, some of which is edible and some preferred by birds. For red fruit, consider the Amur maple, cotoneasters, euonymus, hollies, crab apples, firethorns, roses and many viburnums; for blue fruits, junipers and mahonia; for black fruit, acanthopanax, privets and some viburnums; for yellow fruit, the Russian olive and sea buckthorn, and for white fruit, the Siberian dogwood, grey dogwood and snowberry.

The plant's requirements for soil quality, too, must be considered, although many shrubs will grow satisfactorily in any soil that is not excessively acidic or alkaline, and, fortunately, most developed areas of the North have soils that are more or less neutral (a pH of about 7). Wooded areas, however, often have acidic soils that are a necessity for the successful

Agriculture Canada

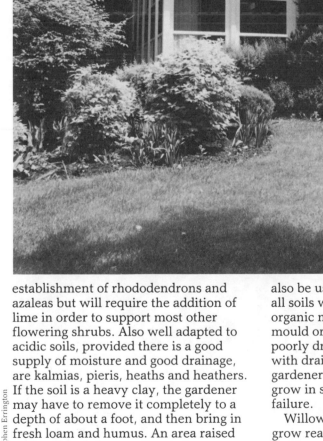

Stephen Errington

establishment of rhododendrons and azaleas but will require the addition of lime in order to support most other flowering shrubs. Also well adapted to acidic soils, provided there is a good supply of moisture and good drainage, are kalmias, pieris, heaths and heathers. If the soil is a heavy clay, the gardener may have to remove it completely to a depth of about a foot, and then bring in fresh loam and humus. An area raised with railroad ties or other timbers can

also be used to contain new soil. Almost all soils will benefit from the addition of organic matter such as peat moss, leaf mould or compost. If an area is very poorly drained and cannot be corrected with drainage (see Chapter 2), the gardener must choose shrubs that will grow in such soils, or risk almost certain failure.

Willows are among the plants that will grow readily in poorly drained soils, but another possibility is the red osier

dogwood, which not only grows well in wet soils but also has colourful red twigs to add winter interest. Various blueberries grow best in wet, acidic soils, and several viburnums can also be depended upon to establish themselves well in similar conditions. Of all the evergreens, the cedars tolerate wet ground best but must not be planted in areas that are continually flooded.

On the other hand, soil that is excessively dry throughout the summer

Foundation plantings are composed of plants, usually shrubs, that are set against the house but do not overpower it. Their natural colours and textures and their varying heights and shapes are pleasing complements to the straight lines and hard building materials behind them.

should be planted only with shrubs known to establish themselves well without a good water supply. Acanthopanax, Amur maple, bearberry, pea shrub, broom, Russian olive, sea-buckthorn, junipers, ninebark, potentilla, sumach, *rugosa* roses, tamarix and yucca will all survive in a relatively dry garden, if they are helped with some added humus and a thorough watering when they are planted.

SHRUB CHOICE AND MAINTENANCE

There are several ways to find suitable shrubs. One, already mentioned, is to select native species that can be transplanted from the wild. Take care to dig and plant them carefully, so that they will survive the arduous change of environment. Also, neighbours, local horticultural societies and other nearby gardeners may have desired species that can be propagated from cuttings: new shoots from plants such as juniper, heather, euonymus, mahonia, potentilla, cotoneaster, and roses can be cut just below a bud, dipped in rooting hormone, and kept in damp potting medium until they sprout. Many more shrubs can be grown from seed, although this is a very time-consuming way of providing landscape plants, and it can be tricky for some species. Easier is the purchase of plants from local nurseries or from mail-order catalogues that stock suitably hardy plants. Buying from a local nursery enables the gardener to select vigorous, well-growing specimens. Establish whether or not the nursery will replace the plants should you run into a problem.

Until a few years ago, most shrubs were sold bare root only for a few weeks during the spring and late fall. Today only deciduous hedging shrubs are normally sold this way. Most other

shrubs are sold already balled and burlapped or in pots, in which case they can be planted from spring through summer into late fall. No longer are gardeners restricted to two very short planting periods. Mail-order nurseries, however, still ship shrubs bare root and so can fill orders only in early spring and, sometimes, late fall.

As soon as the plants are obtained, they should be planted. Balled or potted shrubs, however, can be kept in a shaded location for a few days if the soil is kept moist. It is important that great care be taken in planting the shrubs, to ensure that they will soon become well established and thus provide years of trouble-free growth. Plant them *at the same depth* at which they were planted in the nursery — *never* deeper. Dig a planting hole large enough to allow for the addition of some fresh loam, well-composted cattle manure and, especially on dry soils, peat moss. All acid-loving shrubs benefit from peat moss added to the soil. If the soil is naturally acidic, the gardener should add lime to the planting soil for all except acid-loving shrubs; soil tests done by the local ministry of agriculture will indicate how much lime

should be added. Water the shrubs heavily as soon as they are firmly in place, and thereafter, unless there is ample rainfall, provide about an inch of water a week. Once the shrubs are established in about a year, they should require watering only during dry spells. Give the plants a good soaking, not just a sprinkle and water well in late October if the fall has been dry. New plantings should be mulched with a mixture of peat moss, compost and cattle manure, which can be reapplied every two or three years.

Thereafter, most shrubs require little maintenance, although when they approach the desired size, a regular pruning program can keep them from crowding other plants. As a general rule, spring-flowering shrubs should be pruned as soon as they finish flowering, while summer-flowering shrubs such as hydrangeas and potentillas should be pruned in early spring. Remove a few branches of older, deciduous shrubs to the ground each year to rejuvenate them and in pruning any deciduous shrub, remove all dead, damaged, overly long and crowded growth rather than cutting the tips off all the shoots. Evergreens may be lightly pruned in spring before growth begins or in midsummer after the new growth has matured. Shrubs such as lilacs, which have large, unattractive seed clusters, should have the flower heads cut off as soon as they have finished blooming.

Detailed information on a wide variety of shrubs can be found in Appendix C.

Author of Ornamental Shrubs of Canada *(Agriculture Canada, 1965), Lawrence Sherk is a graduate of the University of Guelph and Cornell University, where he studied ornamental horticulture. Formerly a member of the staff of Agriculture Canada's Plant Research Institute, he is now chief horticulturist at Sheridan Nurseries in Oakville, Ontario.*

Dig a planting hole large enough to accommodate the roots, spread out and allow the addition of some fresh loam, well-composted cattle manure and, especially on dry soils, peat moss. Then plant the shrub at the same depth it was growing in the nursery and water heavily.

9 Green Walls

Hedges, climbers and vines define garden spaces

By Trevor J. Cole

Henry VIII once lived there, and so did William of Orange and Queen Mary II and a procession of other English royalty until the time of George II, but for me, during those first few days on the job, Hampton Court was no place for pomp and ceremony. I was a groundskeeper newly hired from the British Army, and I nursed my blistered hands and aching back after each day I spent raking the gravel paths trodden by tourists. Still, I could take some spiritual comfort in knowing that I had something in common with those monarchs. Like me, they had gazed upon the unusual hedges in the gardens, the complex knot gardens delineated with box only about a foot high and the famous maze composed of yew bushes tall enough to hide an adult.

Among the hedges I have known, those were probably the most noteworthy, and yet, throughout a series of increasingly interesting jobs and a change of continent, I have found that all the green walls I have seen, however humble, have had similar purposes: they define a space, provide privacy, or exclude unwanted animals or people. Some fulfill two or even all three roles. Although their materials and methods can vary greatly — tall or short, natural and unclipped or formal and clipped, deciduous or evergreen, annual or perennial, flowering or not — one thing is consistently true: whether it is designed for a king or a suburban gardener, a well-chosen hedge can provide a lifetime of beauty and use. Where hedges are not needed or wanted, climbers and vines can decorate already standing walls or fences to provide yet more vertical interest in the landscape.

A surprising range of plants is suitable for use in a hedge. The most important consideration for a perennial hedge is the plant's hardiness — its ability to survive in the gardener's particular climatic zone. Next, the plant must be capable of branching and leafing from the base; the honey locust, (*Gleditsia triacanthos*), for instance, is usually grown as a tree, but if cut at the base when young it will make an acceptable hedge plant. Important in hedge growth is the principle that when the growing tip is clipped off a plant, dormant buds are forced into growth, so that where there was once only one shoot, there are now two or three; the more often the hedge is clipped, the thicker (and probably shorter) it will be. Virtually any plant that does not have a pyramidal shape — which would, unless severely pruned, result in a sawtooth contour — will be adequate for a hedge. Consider, however, that a plant such as lilac can make a good informal hedge but will not provide privacy, because with the passing of time it will develop a bare trunk.

If there is a place in the landscape that would probably benefit from a hedge, the gardener should first realize that it will occupy a certain amount of space, not only in height but also width. Take the eventual height into consideration and then assume that a formal (sheared) hedge will reach approximately half the width of that eventual height: if a formal hedge is going to be 8 feet tall, it can be expected to grow about 4 feet wide and should be planted 2 feet inside the property line. An informal (unsheared) hedge may be as wide as it will be tall, as may a very small formal hedge such as box. When its width is taken into consideration, the planting of a hedge on a small property may not be as wise as, say, the construction of a fence that can be intertwined with climbing honeysuckle or even *Scarlet Runner* beans.

Consider, too, whether a perennial

Public Archives Canada PA 10643

hedge might best be evergreen or deciduous, losing its leaves in winter. Evergreen hedges have the advantage of providing year-round protection, and so they make better windbreaks or winter privacy screens. However, in regions subject to heavy (even if short-lived) snow storms, there is a tendency for evergreen hedges to become bent or broken by the weight of the snow. One solution is for the gardener to go out immediately after every storm and shake the snow off, but there are generally more important or more appealing things to be done, and this cold, wet task is so easily ignored that Northern evergreen hedges often suffer. If the hedge is composed of deciduous plants, the snow can sift through the branches when it falls, so breakage is not as

common. A further bonus with deciduous hedges is that many of them are composed of flowering shrubs that are outstanding when in bloom.

The next decision to make is whether the hedge will be formal or informal. Formal hedges are the ones that usually come to mind when the word "hedge" is mentioned: a close row of plants, regularly sheared to produce a living wall, a very unnatural looking phenomenon, but one that well serves its function, especially in a small space. Formal hedges are labour intensive because they must be hand trimmed at least twice a year, but in certain situations they can provide just the right appearance of tranquil, formal delineation. Informal hedges, on the other hand, are allowed to grow more or

less naturally, and so are more likely to enhance a natural landscape or to act as an effective windbreak. (The subject of windbreaks is treated in Chapter 3.) They are lightly pruned once a year to remove any shoots that are growing out of line and to even up the growth rate of individual plants within the hedge. Their chief drawback is that, because of the type of plants chosen — usually dwarf flowering shrubs — and because these hedges are not sheared, they occupy more space than do formal hedges of similar height. Once the gardener has chosen a suitable species, the only remaining considerations are cost — about one plant per foot will be needed for a dwarf hedge, one every 18 inches for a medium (5-to-7-foot-tall) hedge and one every 2 feet for a tall hedge or any informal hedge — and suitability for the gardener's site and needs.

Hedges do not have to be composed of woody plants. A temporary summer hedge can be produced from upright annuals, such as summer cypress (*Kochia scoparia*) or a tall marigold like *Yellow Climax*, which makes a pleasant, 3-foot-tall summer edging down the side of a driveway without creating winter snow removal problems. In a similar fashion there are many perennial plants that make excellent hedges and can be cut back to almost ground level each fall. Peonies, the obedient plant (*Physostegia virginiana*), phlox, showy stonecrop (*Sedum spectabile*) or day lilies would all be suitable and would cost much less than woody plants. Even vegetables can be used in hedging — a centuries-old tradition in France. Peppers, eggplants or a row of staked tomatoes will all serve to make a barrier and define an area. *Brassicas* such as broccoli and cauliflower will all make good stiff hedges, but they are rather slow-growing

Stephen Errington

and do not form an effective hedge until late in the season.

PRIVACY HEDGES

Plants for privacy hedges should be dense, grow reasonably quickly and grow to a medium or tall height, which they will usually attain, at suitable density, in about five years. Unfortunately, the more quickly a hedge grows, the more frequently it requires cutting, so a plant such as Siberian elm (*Ulmus pumila*), listed in some catalogues as Chinese elm and often recommended as a fast-growing privacy hedge, should actually be used with great caution. It is so fast-growing that it needs cutting every two weeks during the summer to keep it down to the desired height. Siberian elm has the added disadvantage of losing its leaves in the fall, and hence losing its value as a privacy barrier.

The gardener has to strike a balance between speed of plant growth and the maintenance needed. Probably the most commonly used plant for privacy hedging, certainly in the eastern half of the country, is the arborvitae (*Thuja occidentalis*), generally known as cedar. This is virtually the ideal privacy hedge. It does best with three clippings a year, the first as soon as the spring flush of growth is finished, the next in early August and the last in late fall, so that total growth is limited to only about an inch a year. However, the arborvitae is such an amenable plant that a reasonably good hedge will result from only a single cut each year, although this hedge will not be as thick as one more frequently cut.

In milder parts of the country, where winter temperatures do not drop below about 23 degrees F (zone 7b), the Leyland cypress (*Cupressus lelandii*) makes an excellent tall hedge. This interesting plant is a cross between two

different but closely related plant species: the true cypress (*Cupressus* spp) and the false or Hinokai cypress (*Chamaecyparis* spp). If it is grown as a specimen plant, Leyland cypress will produce a tree as tall as 50 feet, but when planted as a hedge, it can be kept considerably shorter. It is very attractive and is a more vibrant green and faster growing than cedar.

Under prairie conditions, on heavy soils, or where rainfall is light, the Siberian pea shrub (*Caragana arborescens*) makes a reasonably good privacy hedge. Like the Siberian elm, it loses its leaves in winter, but for the summer months it will screen out unwanted scrutiny, and it produces small, fleeting, yellow flowers. Because the Siberian pea shrub tends to grow into

a small tree and become bare at the base, hard pruning, almost back to ground level, is necessary every few years to keep the base well furnished. An established plant will regrow rapidly.

These four plants, Siberian elm, arborvitae, Leyland cypress and Siberian pea shrub, will all grow more than 6 feet tall, so are useful where a complete screen is desired. The following plants will make a good dense hedge about 5 feet tall. There are several privets, for instance, excellent dark green, oval-leaved hedge plants grown a great deal as medium-sized hedges in England, but less used in Canada because they are hardy only in the southern parts. They vary in hardiness, so take care to choose one that will survive local winters. Amur privet (*Ligustrum amurense*) is one of the toughest of them all, reliably hardy to zone 5. In colder regions, there is increasing winterkill, and the entire hedge may be killed back to the roots during unusually cold winters. Gardeners who want a yellow-leaved privet, so much used in Britain for hedging, should choose the Vickary golden privet (*L. vickaryi*), which is hardy to zone 6, rather than the golden form of the common privet (*L. vulgare Aureum*), which tends to burn badly during summer heat waves.

Both yew (*Taxus* spp) and holly (*Ilex* spp) will make attractive evergreen hedges. Yew is a dense, low-growing plant which, if not clipped, has bright red berries with edible flesh and semi-poisonous seeds. The foliage of yew is poisonous to cattle so it should be used with caution around the farm. But because yew is shade tolerant, it can be used in places where other species will not grow. The noted English landscape artist Gertrude Jekyll wrote early in this century, "Compared with the yew no tree is so patient of coercion, so

The use of vegetables to define a garden boundary is a venerable French tradition. Even a row of staked tomatoes can serve to delineate an area with a temporary summer barrier that is useful as well as attractive.

protective in its close growth, or so effective as a background to the bright bloom of parterre or flower-border. Its docility to shaping into wall, niche, arch and column is so complete and convenient that it comes first among growing things as a means of expression in that domain of design that lies between architecture and gardening." Yew does have one serious drawback, however: it tends to windburn badly in exposed sites during the winter. If this proves to be a problem, a screen of burlap on the windward side will usually be sufficient to stop browning. There are both upright and prostrate forms of yew, so be sure to buy an upright form suitable for hedging. Holly, with its dark green leaves and brilliant red fruits, makes a particularly attractive hedge in zone 7, but it is very slow growing and not recommended for impatient gardeners. Both yew and holly have separate male and female plants, and some of each sex are necessary to ensure a fruit set. One male will suffice for several females.

Although a well-selected plant species can provide some protection against animal invasion, there is no hedge, however dense and spiny, that will keep out all animals; mice and voles may still get through to eat the bark of young trees. A gardener can, however, keep out the worst of the animal population as well as the neighbourhood toddlers by the use of the right type of hedge plants, among the best of which are the shrub roses. Many of these are extremely hardy, and if closely planted will form a thorny, informal barrier few animals will tackle. Since many shrub roses are naturally upright in habit, little pruning is needed. Many of the named forms of the Japanese fruiting rose (*Rosa rugosa*) are suitable, as is Harison's Yellow rose, (*R.* × *harisonii*). They should be cut down quite hard, to within about a foot of the ground, each summer after flowering for the initial three or four years, so that they will branch out from the base to produce a dense, impenetrable jungle.

Hawthorn (*Crataegus* spp) is another plant often effectively used as a wildlife barrier, although its location should be carefully considered. The long, vicious spines on many species preclude their use close to pathways where people may come into contact with them. In addition, hawthorns are members of the same plant family as apples and can act as reservoirs for various apple diseases unless they are sprayed along with the fruit trees. In *The New American Gardener* of 1843, a Mr. Quincy of Massachusetts directed that where a hawthorn hedge is to be planted the gardener should plough a course 6 feet wide and plant it with potatoes for a year. Then "set the thorns 8 inches apart. This is near enough in a country like this, where hogs are not permitted to run at large . . . . Keep both sides of the hedge planted with potatoes during the whole six years that the hedge is coming to perfection. The potatoes will nearly pay the cost of the labour. The manure for the potatoes benefits the hedge; and, while hoeing the potatoes, keeping the hedge clear of weeds is easy." Hawthorn is very tough and can be cut part way through and layered if it gets too tall, a once common system called "plashing." One turn-of-the-century book noted that with this system "the bent stems soon send out shoots; and if the plashing has been done with care, and that on moderately young and pliant branches, it will be found to be a cheap system."

QUINCE BORDERS

Flowering quince (*Chaenomeles speciosa*) and its various named forms will do much the same job as hawthorn, but on a smaller scale. If allowed to grow, hawthorns will become trees, but they can be grown as hedges as short as about 4 feet, while quinces, low-spreading shrubs that do best as informal hedges, rarely reach this height. The flowering quinces are hardier than fruiting quince (*C. japonica*) and also produce beautiful blossoms and edible fruits, although these are so tough that they are best used in wines and preserves.

All the forms of honey locust (*Gleditsia triacanthos*) will make good hedges. The named forms such as *Sunburst* and *Skyline* have been bred without thorns, but the original species is well armed and, again, should not be planted close to walkways. Buy whips rather than more mature trees and cut them back to make them branch out from the base. Also thorny is the native prickly ash (*Zanthoxylum americanum*), which is occasionally used by farmers to contain their cattle. It grows about 15 feet tall and tends to be quite wide — perhaps 8 or 10 feet — making it unsuitable for all but the largest gardens, and even there it can become invasive, with seedlings

Trevor J. Cole

A formal privet hedge, cedar, dogwood and climbing Dutchman's pipe provide a city residence with several levels of interest yet require very little maintenance.

Stephen Errington

springing up everywhere.

All hedges, of course, define spaces, and so all of the materials already mentioned are suitable for boundaries, but a boundary hedge may be quite small if it fulfills a role such as dividing the vegetable garden from the living area, or splitting an awkwardly shaped garden into separate units. The choice of plants for this type of hedging is virtually limitless, bound only by the gardener's budget, imagination, climate and needs. Some of the better choices for dwarf formal hedges include privet or yew, either of which can be grown as a dwarf hedge, and dwarf forms of cedar (*Cedrus* spp) such as *Hetz Midget* or *Little Champion*, which require little clipping.

Box or boxwood (*Buxus* spp), an evergreen that is hardy only to zone 6, has a long history of use in hedging and even in topiary, the sculptural shaping of plants. It produces the lowest of all clipped hedges, often less than a foot tall, and so is used extensively in old-fashioned knot gardens, where it is planted in an intricate, woven pattern

Stephen Errington

that surrounds beds of paving or other small plants. In 1911, Walter P. Wright, an Englishman, wrote in *An Illustrated Encyclopaedia of Gardening* that box "harbours slugs and likewise impoverishes the soil, but its Old-World appearance is in its favour, and causes people to plant it in spite of its drawbacks. When allowed to get scraggy and gappy it is not, however, pleasing."

Also suitable for a boundary hedge is the Nanking or Manchu cherry (*Prunus tomentosa*), which produces masses of pink flowers on the old wood, so it flowers well even if clipped. These flowers are followed by sweet red cherries which, although not as tasty as dessert cherries, are still well worth picking for pies, wines and preserves. Ninebark also makes a good hedge, but both the species *Physocarpus opulifolius* and the golden form *P.o. luteus* are better as medium-sized hedges, while the dwarf *Nanus* and the recently introduced dwarf golden variety *Dart's Gold* both make excellent low hedges.

Goldstem willow (*Salix alba vitellina*) is one plant that needs regular cutting back. Its name comes from the bright yellow new twigs, so an annual pruning is essential to promote new growth. Since its winter effect is especially pleasing, goldstem willow should be planted close to the house. The arctic willow (*S. purpurea gracilis*) also makes a good low hedge but lacks the bright new growth. Both willows are very hardy, to zones 3 and 2 respectively.

Alpine currant (*Ribes alpinum*), much planted in the Montreal area, makes a good formal hedge 3 feet tall or more. It can be kept shorter than the golden currant (*R. aureum*), but the flowers lack the powerful scent of those of the golden currant. The Mohave firethorn (*Pyracantha mohave*) is smothered in brilliant, inedible orange fruit in fall.

Among other flowering plants that can be used as hedges are the lilacs (*Syringa* spp), mock-oranges (*Philadelphus* spp) and various forms of pink flowered spirea (*Spiraea × bumalda*) such as *Anthony Waterer*, *Froebeli* and *Goldflame*. Other good choices are the shrubby cinquefoils, forms of *Potentilla fruticosa*, Turkestan euonymus (*Euonyumus nanus Turkestanicus*), bridal wreath (*Spiraea × arguta*) and some of the new hardy roses such as *Champlain*, recently released by Agriculture Canada.

HEDGE PLANTING

Since hedges will generally be in place for many years it makes sense to spend time preparing the site before planting. Dig out a trench to full spade depth and work some old compost or manure into the base of it. If the soil is chiefly clay, be careful not to step in the trench, packing the base down, for this could result in the plants sitting in water.

Planting can take place in spring or fall, but spring is generally preferable in areas with cold winters. Set the plants just a little lower than they were in the nursery — you will see the colour change on the stem that marks the previous soil level — and then carefully fill in between them, taking care not to leave any air pockets in the soil. It is a good idea, at this time, to add a soluble fertilizer high in phosphorus, which plants need to make new roots.

Once the planting is complete, it is time to make the most important cut in the life of the hedge. Step back and look at the row of plants. Find the shortest one and cut all the plants back to below the top of this one. Failure to do this, if you hope that shorty will catch up in a couple of summers, will result in a hedge that is uneven for many years. As 19th-century gardener John Loudon wrote, " . . . the strong plants very soon outgrow such as are weaker, and not only overtop them, but also deprive them of that nourishment which they so much require. As the hedge advances in age the evil becomes greater; small, stunted plants and innumerable gaps appearing throughout the whole line of the fence, interspersed with others remarkable for their strength and luxuriance." It is far better to cut plenty off the top of a hedge at planting time than to plant, say, 5-foot cedars and only cut them back to 4½ feet. Trimming back by 25 percent is not excessive. A hedge that is hard pruned at planting time will grow dense more quickly than one that is only lightly cut.

Once the plants have been cut to an even height, they should be shaped with ordinary garden shears or special hedging shears. Buy good quality shears, not inexpensive ones that will soon need replacing. For a long hedge, you may want to invest in electric hedge trimmers, which cost $30 to $50 depending upon the blade length. Most plants have a natural taper toward the top, and this should be the way the hedge is trimmed. Flat-topped evergreen

TRIM NEWLY PLANTED HEDGE BACK TO BELOW TOP OF SHORTEST PLANT

As soon as the hedge plants (right) are in place, they must all be cut to a height shorter than that of the shortest individual. Then, if the hedge is going to be formal, it must be shaped into a suitable conformation to shed snow (left). Any shape that is narrow at the top and solid and wide at the base will be suitable, whereas hedges that are widest above the base invite snow breakage.

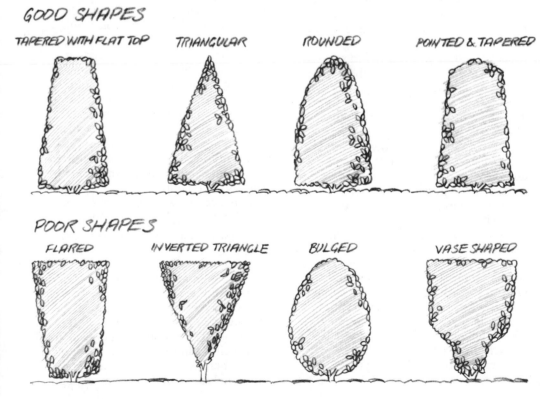

GOOD SHAPES

TAPERED WITH FLAT TOP   TRIANGULAR   ROUNDED   POINTED & TAPERED

POOR SHAPES

FLARED   INVERTED TRIANGLE   BULGED   VASE SHAPED

hedges are permissible in regions that receive very little snow, but in most of the North, hedges should be cut to have a sloping or rounded top, so that snow is easily shed down the sides. With shorter, deciduous hedges this is not as important, since the snow rarely settles on top. The other point to keep in mind while trimming is that if there is to be base growth, the bottom of the hedge must receive sunlight. If the top of the hedge is allowed to become wider than the base, light intensity is reduced and basal growth becomes thinner and thinner as the years go by. Eventually the hedge will have a green top and bare trunks.

Yearly maintenance will consist of at least one clipping a year for a formal hedge, and one pruning of unwanted growth for an informal one. Weeds will not be a problem under most hedges, where so little light penetrates that the ground may be bare. With an informal hedge, it may be necessary to create a clean edge on the ground covers that approach the hedge, while the space under the hedge can be mulched with leaves or bark chips. With a deciduous hedge, allow the fallen leaves to stay in place for mulch and added soil fertility.

CLIMBERS AND VINES

Although they are not freestanding in the manner of hedges and are more often used to decorate walls and fences, climbers and vines can also be used to delineate boundaries, provided they are given some support. They are generally planted about a foot away from a building wall; closer than that, and the plant will be in a rain shadow that will necessitate frequent watering until its roots extend further out in the garden. Most gardeners would be hard pressed to name more than two climbers – only clematis and roses come immediately to most minds – but in fact a look through any of the larger nursery catalogues will reveal a large selection of climbers, some noted mainly for their flowers, others for their foliage. Add to that the many annual vines that can be grown from seed, and the possible selection of vertical decorations becomes quite extensive.

Both clematis and roses are climbers that need some form of trellis to give them support. Clematis species climb by twining their stems and leaf stalks around something, while roses climb by means of their stout, recurved thorns which, in theory, hook on to other vegetation and hold the plant relatively upright. In practice, it is usually necessary to tie up climbing roses, as their thorns do not support them on artificial trellises. Both roses and clematis require full sun to grow and bloom well.

Most gardeners think of clematis as those climbers with the large pink or purple flowers. Few are aware of the many excellent small-flowered species with red, white or yellow blossoms. Clematis are typically grown on a trellis attached to the house wall, probably the best way to display the well-known, large-flowered hybrids. But both these and the small-flowered, less known types can be grown in other, more imaginative ways, such as covering old tree stumps, climbing a wooden fence, or rambling up through a large shrub.

The golden rule for success with clematis is "cool roots and warm tops." The root systems will not thrive in warm, sandy soil, while the top growth will suffer in a shady, cool situation. Always plant clematis in a place where the roots will be protected from the heat of the sun. This can be achieved by planting a second shrub to provide shade, by growing annuals around the base of the vine, or by covering the area around the plant with patio slabs or natural stones. In addition, clematis demand an alkaline soil. Plants which do not seem to be thriving in midsummer will often respond almost magically to being watered with a slurry of 1 cup of lime in a gallon of water. It does not dissolve, so keep it well stirred.

The parentage of clematis is rather complex but important to understand, since it governs the way in which the plants flower, and thus the way in which they should be pruned. Varieties derived from *Clematis jackmanii* flower on the new wood in July and continue to bloom until frost. They should be cut back hard each spring, almost down to the base in areas where winters are severe. This group includes some of the most popular varieties such as the pink *Comtesse de Bouchaud*, the red *Crimson Star*, the purple *Gypsy Queen*, the purple-flowering species *C. jackmanii* itself and the light pink *Pink Chiffon*, also called Hagley hybrids. A similar group is derived from *C. viticella*, the Italian clematis. These also bloom on the current season's growth and can be cut back hard each spring. They will produce a woodier stem and, where greater height is required, may be pruned to within 6 inches of the previous year's wood. This gives a larger

framework each year. Popular varieties in this group are the red-violet *Ernest Markham*, the blue *Lady Betty Balfour*, and the lilac *Ville de Lyon*.

The next group, derived from *C. lanuginosa*, requires a portion of the old wood to be left. Cut the plants back to within 2 to 4 feet of the ground each spring. Flowers will be produced on both the old and new wood starting in June, earlier than the previous two groups. This group also contains some of the more popular hybrids, the red *Crimson King*, the white *C. henryi*, the

deep blue *Lord Neville*, mauve-pink *Nelly Moser*, and lavender-blue *Ramona*. The double white *Duchess of Edinburgh* is the only selection readily available from another group, the *C. florida*. It is characterized by flowers in late spring on the previous year's growth, so should not be pruned until flowering is over. Early spring pruning will remove the flower-bearing wood, while later pruning will give the plant a chance for the new growth that will produce flowers the following year.

The final group, based on *C. patens*,

A New Brunswick house that might otherwise seem to be a visual intrusion upon the landscape is softened and given grace by a summer blanket of green ivy.

There are two types of wall roses, climbers and ramblers, either of which can be tied against a fence, trellis or pergola in a suitably moderate climate. Climbing roses are pruned in spring before growth starts, while rambling roses must not be cut back until they are finished blooming in summer.

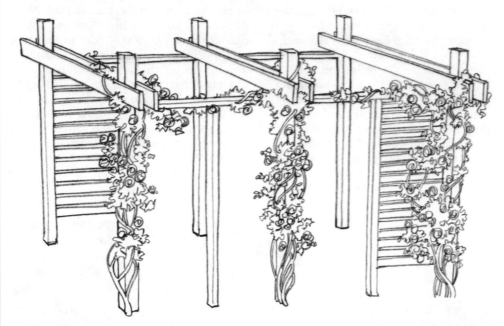

should be grown only in warmer gardens. These clematis flower on the old wood, but in cold areas, where they are winterkilled back to the ground, they may produce a few small flowers late in the season but are most disappointing. I know this from experience, as I had a *Lincoln Star* here in Ottawa that grew 8 feet high every year and in late August or early September would have two or three flowers right on the top. This is when I came to realize that this group in particular is just not quite as hardy. This group includes the rosy violet *Barbara Dibley*, the pink *Bees Jubilee*, the deep violet *The President* and *Lincoln Star*, which is pink with a dark stripe on each petal.

There are also smaller-flowered clematis that are ideal for growing in more natural situations, or for planting under a spring-flowering bush such as lilac to make it appear to bloom twice. Not so much climbers as sprawlers, they grow tall and sort of lean on things, and are thus equally useful when allowed to trail down a steep bank or rock pile. These include the sweet autumn clematis (*C. paniculata*), a native of Japan that is a vigorous grower, climbing on almost anything and ideal for covering old tree stumps. It bears a profusion of small white, sweetly scented blooms in August. The very hardy golden clematis (*C. tangutica*) has solitary flowers of the brightest yellow in June and July. Scarlet clematis is the name given to *C. texensis* which, as its name suggests, comes from Texas. The flowers are vivid red, about an inch long and shaped like upside-down urns.

ROSES

Growing climbing roses in much of Canada is simply a labour of love. They are not reliably hardy in areas cooler than about zone 6, and yet Northern gardeners still insist on growing them. Some of the newer varieties being produced by Agriculture Canada in Ottawa are much hardier than older types and are now becoming available in nursery catalogues. Look for *John Cabot*, *William Baffin* and *Henry Kelsey*.

There are two types of wall roses, climbing and rambling, and as is the case with clematis, it is important to know which type your plants are so that the proper pruning can be done. So-called climbing roses, the ones most commonly grown, flower on the new wood and should be pruned in early spring before growth starts. Typical of this type are *Blaze* and *Golden Showers* (the best of the yellow forms for colour, but also more tender than many others) and *New Dawn* which is one of the best of the pinks. Rambler roses bloom on the previous season's wood and must not be cut back until the blossoms are finished. The pink *Dorothy Perkins* is probably the most widely grown of the rambler group. Because in most areas roses suffer badly from winterkill, and thus have to be cut back in spring, rambler roses are not as frequently offered in Northern catalogues and should be grown only where winter injury is rare.

In regions where roses are not reliably hardy, it is best to take them down from their trellis each fall, tie the canes together in a bundle for ease of handling, and, if possible, wrap them in burlap. In very cold areas it is necessary to dig a trench, lay the bundled-up roses in it, and cover the plants with 9 to 12 inches of soil. In marginal areas, however, it is sufficient if the bundle of canes is given the protection of a layer of straw or leaves and then A-frame boards to keep the straw dry. Remember that wherever straw or leaves are used for protection, you are inviting mice to come and visit. Make sure you include a few packets of mouse bait in your straw cover or there may be no bark left on the roses come spring.

In spring, once the danger of hard frost is past, the roses can be uncovered. Remove the boards or half the soil one weekend and the rest of the soil or the leaves a week later. This gradual uncovering allows the wood to acclimatize itself to outside conditions. Unwrap the vines and tie them loosely to the trellis. Do not be in a hurry to prune at this stage; it is amazing how often seemingly dead wood will recover and break out into growth given time. After a couple of weeks, you should be able to see clearly how much winter

damage there was, and know how far back to cut your canes. All dead growth should be removed. If winterkill was light, prune the canes back by about one-third.

Another important group of climbing plants is the honeysuckles (*Lonicera* spp), a family that includes many fine woody shrubs of varying hardiness. All of the vining species twine around some form of support and so can cover a house wall, weave through a chain-link fence or blanket a tree stump with equal ease. Do not expect rapid growth in the first

year; these plants usually take a couple of years to become established, but they then grow quickly to about 8 or 10 feet in the North. The leaves are dull green, nothing very exciting, although there is a variegated form whose veins are picked out in white. That species is, however, fairly tender, while gardeners in cold areas are more or less limited to the *Dropmore Scarlet Trumpet* honeysuckle (*L.* × *brownii Dropmore*), developed in Dropmore, Manitoba. The flowers, scarlet outside with orange interiors, are produced from midsummer until frost.

Next in hardiness, capable of surviving in zone 4, is the plant usually called goldflame honeysuckle (*L. heckrottii*) which is similar in habit and flower to the Dropmore scarlet except that the flowers are pinkish outside with yellow interiors. The early Dutch honeysuckle (*L. periclymenum belgica*) is often listed in Prairie catalogues although it is a zone 5b plant that has not been reliably hardy in Ottawa. The flowers are smaller and more open in shape than those of the previous species, but they have a strong perfume.

The last honeysuckle species should be tried only in Southern Ontario or coastal British Columbia (zone 6b). This is Hall's Japanese honeysuckle (*L. japonica Halliana*), which has sweetly scented, small, white flowers that turn yellow with age. The form with variegated leaves (*L. j. Reticulata*) is attractive all year round but is slower growing.

One of the most spectacular of all climbers is surely the wisteria (*Wisteria* spp) which has very large, compound leaves as long as 9 inches and produces long trusses composed of several dozen individual blue flowers. Wisteria climbs by twining around its supports and can be used on a house wall if a strong trellis is firmly attached to the wall. Where

Unreliably hardy beyond zone 6, climbing and rambling roses can be coaxed to flower in slightly cooler areas if they are untied and covered in winter. In the warmest corners of the North, however, they dependably provide the sort of spectacular display that colours the garden behind Victoria's Empress Hotel.

space permits, however, probably the most spectacular use of wisteria is to grow it on a pergola or arbour, so that the flower trusses hang down overhead and can be seen to perfection. Unfortunately, wisterias are not hardy enough for most of Canada, and can be grown only where winters do not get colder than about minus 4 degrees F (zone 6). In other areas, the best chances for survival will come with the Japanese wisteria (*W. floribunda*), which is slightly hardier than the Chinese (*W. sinensis*), and a form of the Japanese wisteria called *Lawrence*, which was found growing on Lawrence Street in Brantford, Ontario and should be appearing in nursery catalogues soon. This form is the hardiest of them all and flowers most summers at the Central Experimental Farm where it has survived temperatures approaching minus 40 degrees F.

HOLDFASTS

The closely related Virginia creeper (*Parthenocissus quinquefolia*) and Boston ivy (*P. tricuspidata*) are true climbers, since they support themselves with the aid of tendrils, and yet I always think of them as vines. Both are very useful plants since not only will they quickly cover the wall of a house or smother an old tree stump — Virginia creeper will grow as much as 25 feet in a year — they will also act as ground covers and spread over a large area if not given support. The tendrils on these plants are so sensitive that they can twine around the smallest objects, even stucco. Unless the vines are pulled off when young, they will remove many of the stones with them later. Virginia creeper which has leaves divided into five leaflets, is the hardier of the two, surviving even in zone 3 on the Prairies. Its chief attraction is its brilliant red fall colour, but

unfortunately it is attacked by the grape flea beetle, which chews numerous small holes in the leaves and renders them unsightly. The small-leaved form known as Englemann's ivy (*P. q. engelmannii*) has, in addition to the tendrils, small discs on the tendril ends. Known as holdfasts, these discs act as suction cups that enable the plant to climb almost smooth surfaces. Boston ivy, which does not resemble the true ivies (*Hedera* spp), is more tender than Virginia creeper, and cannot be grown in areas colder than zone 5b. It is distinguished from Virginia creeper by having leaflets in threes rather than fives, so that is is easily mistaken for poison ivy in areas where both are native.

Although most gardeners are familiar with the Peegee hydrangea (*Hydrangea paniculata Grandiflora*), with its heads of white summer flowers that later turn pink, few recognize its climbing relative, *H. anomala petiolaris*, which is hardy to zone 5 in most years. However, one plant that had covered the side of the Arboretum building in Ottawa since 1952 was killed in the winter of 1980-81 when the temperature dropped to minus 39 degrees F. In harsh climates such as

this, the climbing hydrangea should only be grown on the east side of a building, so that it receives early morning sun in winter. If grown on a south or west wall, it will warm up too much during the day and will be damaged by the sudden drop in temperature when evening comes. In warmer climates, this caution does not apply.

One of the fastest growing of all climbers is generally sold as the Tara vine, also called bower actinidia (*Actinidia arguta*), a close but far hardier relative of the kiwi fruit (*A. chinensis*) that is now receiving a great deal of attention along with all the other *Actinidia* members. Although *A. arguta* will also yield edible fruit, I have never seen fruit produced in this region. At Boston's Isabella Stewart Gardner Museum, however, two vines in the courtyard yield more than 10 gallons of fruit every year. Further north, the plant is noted mainly for its green leaves that are edged with pink if exposed to sunlight. It will grow 15 to 20 feet in a season and can become invasive if not pruned back severely each spring. The white, scented flowers are produced only in the warmer parts of the country, but the plant itself is hardy to zone 4.

The following two species are better grown on an arbour or on some form of trellis enclosure rather than as wall plants. They are also useful for clothing banks, rock piles and similar awkward locations. Hardy to zone 6 is the white-flowered silver lace or silver fleece vine (*Polygonum aubertii*), a rapid grower that will extend 9 feet in a season. The individual flowers are very small, but they are borne in large trusses. One of the best climbers for providing deep shade is the Dutchman's pipe (*Aristolochia durior*), often listed as *A. sipho*. It is hardy to zone 5. When grown in rich soil this vine will produce leaves that are as large as 8 inches by 6. The small, inconspicuous flowers that have been described as resembling a meerschaum pipe are produced in early summer.

There are two different bittersweets grown as climbers, preferably on some sort of arbour. The Chinese bittersweet (*Celastrus rosthornianus*) is hardy only as far north as zone 5, while the American bittersweet (*C. scandens*) will survive on the southern Prairies in zone 3b. Both are grown for their very attractive fruits which give winter colour, and both have some plants that only produce male flowers and thus do not set fruit. It is therefore wise to plant several vines to increase your chances of planting at least one of each sex, ensuring good cross pollination and fruit set.

One of the best shrubs for covering old tree stumps is the trumpet vine (*Campsis radicans*), not to be confused with the scarlet trumpet honeysuckle. This is often listed as a zone 6 plant, but it is hardy in sheltered locations in Ottawa, zone 5, where it produces masses of brilliant red trumpets in midsummer. It climbs by means of small rootlets which anchor themselves particularly well to bark, but which will also cling to brickwork, as will true ivy. English ivy (*Hedera helix*) is hardy only in the mild zone 6b, while Baltic ivy (*H.h. Baltica*) will survive and climb in slightly cooler regions, zone 6. Being evergreen, ivies add a layer of insulation to the walls, as well as providing a good hiding place for spiders and a winter roost for sparrows. Gardeners who do not like spiders or being awakened by birds should probably not grow ivy on their walls.

Grapes are also climbing plants worthy of consideration. They can be grown along wires against a wall or, more usually, can be allowed to romp over a trellis or arbour. The forms suitable for table use or for making

Favoured vines of Old-World gardeners, grapes produce fruit and summer shade in regions as cold as zone 2, although the cultivars with higher fruit quality, such as *Concord*, thrive only in zone 5 or warmer gardens.

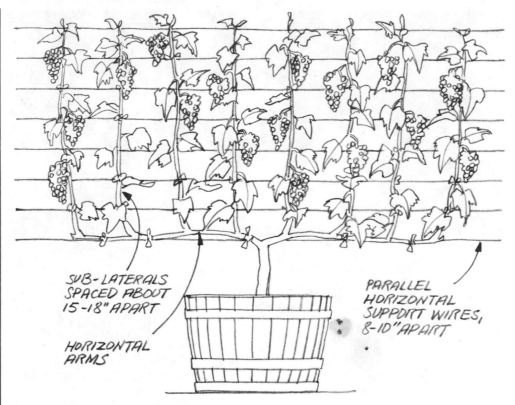

SUB-LATERALS SPACED ABOUT 15-18" APART

HORIZONTAL ARMS

PARALLEL HORIZONTAL SUPPORT WIRES, 8-10" APART

quality wine are hardy only to about zone 5, but in regions as cold as zone 2, some of the native grape species can be trained to cover a wall or arbour. Although these do not yield table grapes, their fruit will make good jellies and drinkable wines. Both the riverbank grape (*Vitis riparia*) and the frost grape (*V. vulpina*) are available commercially.

There is one final, ancient way of covering walls, and that is with trees, either ornamental or fruit. Known as espaliers, or what Aldous Huxley called "crucified fruit," these trees are pruned to lie flat against the wall, and the branches are tied down to wires or wall spikes to give the desired shape, usually with the branches parallel to one another and equidistant from each other. In small gardens, this is an ideal way of growing fruit without taking up much space. If they are trained against a south wall that reflects heat, espaliered trees can often be grown beyond their normal range. My father-in-law had an espalier peach on his house in central England, well beyond the normal peach-growing range, and picked fruit off it most years. While there is more skill needed to grow fruit trees in this way, many books specializing in fruit growing provide instructions. Non-fruiting trees are relatively simple to train this way.

Espaliers do not have to be grown against a house wall. They can also be trained along wires strung between posts, to take on many of the functions of a hedge. Many trees and large shrubs are suitable for this treatment, but normally only fruit trees and bushes such as black currants, gooseberries and figs (in very mild areas) are grown in this manner. The amount of fruit produced per bush is smaller, but the area of land needed is also much less.

ANNUAL VINES

Several annuals will serve duty as climbing vines. Generally these are grown on some form of fence or trellis rather than on a house wall, but there is no real reason to be bound by this rule. In either case, the dead vines will have to be pulled off their supports after they die in fall. Because they grow quickly, annuals are probably most useful as a temporary cover while more permanent plants are getting established, but they can also be used to provide a screen year after year.

When I was a teenager, my father was bitten by the sweet pea bug and actually used to get up an hour early each morning during the summer to allow time to tie up his sweet peas before going to work. The vines grew about 16 feet tall and the flowers had as many as nine blooms on a stem 15 inches or more long. It is not necessary to go to such lengths to grow acceptable sweet peas, however. The secret of success is to start them early and get them into the ground while the soil is still cool. Providing they are given plenty of water during the heat of summer, and the flowers are kept picked, they will bloom freely. There is also a perennial sweet pea that will come up anew each year, but the flowers on this are smaller and the colour range is not as great. Sweet peas are easiest to grow on a chain link fence or on bean netting stretched between two poles.

Beans themselves can provide attractive and useful screening. The *Scarlet Runner* bean even has the bonus of brilliant red blossoms. Some gardeners maintain that *Scarlet Runner*

A euonymus hedge and climbing clematis complement the white and green colour scheme of a house and its surrounding picket fence.

Derek Fell

Northern Gold forsythia (left), which has proved hardy on the Canadian Prairies, is one of the most important recent developments in shrubs for Northerners. Foundation plantings (right), which allow the vertical lines of buildings to meld into the horizontal contours of neighbouring ground covers, can consist of annual or perennial flowers, shrubs or trees.

Evergreen azaleas (overleaf) are hardy only in Agriculture Canada climatic zone 7b and warmer gardens, but where they are successful, they can provide spectacular early summer colour and broadleaf winter greenery. Here, they grow in the company of grape hyacinths, silver dollar plants and yellow alyssum.

Among popular and easily raised perennials are poppies and irises (top), which come back from the same roots or rhizomes each spring, and tulips and grape hyacinths (below), which arise from fall-planted bulbs that will renew themselves and continue to bloom from year to year if they are planted in favourable circumstances.

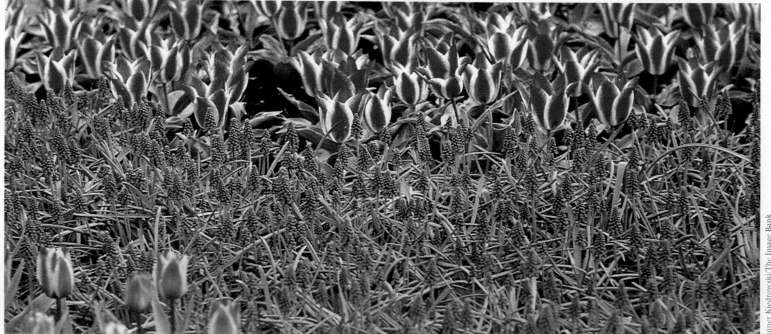

Where grass would have been difficult to plant and tend, a ground cover of creeping phlox in various shades imitates a wild mountain meadow and requires no ongoing maintenance at all.

Virginia creeper is a relatively cold-hardy vine that loses its leaves in winter but quickly forms a thick mat in spring. Like its smaller relative, Boston ivy, it climbs, with the use of tendrils so sensitive that they can twine around the individual stones of stucco.

beans are not edible — I have even heard rumours that they are poisonous — but in fact the young beans are perfectly delectable, although they may not be very appetizing if allowed to become too old before harvesting. Like all beans, bush or pole, *Scarlet Runners* are tastiest when young and tender. Cucumbers, too, will climb on a net or on string to produce attractive vines with edible fruit. Although they cannot be planted until the soil is warm, cucumbers will quickly climb a fence or net where they will produce crops until frost. Be sure to purchase a vining, not a bush cucumber. Grown in this way, the cucumber plant needs little ground space, while its fruit is kept clean and ripens evenly.

Morning glories (*Convolvulus* spp) and moonflowers (*Ipomoea* spp) are closely related climbers that are most often seen decorating strings around verandahs in summer. They are unpredictable plants, however, that seem to be very dependent upon the weather conditions shortly after planting. I have seen some fantastic displays in home gardens, followed the next year by plants that never grow more than 3 feet high.

One native vine that is very useful for covering stumps, old fences and similar eyesores is the native wild cucumber (*Echinocystis lobata*), which will grow as tall as 15 feet in a summer and can almost completely hide whatever it is climbing upon. Its arching sprays of white flowers appear in August, and the seed pods that follow can be used for winter decoration. There are many other vines, both annual and perennial, that can be used. Keep in mind that variety is the key to interest in the landscape and, while a hodge-podge of plants looks disorderly, a well-thought-out scheme calls for a diversity of plant materials. Even at Hampton Court, one of the kingliest of gardens, there are hedges, tall and short, dividing areas of trees and flowers, and even a venerable climbing grape vine still provides interest for tourists and work for the humble groundskeepers.

Trevor Cole received his horticultural training in England, graduating in 1960 from the Royal Botanic Gardens at Kew. After working in several English nurseries, he emigrated to Canada in 1967. He is now Curator of the Dominion Arboretum at the Central Experimental Farm in Ottawa.

In Vancouver (facing page) brilliant tulips and self-seeding forget-me-nots are especially beautiful when they grow in a bed that has a gracefully curving boundary.

10 | Tree Lines

Shade, flowers, fruit and year-round beauty

By Jennifer Bennett

For poets, they are even more inspiring than flowers. Trees moved Robert Frost to swing from birches and stop by the woods on a snowy evening, sent A. E. Housman into the forest "to see the cherry hung with snow," and, in rhyming couplets remembered by generations of school children, allowed Joyce Kilmer to compare his ability to write foolish poems with God's ability to make trees. Along similiar lines, Ogden Nash wrote:

I think that I shall never see
A billboard lovely as a tree;
Perhaps, unless the billboards fall
I'll never see a tree at all.

Scientists find trees equally intriguing if less romantic. What one author called "woody plants with a trunk" are not only the most massive examples of an almost miraculous vegetal ability to transform sunlight into cells and oxygen but are also devices capable of filtering pollutants out of the air, keeping the air on the forest floor as much as 25 degrees F cooler than that above the forest, directing or decreasing wind and preventing light rainfall from ever hitting the ground.

Both poetically beautiful and scientifically practical, trees can share equal billing with houses and other buildings as the focal points of any landscape, rural or urban. For the property owner, however, trees can also be the focal points of a frustrating exercise in fighting the elements and discovering the limits of one's arboreal expertise. Working with trees demands not only some knowledge and skill, but also patience and a certain amount of vision. Here, more than in any other aspect of landscaping, one has to take into consideration the long view of both space and time. Acorns do indeed produce mighty oaks but can require a generation to do so. The properly selected tree may be a gift for yourself, your children, for the neighbourhood or for the city, but a poorly chosen or poorly planted tree will cause only disappointment.

For the North, the majority of landscape architects and horticulturists agree that the most important consideration in choosing a tree is hardiness – its ability to survive the winter. Trees planted beyond their area of survival will weaken, falter and probably die – and few things are as disheartening as a dying tree. Fortunately, climatic zone maps (pages 20 and 21) and lists of species and cultivars classified according to their coldest zone of survival have been created. State departments and provincial ministries of agriculture can supply lists of preferred trees for their own areas. Buying a plant from a local nursery that has overwintered its own stock is some assurance that the plant will survive in your garden – as is, of course, the growth of the same type of plant in a neighbouring yard or field.

Native species are often the hardiest, while imported species of the same tree are usually more tender. For instance, the native black walnut is hardy to zone 3b, while the English walnut is hardy to only zone 7, which restricts its growth to the warmest corners of Canada. The native American elm can be grown in zone 2, while the Chinese elm is hardy to zone 5 and the English elm to zone 6. In addition, green-leaved cultivars or species are generally hardier than those with variegated or differently coloured foliage: the native box elder, for example, is hardy to zone 2, but the silverleaf form can be grown only in zone 7 or warmer areas. Often, however, cultivars – that is, cultivated varieties – of native species may

Ontario Ministry of Agriculture and Food

represent improvements over the originals in plant shape, colour, disease resistance and such, sometimes without a loss in winter survival, so the choice of a native for the landscape may not always be the wisest option.

If hardiness is the first consideration in choosing a tree, the second is the gardener's own preference. There is no sense in planting a Blue Colorado spruce simply because every front yard on one's street has proved its viability. Remember that a tree is a long-term proposition; a short-lived birch may last 20 years, an oak, hundreds. Eager for fruit, my husband and I planted both a McIntosh apple and a Cortland on our Ontario property soon after we moved there. Disease-prone and demanding, the two trees have never thrived, yet we haven't the heart to cut them down, and only wish we had considered a few of the more unusual apples before buying so quickly. Do you want shade? Edible fruit? A tree that looks attractive in winter? Scented blooms in spring? Red or golden or weeping foliage? All of these options are available. Take time to choose wisely.

Next, consider the limitations of the potential tree-planting site. Its soil quality (heavy or light, sandy or loamy or clay) is important, and so is its dryness or wetness. A wet spot, which will probably be low enough to be a frost pocket as well, can be expensively drained or more inexpensively planted with trees that will tolerate wet soil: willows, red or silver maples, alders, river or paper birches, tamaracks, white spruce, poplars or pin oaks, to name a few. On the other hand, a dry spot could receive a honey locust, pine or spruce. Other factors to consider are whether the site offers full shade, partial shade or full sun, whether it is exposed to strong winds, whether it will be sprayed with

road salts or receive pollutants from nearby chimneys or passing trucks, whether there are overhead wires or underground pipes, and how much space is available for tree roots and branches. An oak, maple, elm, white ash or linden needs a tree-free space 40 to 50 feet in diameter. In fact, to allow for branch and root spread, no large tree should be planted within 25 feet of a house.

Oaks, maples and elms are also relatively slow growing, becoming good shade trees only after about 10 years of growth. A birch, willow or poplar, on the other hand, could reach the same height in three or four years, perhaps even less. Today's landowners are often transient enough that they do not choose to plant the more beautiful but slower-growing hardwoods.

Trees are generally the largest living elements in a landscape, and therein lies their weakness and their strength. While gigantic trees provide both shade and beauty, a 50- or 75-foot-tall chestnut, oak or beech is too big for most lots. Useful in almost any situation however, are smaller trees, many of which can be considered either shrubs (multi-stemmed) or trees (single-stemmed) depending upon how they are pruned. Excellent small trees or large shrubs, none of which normally exceeds 30 feet in height, include crab apple (*Malus* spp); hawthorn (*Crataegus* spp); cherry (*Prunus* spp); serviceberry (*Amelanchier* spp); mountain ash (*Sorbus* spp); Japanese, mountain and Amur maple (*Acer* spp); hop-hornbeam or ironwood (*Ostrya*

Agriculture Canada

virginiana); dogwood (*Cornus* spp); Eastern redbud (*Cercis canadensis*); common witchhazel (*Hamamelis virginiana*); staghorn sumach (*Rhus typhina*); nannyberry (*Viburnum lentago*); Russian olive (*Elaeagnus angustifolia*); magnolia (*Magnolia* spp); laurel willow (*Salix pentandra*); Japanese tree lilac (*Syringa reticulata* formerly *S. amurensis japonica*); common smoketree (*Cotinus coggygria*); rose of Sharon (*Hibiscus syriacus*); Carolina silverbell (*Halesia carolina*); Goldenrain tree (*Koelreuteria paniculata*) and the Laburnum or Goldenchain tree (*Laburnum × watereri*).

What about fruit trees in the landscape? Even on a small city lot, these are often sensible options. Although older landscaping books advise against purchasing species that "litter the lawn with fruit or flowers," most landowners now would rather be practical than immaculate. The fruit tree, although capable of littering, requires relatively little space, flowers in spring and, provided its pollination requirements have been met, produces useful fruit in summer or fall. Keep in mind however, that most popular fruit trees are quite tender. They can survive high temperatures if they have sufficient water, but low temperatures usually limit their northward range. Peaches and sweet cherries are more or less limited to zone 6 and warmer, while sour cherries and plums will struggle beyond zone 5. In colder areas, choose fruit bred for survival there: cold-hardy apples, apple crabs, crabs, pears, cherry plums and apricots. Many fruit trees need a mate for best fruit production. On a small city lot there may not be space for two fruit trees, so, unless a next-door neighbour has the same type of fruit, the gardener might best choose a tree that can self-pollinate – a sour cherry, say, or an apricot, or one of the self-pollinating

plums. Another option is to choose two plants from related groups: a crab apple with an apple; a sand cherry with a late-blooming plum. Fortunately, fruit trees, unlike most ornamental trees, are available grafted onto a variety of different rootstocks that affect the eventual size of the tree. While the really small dwarf trees, those that reach only a few feet at maturity, will not survive in colder areas, there are many semi-dwarfs – trees that are 50 to 85 percent the size of a standard – well suited to most Northern gardens. For the best selection and for reliable information, patronize a local or mail-order nursery dealer who specializes in fruit trees. See Appendix E for tree sources and ordering information.

OLD TREES, NEW TREES

In renovating a landscape, think at least twice before removing existing trees – they may take generations to replace. Should you wish to alter the landscape around an existing tree, try not to raise or lower the soil level close to the trunk. Roots grow to a specific depth because of the availability there of soil microorganisms which supply them with nutrients. If soil is taken off the roots, they are left vulnerable to drought and quick temperature changes. If soil is added to the root area, the microorganisms die or move into higher soil, and the tree may die. Complex and expensive procedures such as walling off the root area so that the surrounding garden may be raised or lowered without affecting the tree may or may not be successful. Certainly the roots that grow beyond the wall will still be bared or buried.

There are basically two tree-planting seasons and, for that matter, only two seasons when most Northern nurseries will sell trees: in spring before growth

The Russian olive is among the trees recommended for smaller sites, as it is less than 30 feet tall when mature. The tree form of a popular, silver-leaved shrub, it produces sweetly scented yellow flowers in late spring, followed by silver berries.

begins, and, more controversially, in autumn from leaf fall until about six weeks before the ground freezes, after which most root growth ceases. Fall planting allows little leeway for the tree to become established before winter, making frost heaving and winterkill a possibility, but it does mean that the plant has the full advantage of the previous year's growth in an established site. Evergreens have proved most successful in fall planting, and work at Cornell University in northern New York State has shown that late summer and early fall are suitable times for planting all balled and burlapped, (B & B) plants in fairly sheltered sites, because at that time there is reduced moisture stress, and the trees are gearing down for winter. Riskier for fall planting

Agriculture Canada

are deciduous trees, especially red maples, birches, beeches, hawthorns, dogwoods, poplars, fruit trees, oaks and willows. Deciduous trees in general, and in particular marginally hardy species and any trees purchased "bare root," are best planted while they are still dormant in spring: warming weather and plenty of watering will allow them to become gradually and securely settled in their new locations before the onset of the most trying time for all Northern plants, winter. Larches, deciduous conifers that lose their needles in fall, should be treated as other deciduous trees.

Bare-root trees, those dug from the soil of the nursery or received in the mail wrapped in damp moss in plastic bags, should be planted as soon as possible. Fifteen minutes of sun on bare roots, especially of conifers, can be deadly. If the trees cannot be planted right away, the roots should be soaked in cool water for half an hour, and then the trees should be "heeled" into a moist, shady,

If it cannot be planted immediately, a bare-root tree should be heeled in (left), a temporary measure in which the roots are placed in a hole and covered with damp soil in a shady location. As it is planted, a large tree or one in a windy site may require the insertion of a stake between the roots, 4 to 6 inches from the windward side of the trunk. The stake is tied to the trunk with figure eights of soft cloth or wire threaded through an old hose or bicycle tire (right).

sheltered spot outdoors. "Heeling in" is a temporary measure that consists simply of digging a hole just large enough to accommodate the roots, covering and tamping them lightly and watering. The tree need not be upright. Then, dig a hole at least a foot wider than the width needed to easily hold all the naturally

spread roots, and just deep enough to keep the tree at the previous soil level — too little soil over the roots will expose them to changes in temperature and moisture, while even a couple of inches too much soil can smother them. Keep all the removed soil next to the hole. Break up the subsoil at the bottom of the hole. Have an assistant hold the tree vertically in the hole and check that the depth is correct according to the soil line on the trunk. With fruit trees, the graft line on the trunk should be above the soil level. Recent research has shown that the formerly recommended addition of soil lighteners such as peat moss, pine bark, sawdust, perlite or vermiculite to a tree or shrub planting hole not only does not help the plant but can hinder it, producing a dish of lighter soil that can collect water and restrict the growth of roots into the surrounding, heavier land.

Only if the soil is very poor should it be amended. In this case, the planting hole should be made about twice as deep and wide as the root ball, the base soil should be broken up with a spade, enough topsoil replaced in the hole to bring the tree to the correct planting height, and one part good-quality soil should be mixed with three parts of site soil to fill the remainder of the hole.

A stake, carefully inserted into the ground between the roots, should be used to support the tree only if the site is windy or if the tree has a trunk more than 2 inches in diameter. For smaller trees, the use of a stake can actually hinder normal strengthening and root growth. If a stake is necessary, have your assistant hold a strong post about 4 feet long 6 inches from the windward side of the tree while you fill the soil in around both. Later, the tree will be tied to the stake with figure eights of thick twine or strips of cloth. Really large transplanted trees can be held in place

with a tepee of guy wires staked to the ground around the tree. Remember to check all such ties the following spring, replacing them if there is little space left for trunk growth. In any case, stakes or guy wires should only be necessary for two years.

Balled and burlapped trees, chiefly conifers, are planted similarly. If it is

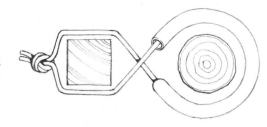

dry, water the ball before planting. Then, leaving the burlap in place — conifers need to retain soil around the roots throughout the planting process — set the root ball in the planting hole. Untie and cut or fold away as much burlap as possible from around the sides of the root ball before filling the hole as usual. If the tree has been purchased in a pot, water it, carefully loosen it from the pot, retaining as much soil as possible around the roots, and then plant as usual. In all cases, the more soil there is around the roots, the more successful the transplanting is likely to be.

Once any type of tree is in place, fill about three-quarters of the hole with soil, tamp it down fairly firmly with your foot, pour in enough water to fill it, let the water soak down, and then finish filling the hole with the remaining soil. The earth around the tree should now be just above the surrounding soil level, as it will settle down during the next few weeks. Tamping down this added soil is not necessary and can result in overly compacted soil and root suffocation. A few hours after planting, give the tree another thorough watering. Over the loose soil, a mulch of bark chips, gravel, leaves or grass clippings will help keep the soil moist while discouraging competing weeds, which should be kept from the root zone for at least the first two years. Do not use a plastic mulch, as it will shed water and exclude air from the roots.

Some pruning of the tree may now be necessary, but the old rule that recommends cutting back one-third of the top growth of a newly planted tree is no longer considered wise. Conifers need not be pruned at all, although in spring new growth can be pinched off, forcing the tree into a bushier shape. Conifers do not recover from pruning as deciduous trees do, and an ugly, permanent hole can be left from an injudicious cut, so other than tip pinching, only broken or dead growth should be cut away. The tree may be sheared lightly to shape it. Shade trees, too, need only have damaged growth removed, although you may also wish to remove very low or unattractive branches. Thereafter,except in the case of bleeders such as birches, dogwoods, elms and maples, which should be pruned only in summer, any pruning of deciduous trees should be carried out after active summer growth is finished and before the sap starts to run in spring. At this time, removal of diseased, damaged, dead or seriously infested branches will lessen disease problems. After working on each tree, disinfect the pruning tools in a solution of one part household bleach to four parts water.

Wound dressings are unnecessary for pruned limbs. As the University of California cooperative extension states, "Research and observation have shown that commercial tree wound dressings are primarily cosmetic. While they may delay the entry of disease organisms, in most cases they do little if anything to

Properly situated trees do not block the house. They frame the building as seen from the most common outdoor vantage points and provide attractively arranged views from indoors as well.

prevent the development of wood decay in the long run." Fruit trees have complex, lifelong pruning requirements that cannot be entirely described here. Refer to a library or the local department of agriculture for publications about the pruning and care of fruit trees.

WILD TREES

In some places, trees may be gathered from government land with permission, and they can be taken from the private property of a generous friend, or even moved about on your own land. Check

with the local department of forestry about the transplanting of wild trees. In Michigan, for instance, woody plants must be inspected by the department of agriculture before they are moved. The selection of wild trees follows the same criteria as does that of purchased trees — the fact that it is free is not sufficient reason to plant it. You will, however, know it to be sufficiently hardy if it is growing near the intended planting site, and you can easily check its preferences for sunlight, soil, moisture and space by checking the surroundings of a healthy specimen. That does not mean, however, that it will necessarily transplant successfully. Tap-rooted trees such as black walnuts, oaks and hickories are difficult to move unless very young, and all wild trees, their roots far less constrained than those of nursery-grown trees, can present difficulties. Purchased trees have had their roots confined, making them relatively easy to move. The younger the tree is, then, the better chance you have of keeping it alive, although even the best move will cause the tree some trauma. Alberta Agriculture lists the following maximum heights for successful transplanting by amateurs:

6 feet or less:
  Acer negundo (Manitoba maple)
  Betula spp (Birch)
  Elaeagnus angustifolia (Russian olive)
  Populus spp (Poplar)
  Salix spp (Willow)
  Ulmus americana (American elm)
  Ulmus pumila (Siberian elm)

4½ feet or less:
  Crataegus spp (Hawthorn)
  Fraxinus pennsylvanica subintegerrima (Green ash)

Larix sibirica (Siberian larch)
Picea glauca (White spruce)
Picea pungens glauca (Colorado spruce)
Prunus padus commutata (Mayday)
Prunus virginiana (Choke cherry)

4 feet or less:
  Quercus macrocarpa (Bur oak)

3½ feet or less:
  Malus spp (Apple, flowering crab apple)

3 feet or less:
  Malus spp (Fruiting crab apple)
  Pinus contorta latifolia (Lodgepole pine)
  Pinus sylvestris (Scotch pine)

For larger or difficult specimens, choose the tree a year ahead of the transplanting year. During the first spring, dig a circular trench around the trunk with a sharp spade, cutting through the roots. For every inch of trunk diameter the circle should be 12 inches from the trunk — that is, a tree with a trunk 1½ inches across at the base will have an encircling trench 1½ feet out from the trunk. Dig the trench about 18 inches deep, or below the level of the main roots, and fill it with loose earth. The tree is now left for a year,

during which time it will form new roots within the trench. Because the bottom roots have not yet been cut, the trauma to the tree is lessened.

The actual transplanting operation is best done on a cool, overcast, even rainy day. For all trees the procedure is now the same. First, tie the branches up toward the trunk to reduce potential damage. Unless the distance travelled to the new site is short enough to allow the tree to be moved by hand or in a wheelbarrow, the newly dug roots should be balled and burlapped. Consider at this point that soil weighs about 110 pounds per cubic foot, so it may be necessary to have several friends help in the operation.

Water the soil around the tree and, after digging the trench, tip the tree toward one side so that the roots underneath can be severed with a spade. This may take considerable chopping and tipping. Now push the wet burlap down one side of the trench, tip the tree against it, unroll the burlap up the other side of the trench, gather the burlap together at the trunk, and tie it securely. Ropes should extend under the root ball to hold it to the trunk as well. Once in

On-site trees must be carefully transplanted to minimize trauma. Transplant large or difficult trees over a two-year period. The first year (left), dig a trench in a circle around the trunk; the following spring (centre), sever the entire root ball, and fit burlap down in the hole. Wrap the root ball in burlap and tie before moving (right).

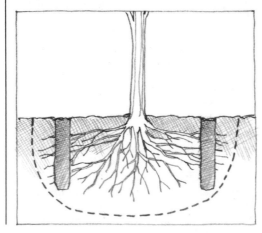
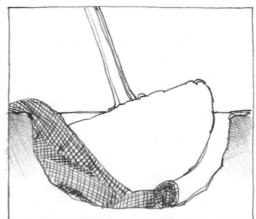

the new location, the tree is planted in the manner of a purchased one.

There is another option for obtaining trees. For the gardener with patience, some species such as junipers and cedars can be grown from seed. White oak acorns often germinate almost as soon as they fall from the trees and can be kept in sandy soil on a sunny window sill until they are planted out in spring. In addition, there are companies listed in Appendix E that specialize in tree seeds and information about growing them. A few, such as cottonwoods or hybrid poplars, may be purchased simply as rooted or unrooted cuttings, as described on page 59.

TREE CARE

For the first two years, all newly planted trees should receive about an inch of water a week during spring and summer, if not from rain, then from the gardener. Sufficient water in the early stages is critical to the establishment of the tree, and unfortunately it is all too easy to forget that a plant with a woody stem needs water just as much as a herbaceous plant that quickly shows its needs by wilting. The tree should not become waterlogged, however; the ground should dry out between waterings. Fertilization, too, can help trees as much as it can help any other plants. While fertilization is not essential unless there are obvious signs of malnutrition or poor growth, the disease-free vigour of a landscape tree often depends on the supply of more nutrients than the soil contains. Fertilization is especially important for gardeners who rake away leaves and grass clippings, the sorts of organic materials that supply nutrients to the roots of trees growing in the wild.

Fertilization of the newly planted tree should not commence until its second

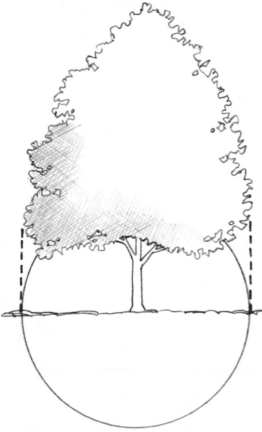

spring, when the tree has begun to establish itself. Then, as soon as the ground has thawed, fertilizer can be placed directly on the ground or mulch under the branches. Alternatively, it may be inserted into the ground around the tree roots. According to the Ontario Ministry of Agriculture and Food, a deciduous tree whose trunk diameter a yard above the ground is 6 inches or less should receive ½ to ¾ pounds of 10 percent nitrogen fertilizer. Adjust the amount of fertilizer according to the percentage of nitrogen: 5 percent nitrogen fertilizer can be applied at twice the rate of fertilization; 2 percent, at five times the rate of fertilization. For trees

more than 6 inches in diameter, apply ¾ to 2 pounds of 10 percent nitrogen fertilizer. Use the minimum amount in the coldest areas, zones 1 to 4. The percentage of nitrogen in any purchased fertilizer is indicated by the first number of the analysis on the label. The area fertilized encompasses the outer half to two-thirds of the ground under the branches. Either spread the fertilizer evenly around this circle, or turn back flaps of sod at 2- or 3-foot intervals around the tree, punch holes about 18 inches deep in the soil, and distribute the fertilizer evenly among all the holes. Replace the sods and water thoroughly.

THE WINTER TREE

In the North, it is most important that trees not be fertilized in summer or fall, for this will encourage the growth of tender new shoots that may not harden properly before the winter. From summer onward, the tree prepares itself for the oncoming winter, storing nutrients and producing seed, then beginning the process of hardening itself off so that it can survive temperatures far lower than it could tolerate in summer. Unneeded leaves are sloughed off in fall, often providing a spectacular show. Even conifers shed many of their needles in autumn, a process disturbing to some gardeners. Some, such as Scotch, Lodgepole and Austrian pines drop their needles every three or four years, while spruce and fir may retain theirs for more than five. While this process is normal, needle drop can be increased by stresses such as drought, wet soil, transplant shock, poor fertility, soil salinity or pesticide damage. Normal growth should resume when the shock subsides.

Thoroughly watering trees just before freeze-up used to be recommended as an aid to winter survival, but recent

The ''drip line'' is an imaginary circle circumscribed directly underneath the outermost foliage of the tree. Fertilizer, if necessary, is applied only to the outer half or two-thirds of the ground within the drip line.

137

evidence has shown that trees benefit from watering only when it is really needed – during the summer, especially during a drought. The tree can make little use of water added just as it is becoming dormant. On evergreens, sunscald, caused by the needles expiring more water than the roots can take up, creates scorched-looking yellow or brown needles on the sunny side of the tree, especially if it did not receive enough water the previous year. Exposed evergreens or trees planted on the sunny side of a reflecting building can be protected during winter under a tripod of posts covered with burlap, or behind canvas, plastic or burlap screens placed on the south and west sides. Sunscald on deciduous trees takes the form of cracks on the trunks, whose wood warms and becomes active during the temperate days of late winter, and then freezes and ruptures when the temperature plummets again at night. The wood under the bark on the sunlit side of the tree may be 15 degrees (F) warmer than that of the surrounding air. Trunks can be protected from sunscald with plastic tree guards, heavy paper, boards or with a coating of exterior white latex paint, which reflects heat away from the tree.

WINTER HAZARDS

Winter root damage is worst on poorly drained soils or where there is little snow cover or mulch, and is evident in spring when the tree dies down at the the branch tips. Trees that are only marginally hardy may suffer damage during even the mildest winters, displaying tip dieback every spring until a test winter finally kills them outright. If the tree dies to the snowline, frost damage is the culprit, and the tree was evidently not sufficiently hardy for the area. Even when winter is over, winter damage can persist. Late spring frosts will inflict more damage on flower buds than leaf buds, cancelling that year's blossoms and fruit. Frost that occurs just as buds are breaking can produce puckered or distorted leaves.

Mechanical injury by snow and ice can be prevented by planting trees away from roofs and snowplough routes, by tying up the branches of evergreens and supporting those of some of the more brittle deciduous trees, and by gently brushing snow off vulnerable branches as it collects. In Japan, some of the most venerable, centuries-old trees have every branch supported by overhead wires throughout the winter; an ice coating may increase the weight of a branch by a factor of 40.

Animals can also cause winter havoc.

Mice, rabbits, porcupines and deer, all vegetarians, will eat the bark and branches of sweet-wooded trees unless they are prevented from doing so. Plastic tree guards that extend several inches above the snow line will protect the most vulnerable young trees from mouse damage. Tamp down the soil close to the trunk to prevent their tunnelling to the trees. A 4- to 8-inch wire screen cage set 3 to 4 inches into the ground around the trunk and extending 20 inches above the snow line will repel not only mice, but also rabbits. Such a cage will not prevent deer from eating the branches, but it will prevent their ringing the tree base, the most dangerous practice. Chemical repellents such as Skoot and Arborgard Rabbit Repellent, which contain bitter-tasting thiram, can be painted on dry trees to a level about a yard above the snow line just after the leaves fall in autumn.

SALT TOLERANCE

Salt damage is also especially prevalent in winter, when trees planted close to treated roads can lose needles and, later, spring growth on the side facing the traffic. Saline soils or the spillage of household wash water or grey water onto the garden can also cause salt damage to trees. If trees must be planted in such conditions, consider any of the following salt-tolerant deciduous species: Russian olive (*Elaeagnus angustifolia*), honey locust (*Gleditsia triacanthos*), mulberry (*Morus* spp), white poplar (*Populus alba*), white oak (*Quercus alba*), red oak (*Quercus rubra*), bur oak (*Quercus macrocarpa*), black locust (*Robinia pseudoacacia*), willow (*Salix* spp), Siberian elm (*Ulmus pumila*). Among evergreens, the arborvitaes (*Thuja* spp) are tolerant to salt in the root zone but not to salt spray, while three species are tolerant to salt spray but not to soil salts:

white spruce (*Picea glauca*), Colorado spruce (*Picea pungens*), and Austrian pine (*Pinus nigra*).

If winter is a time of peril for the landscape tree, it can also be a time of beauty and a time when the landowner has leisure to appreciate it. Now, bark textures and colours become apparent — the silver of the birches and brownish yellow of the Amur cherry. Evergreens assume an important role previously held by the leafy deciduous trees. And those trees, too, display new aspects. Gertrude Jekyll, the famous English garden designer, wrote in her book *Wood and Garden* in 1899, "In summer-time one never really knows how beautiful are the forms of the deciduous trees. It is only in winter, when they are bare of leaves, that one can fully enjoy their splendid structure and design, their admirable qualities of duly apportioned strength and grace of poise, and the way the spread of the many-branched head has its equivalent in the wide-reaching ground-grasp of the root."

The Northerner should take winter beauty into consideration in choosing suitable trees — winter is, after all, a goodly proportion of the boreal year. But there are many other considerations involved, and hundreds of species and cultivars of trees that will grow successfully in almost any area. Only a few, however, have proved themselves outstanding in almost any situation. Following are descriptions of ten good landscape trees for most Northern situations. They are winter hardy throughout most of Canada and the northern United States, attractive or durable in winter, relatively fast-growing, and possess other qualities that give them the upper edge in landscaping. Naturally, there are scores of other trees that might be better in a particular

Ontario Ministry of Agriculture and Food

situation. Refer to plant nurseries or government departments of agriculture for more information.

THE TOP TEN

ACER spp (Maple)

The maple genus includes trees that are virtually shrubs and trees that are giants. The Tatarian maple (*A. tataricum*) grows only 12 to 20 feet tall while the bigleaf maple of the Pacific coast (*A. macrophyllum*) can top 60. Maples vary too, in hardiness, from the native box elder or Manitoba maple (*A. negundo*) and the shrubby mountain maple (*A. spicatum*), which will survive in zone 2, to several, such as the bigleaf maple and the trident maple (*A. buergeranum*) that are most comfortable in zone 7 or warmer areas. Agriculture Canada's *Checklist of Ornamental Trees for Canada* (see Appendix D) includes 23 species and many more cultivars of maple, one to suit anyone who wants beauty of form and leaf colour, shade, perhaps some good lumber and maybe even maple

syrup, which can be had from the lordly sugar maple (*A. saccharum*).

The box elder or Manitoba maple (*A. negundo*) is a tall-growing, 40- or 50-foot native that is something of a nuisance in the east, where it seeds itself freely, producing very hardy drought-tolerant specimens with weak wood that breaks easily. On the Prairies, however, it is one of the few maples that will survive dependably, and thus is valued as a specimen tree and for shade.

The Norway maple (*A. platanoides*) is extensively planted in cities, although it is somewhat disease susceptible. It is adaptable to a wide range of soils, tolerant of drought, salt and air pollution and easy to transplant and prune. There are dozens of cultivars, among the best of which are the 10- or 12-foot-tall lollipop-shaped globe maple, *Globossum*; the *Emerald Queen* whose oval crown may top 50 feet; *Crimson King*, the most popular red-leaved maple; *Royal Red*, which is similar to *Crimson King*, but more cold hardy; and *Schwedleri* whose

Edible tree fruit is possible even in small gardens, thanks to new, hardy cultivars and dwarfing rootstocks that limit the size of the mature tree. The fruit tree owner must ensure, however, that the tree's pollination needs are met.

bronze spring foliage becomes bronze-green in summer.

BETULA spp (Birch)

Although short-lived, many surviving only a generation, the birches grow very quickly into some of the most graceful of Northern trees, adaptable to many soils and climates. All have attractive white or light-coloured bark and foliage that turns yellow in fall. They will tolerate moist or wet sites better than many trees. The shade they cast is light, but they are perfect accompaniments to dense, more slow-growing shade trees, and their white bark shows well against evergreens. As one book of 1874 noted, the birch "has a beautiful and elegant contour, on which account it is introduced into ornamental scenery, especially if water be in the picture." Little available in Canada, the *Monarch Island* birch (*B.maximowiczii*), which has apricot-coloured bark, was called the most beautiful birch by plantsman and author L.H. Bailey. On the negative side, birches have soft, easily broken branches, and they are prey to birch leaf miners, sawfly larvae that attack birch leaves, producing small, pale patches that later turn brown. More destructive is the bronze birch borer, which tunnels under birch bark to cause the top of the tree to die back. These pests make the most headway in trees already weakened by drought, too little fertilizer, or attacks of birch leaf miners. The yellow birch (*B. alleghaniensis*) has some resistance to bronze birch borers.

B. papyrifera — "There is scarcely a more beautiful or easily grown tree than the canoe birch," wrote Samuel Maynard, in his 1911 book *Landscape Gardening*: "It succeeds in nearly all kinds of soil and is transplanted without much difficulty if trees of too large size are not attempted, those of one to one

and a half inches being the best. It is especially beautiful when planted among evergreens or in contrast with trees and shrubs with bright yellow or red shoots for winter effect." Also known as the paper birch or white birch, this native, with its characteristic peeling, white bark, will thrive in shade and is hardy to zone 2, where it grows 30 to 50 feet tall. The European silver birch (*B. pendula alba*) is more effective for shade purposes, as it produces its leaves earlier and drops them later than the native birches.

B. pendula (*B. verrucosa*) *Gracilis* or *Laciniata*, the cutleaf weeping birch, is a beautiful form of the European birch that has fine, lacelike foliage on long, drooping branches. The true weeping birch, *Youngii*, Young's weeping birch, grows about 30 feet tall and is hardy to zone 2b. Another cultivar, *Purpurea*, has purple leaves.

The native grey birch (*B. populifolia*) grows in clumps, and is easily transplanted to even the poorest soil. Although it is easy to grow and highly resistant to air pollution, it is usually considered a weedy alternative to the more desired types listed above.

GLEDITSIA triacanthos (Honey locust)

A tree whose delicate, fernlike foliage casts only light shade and disappears into the grass in fall, the honey locust is a superb lawn tree that is also increasingly being used along roadsides, where its tolerance to drought and salt and its height of 45 to 100 feet make it ideal. The variety *inermis* has been bred into several cultivars that are, like the parents, hardy to zone 4, and, unlike the native *G. triacanthos*, do not have thorns or pods. The seed-filled pods that appear on *G. triacanthos* in summer may have some value as livestock feed, but are certainly relished by squirrels and birds. The honey locust transplants well, will tolerate both wet and dry soils, is disease resistant, pollution tolerant and thrives in full sun. Honey locust foliage appears late in spring and drops in early fall.

G. triacanthos Shademaster and the even more upright *Skyline* are considered good replacements for the declining American elms. Both are hardy to zone 4, and grow about 45 to 50 feet tall.

JUNIPERUS spp (Juniper, red cedar)

These cedar-like evergreens are most distinctive in their horizontal, bushy forms, which are ideal for foundation plantings and in flower beds, and which are described in chapter 8. But there are also vertical junipers, from the 10-foot-tall *J. chinensis Ames* and *J. scopulorum Grey Gleam* to the 20-foot Chinese juniper (*J. chinensis*). All have greyish-blue, fragrant berries, used as a garnish and in the production of gin. Junipers are considered among the easiest to grow of all evergreens, tolerating dry, windswept sites, low temperatures and neglect. Best known of the uprights is *J. chinensis Mountbatten*, grey-green, growing to about 12 feet. The red cedars (*J. virginiana*) have pleasantly aromatic foliage. Compact,

Agriculture Canada

ornamental and capable of growing year-round in shady or sunny locations, junipers have bluish, gold-tipped or dark green foliage that suits them for many landscape situations.

MALUS spp (crab apple, ornamental crab apple, apple, apple crab)

Requiring a certain amount of cold to flower and produce fruit, apples and their kin are ideal landscaping trees for almost every Northern situation. Most are small to medium-sized, about 18 to 30 feet in height. Provided the site is not too exposed or too cold, but does allow the tree full or almost full sun and reasonably well-drained, good soil, the gardener can expect a beautiful show of white, pink or red spring blossoms, followed by red, purple, orange, pink or yellow fruit. Several crabs such as *Royalty*, *Thunderchild* and *Profusion* have purple or bronze foliage. The form of a crab apple tree may be low and wide, such as the 6- to 8-foot-tall *M. sargentii*, or narrow and upright, such as *Van Eseltine*, or weeping, like *Red Jade*. Before purchasing an ornamental crab, try to see it in bloom, so that you can find exactly the type of tree and the size and shade of blossoms you prefer. All of them produce edible fruit, though the smallest, sourest crab apples are best confined to delectable jellies.

For the best quality fruit select the larger-fruited crabs, or one of the apple crabs or apples, the latter being available on different size-controlling rootstocks. Purchase two trees, or ensure that a single tree is growing within 50 feet of an existing apple or crab. Apples and their crab apple crosses, the apple crabs, yield a wide variety of fruits of varying quality for fresh eating, long storage, cider or cooking. For more information about edible apples, order the nursery

catalogues listed in Appendix E.

The showy crab apple (*M. floribunda*) grows 15 to 25 feet tall and has cultivars that will survive in zone 2b. The flowers are very profuse and the fruit is about ⅓ inch across.

M. ioensis Maybride, is a 15-foot crab developed in Ottawa and hardy to zone 4. The showy flowers are double white, the fruits dark red.

Sargent's ornamental crab apple (*M. sargentii*), is actually a shrub, growing in a mound shape to only about 6 feet tall.

Hardy to zone 5, it is able to retain its tiny fruit throughout the winter, a bonus for those who do not want the edible harvest.

PICEA spp (Spruce)

The spruces are beautiful evergreens that are well suited to use as specimen trees or shade trees. Wind-tolerant species, such as the native spruces and the Norway spruce (*P. abies*), can be used in windbreaks. Once established, the spruces grow quite rapidly. Native

Some crab apples such as *Maybride* and *Betchtel* produce showy double flowers followed by fruit that is inconspicuous but as edible as that of all crab apples, producing delectable preserves. Maturing at 20 feet tall, the *Betchtel* crab is one of the last to bloom. Its large, pink flowers unfold in late spring.

species such as the white spruce (*P. glauca*) and the western white spruce (*P. albertiana*) are hardy to zone 1, while others require warmer conditions. All do best in well-drained, even dry soils.

The native Engelmann spruce (*P. engelmannii*), hardy to zone 3, produces dense shade from a beautiful, bluish-green tree that grows 30 to 50 feet tall.

The dwarf Alberta spruce (*P. glauca albertiana Conica*) forms a dense pyramid only about 6 feet tall. It is hardy to zone 4.

The Colorado spruce (*P. pungens Koster*) is probably the best known of landscape spruces. Because it is grafted, it is expensive, and it is somewhat overused, but in the proper place, especially in a group of other trees, its medium blue to blue-green foliage can add a beautiful contrast. It grows about 30 to 50 feet tall and is hardy to zone 2. The cultivar *Hoopsii* has silvery-blue foliage.

PINUS spp (Pine)

There are pines that thrive in areas as cold as zone 1 — the coldest region where trees can normally grow at all — and there are pines too tender to survive beyond the Pacific coast. Many are tolerant of dry soils, and all are attractive evergreens that provide good quality wood, shade, windbreaks and fence posts. The fast-growing native white pine (*P. strobus*) is susceptible to white pine blister, which produces a stem canker that can kill the trees. To avoid the blister, do not plant white pines in a garden that also includes currants or gooseberries, carriers of the disease.

The bristlecone pine (*P. aristata*) is hardy to zone 3, where its 10- to 30-foot height lends itself to use in flower gardens and small lots.

The mugho pine (*P. mugo mugo*) is a miniature type of Swiss Mountain pine that rarely exceeds 3 feet in height but has an 8-foot spread. It is hardy to zone 1.

The Austrian pine (*P. nigra*) is an adaptable species that grows in almost any soil conditions in zone 4b or warmer. It grows rapidly to about 50 feet, has dark, glossy, green foliage, and is suitable for windbreaks as well as gardens.

POPULUS spp (Poplar, cottonwood, aspen)

Like the birches, poplars are gratifyingly quick-growing trees. The new hybrids, bred for speedy growth, may skyrocket at the rate of 5 feet a year. Such a rate precludes the production of good quality, strong wood, but it does mean that shade or shelter can be produced quickly enough to satisfy the transient landscape designer or the farmer who needs a windbreak quickly. Poplars vary in hardiness from some that will thrive in zone 2 to others, such as the Japanese poplar (*P. maximowiczii*) that requires a yard in zone 5 or warmer. The flowers, produced as hanging catkins, can be attractive. On the negative side, poplars are often scorned by landscape architects because of their limited longevity, their overly tall size for a city lot, and their weak, breakable wood. But on a larger suburban or rural lot, they do have a place. When buying cottonwoods, purchase only males to avoid the allergy-provoking "cotton."

The Bolleana poplar (*P. alba Pyramidalis*) is often considered superior to the Lombardy poplar, whose narrow,

Ontario Ministry of Agriculture and Food

vertical growth to 70 feet has made it a standby along rural driveways and shelterbelts. The Bolleana has attractive green bark, and is more compact, growing to about 50 feet. Both are hardy to zone 4.

The trembling aspen (*P. tremuloides*), is hardy to zone 2, grows to 40 feet, and receives its name from the way its foliage quakes in a light wind.

PRUNUS spp (Apricot, cherry, peach, plum, choke cherry, almond and their flowering counterparts)

Like the *Malus* genus, *Prunus* offers some trees that are chiefly practical, some that are chiefly ornamental, and many that fulfill both roles well. These trees, too, tend to be small to medium in size. There are varieties that will survive in areas as cold as zone 2b. The sweet cherries and peaches, however, are limited to zone 5b or warmer, while the plums are chancy beyond zone 5. The Japanese flowering cherries, cultivars of *P. serrulata*, are limited to zone 6 or warmer, but there they provide masses of beautiful white, pink or yellowish blossoms in April. The most ornamental forms have inedible or withered fruit, or no fruit at all. See these trees in bloom before making a choice.

Gardeners who want fruit must allow for pollination. Plant two sweet cherries and in most cases, two plums, two cherry plums, or a single sour cherry, peach or apricot. Cherry plums, small, hardy hybrids that produce delicious, small fruit, can be used to pollinate plums. Apricots hardy enough to survive on the Canadian Prairies have been developed, but loss of fruit may nevertheless follow late spring frosts that kill blossoms.

P. padus commutata is hardy to zone 2, where it grows 20 to 30 feet tall. It resembles a more decorative form of

Ontario Ministry of Agriculture and Food

choke cherry, with larger foliage and earlier blooming, larger white flowers.

The ornamental Sargent's cherry (*P. sargentii*) that has been popular in the North for almost a century, is hardy to zone 5 and produces rose-pink to white flowers and reddish bark on a tree 30 to 40 feet tall. A cultivar, *Columnar*, is oval in shape. Both have reddish-brown fall foliage.

P. cerasus North Star is a self-pollinating sour or pie cherry that is naturally dwarfed and upright in habit, growing to 10 or 12 feet, making it a natural for even a city backyard.

P. avium Stella is the only self-pollinating sweet cherry. Developed in British Columbia, it is ideal for a temperate city lot that lacks sufficient space for two trees.

SORBUS spp (Mountain ash)

Unrelated to the true ashes (*Fraxinus* spp), the mountain ashes, members of the rose family, are medium-sized, 25- to 40-foot trees with showy, fragrant white flowers in May or June and clusters of red, orange or yellow berries that persist through fall. They prefer any ordinary, if slightly acidic soil, and will tolerate dry conditions. Their lacy, fernlike foliage casts shade light enough to permit the growth of grass underneath, while their summer clusters of attractive red or orange fruit are cherished by some cooks for savoury jellies and are certainly enjoyed by the birds. The native *S. americana* has ¼-inch fruit and pointed flower petals and is hardy to zone 3, while the showier European mountain ash or rowan tree (*S. aucuparia*) has rounded petals and fruit almost twice as large, although it, too, has forms hardy in zone 3, including the weeping cultivar *Pendula*. Mountain ashes are vulnerable to fireblight, a bacterial disease that causes young twigs to appear burnt, then turn black and die. All diseased and dead growth should be removed, including a small portion of attached healthy tissue. Pruning shears should be disinfected after treating each tree in a solution of four parts water and one part household bleach.

The Russian mountain ash (*S. aucuparia Rossica*) is a 20- to 30-foot tree hardy to zone 3. Its upright rather than spreading form, bushy to the ground, creates an especially interesting specimen tree for cold areas.

The showy mountain ash (*S. decora*) is an upright, 30-foot native whose dark green foliage and bright red fruit can be seen as far north as zone 2.

The oak-leaved mountain ash (*S. scopulina* × *thuringiaca Fastigiata*) has dense, oaklike foliage. It grows about 25 feet tall, and is hardy to zone 5.

All birches are fast-growing softwoods that add beauty and shade to a large garden. Weeping birches have a more graceful outline than do their more upright counterparts but also produce the drooping catkins typical of the family.

11 | Landscapes of the Midnight Sun

Adversity nurtures ingenuity

By Karen LeGresley

Their home was built on a steep rock slope that left little scope for landscaping, but, determined to make the best of the situation, Gino and Julie Pin of Yellowknife planted annuals and hardy perennials in garden boxes near their front entrance for a colourful summer display and grew squash on the roof of their tool shed. About 8 inches of topsoil and some string running down the side of the shed for the vines to twine around were all that was needed to transform this otherwise waste space into a precious garden area. The couple have been growing rooftop *Ambassador* hybrid and *Aristocrat* squash for four years; they just add the required lime and fertilizer each year to keep the soil nutrients high.

Such is the inventiveness of the landscaper north of the 60th parallel of latitude. In situations such as the Pins', space is one limitation, because the servicing of a large, northerly lot is prohibitively expensive. But climate is even more restricting. On most plant hardiness maps, the Yukon and Northwest Territories are marked by a small, grey-coloured strip labelled zone 0 — if they are included at all. These zone charts, of course, give only a general idea of which plants are likely to survive in a given area, but still, the designation "0" is a discouraging one, suggesting that zero plants can survive here. For many nursery-grown trees and shrubs, that is sadly close to the truth.

The North is a vast tract of land making up more than one-third of Canada and comprised of a myriad of landforms, ranging from tundra in the central portion to boreal forests in the south and mountainous regions in the west, east and polar regions. The real challenge to the Northern gardener lies in trying to coax a yield from the stubborn tracts of tundra that occupy much of the central Northwest Territories. In fact, the word "tundra" is related to the Finnish *tunturi*, treeless hill, and the term "fell fields," which describes the rocky, nearly barren areas typical of the tundra, is akin to the Danish *fjoeld-mark*, meaning rock deserts. The precipitation in such areas is often less than 12 inches a year, and most of what little moisture does exist is locked up in ice, a form unusable by plants for most of the year. Yet it is the frozen subsoil, the permafrost, that allows the Arctic tundra to flourish during its brief but radiant summer. An impenetrable layer that holds moisture above it, enabling plants to exist in the driest of environments, the permafrost is not the enemy that one might expect, and its destruction by excessive warming or deep excavating can mean the end of gardening opportunities.

The three main factors limiting plant growth in the Far North are: temperature (too low); soils and soil nutrients (too little and too few); and water (too little). Aside from building an often unattractive-looking greenhouse, gardeners can do little to influence the major plant hardiness limitation, temperature, but they can choose plants wisely, and they can provide additional moisture, soil and nutrients, which will increase hardiness. Much of the land was scraped bare by glaciation, and although soil washed down the mountainsides into valleys, such as the Mackenzie Valley, which offer ample possibilities for gardening, not everyone lives in these fortunate areas.

The depth and quality of the soil play major roles in the growth rate and productivity of Northern plants; for instance, there are isolated clumps of willow trees growing near Holman and Bathurst Inlet, communities well north of the tree line. In areas such as these,

which suffer from the same general climate as the surrounding tundra, trees have nevertheless been able to establish themselves in small, low-lying pockets of soil. Water drains into the pockets, sustaining the plants and bringing enough soil particles downslope to develop a thicker organic layer above the permafrost table. Similarly, other places on the "treeless hill" can, with a little coaxing, be enticed to yield an interesting landscape.

The capital and largest population centre of the Northwest Territories is Yellowknife, a city built largely on rock and lacustrine (lake) deposits of clay and silt. Unfortunately, good topsoil is a rare commodity. Most landscape contractors conjure topsoil out of peat, sand, clay, lime and fertilizers, all but the last being available in the North. This same mixture can be prepared by any strong-backed landscaping enthusiast, too, but if you are trying to seed a lawn, commercial preparation is well worthwhile. But the obvious solution is to use as little topsoil as possible — by planting in garden boxes, pots, cold frames and greenhouses. One attractive and clever solution to soil and space limitations is in evidence around a cabin at Willow Flats, an area of Yellowknife, where the owners have successfully grown annual flowers in tin cans filled with soil and nailed to the cabin wall. Around the cabin grow native grasses, which have lovely, delicate forms in subdued shades of beige, gold and green.

In fact, before despairing, the hopeful Northern landscaper should remember three things. One, there are many native species, absolutely hardy, that can be used to good advantage. Two, many plants are not "proven hardy" simply because no one has done much experimentation with those species this far north; it is up to individual gardeners

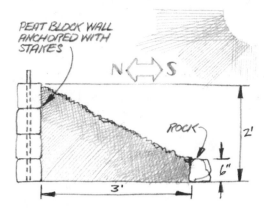

PEAT BLOCK WALL ANCHORED WITH STAKES

N ⟷ S

ROCK

2'

6"

3'

to do their own trials. Worthy of an attempt, for instance, is the European bird cherry (*Prunus padus*) whose small cherries can be used for jams, as can the fruits of various roses such as *Rosa rugosa*. However, do realize that when such fruiting plants are grown under stressful Northern conditions, they will often not start producing as quickly as their southern counterparts, nor will they yield as abundantly. But patience, especially in Northern landscaping, is a virtue. The third thing to remember is that the creation of small microclimates can give plants a hospitable environment, if only a few inches square.

Peat can be used as a soil substitute or to enhance the existing quality of almost any landscape soil. It can be obtained locally from tundra or boreal forests or purchased from nurseries. The important part of a peat garden is preparation. While it would be possible to make a garden of pure peat, the addition of some sand or soil will improve drainage sufficiently to allow for the growth of more plant species. The depth of the ornamental peat garden should vary with the plants that are to be grown. A southward-sloping bed, with about 2 feet of peat in the rear sloping to 6 inches at the front, will warm up

earlier in the spring, though it may dry out quickly in the summer if not dutifully watered. Taller, more deeply rooted plants can then be placed at the back of the bed and smaller ones at the front. Blocks of natural peat, which include the roots of native vegetation, can be used to build up a wall behind which additional peat can be piled. The peat blocks should be locked together with stakes driven through the wall into the ground. Logs or large rocks could also be used to build the wall. Suitable native plants for such a bed include sheep laurel (*Kalmia angustifolia*), which produces pink flowers on shrubby colonies of green leaves; the closely related Labrador tea (*Ledum groenlandicum*), a small evergreen shrub that grows in patches, produces white flowers in late spring or early summer and produces a usable tea; and cranberry (*Viburnum trilobum*). Possible introduced plants for the bed include iris, violets such as *Viola pallens, V. incognita* or *V. cucullata* and such lilies as *Lilium elegans* or *Erythronium grandiflorum*. The dwarf willow (*Salix reticulata*) has many virtues in the ornamental garden, and should not be overlooked. Too often, native Northern species are not given their full due in our backyards.

Look, too, for native species that are not only ornamental but useful as well. Northerners have traditionally gathered wild fruits and vegetables, many of which are very high in nutrients and delicious as well. In removing specimens from the wild, take care to obtain an adequate root ball to increase your chances of successful transplanting — because of the permafrost, many wild plants have a shallow and widespread root system. Trench around trees a season in advance, as described on page 136.

Even native mosses and lichens can be

used to advantage in a landscape. There is an abundance of rocks and gravel here — so why not try a garden that employs some of the ideas of the Japanese? A couple of well-placed boulders can create a perfect microclimate for small wildflowers and mosses, while enclosing a beautiful, intimate garden space. Using small lichen-covered rocks for detail will create a lovely garden without the gardener's having to wait years for a spruce tree to grow.

In fact, if it is imported, you may have to wait quite a while simply for the spruce to arrive; distance is another constraint in the North. Gardeners are far from established nurseries, and shipping plants is very costly. Ordering from southern growers such as Beaverlodge Nursery in Alberta needs to be done early in April, when conditions here are still snowy and wintry. Material from southern nurseries is dug and shipped earlier than Northerners can plant it, so we must be prepared to store the trees or shrubs when they arrive. This is not especially chancy for balled and burlapped or potted plants, for their root systems are protected and can be easily kept moist, but for bare-root plants, extra planning is needed before they arrive. Heel these into sawdust in a cool (not cold) location, such as in a box in a porch. Water the plants every day until planting time arrives — the sooner the better.

If you are going to experiment with an unproved species, remember to buy from the most northerly source possible. Just because two nursery catalogues list the same species does not mean they are exactly the same. The more northerly genotype has a better chance of surviving the harsh winters, especially if it is a native plant or a hardy prairie or alpine species. Even if you cannot get

the actual plant, the seeds of many species are available commercially or from other interested gardeners or local garden clubs. As with all Northern gardening, a bit of scrounging and ingenuity can create unexpected yet wonderful results.

Vegetables and other annuals, the easiest plants to grow from seed, should be chosen for their ability to grow quickly. For instance, the *Shepody* potato, a cultivar developed in Morden, Manitoba, is early, white, and very suitable for Northern gardens. In Yellowknife, close to 5 pounds of potatoes per plant can be harvested with no special mulches, pregrowth or preparations. Potatoes also keep well, and so there should be no problem growing enough to last throughout the year.

Food gardening in the North is not a recent phenomenon. Indeed, its popularity seems to have declined since the early years of white settlement, when a vegetable patch was more of a necessity than a convenience for Euro-Canadian survival. In 1789, Alexander Mackenzie described an excellent garden at the mouth of the Athabasca River where potatoes, turnips and barley were cultivated by Peter Pond, a fur trader. When George Simpson, governor of the Hudson's Bay Company, established district headquarters at the confluence of the Liard and Mackenzie Rivers (now Fort Simpson) he realized how scarce provisions were and how difficult it was to transport goods to his remote outpost. The gardens he subsequently established in the rich alluvial soils yielded, according to the Fort Simpson journal of 1828: "18 kegs of barley, 42 of potatoes, 40 of turnips, cabbages, carrots and onions, and a few quarts of peas."

Missionaries, reluctant to pursue the nomadic existence of the natives they sought to convert, also saw the wisdom of establishing subsistence gardens. In 1922, the Reverend A. Vale of the Anglican Mission at Hay River on the south shore of Great Slave Lake reported that 6 acres of land were under cultivation. "This year we took up over 1,000 bushels of potatoes besides a good supply of cabbage, cauliflower, turnips, tomatoes, cucumbers, onions, beets, carrots, etc." During the Klondike gold rush of the late 1800s, the Yukon too had its share of gardens, as miners, aware that it was cheaper to grow vegetables than to pay the exorbitant prices charged for imported food, devised ways of storing the produce from their gardens in sawdust to preserve them during the long winter.

The early settlers found relatively deep, fertile soils situated on deltas created where major rivers flow into

In the early years of white settlement in the North, food gardening was more necessity than convenience, but the tradition of growing large crops of cold-tolerant vegetables such as potatoes has continued, especially in the rich alluvial soils of river valleys.

Great Slave Lake and the Mackenzie River. Gardening in the alluvial deposits of the communities of Fort Providence, Hay River, Fort Simpson, Fort Norman and Fort Good Hope is still done in much the same way. Just wait (and wait, and wait) for the snow to disappear, and the midnight sun to reappear, then plug in your seeds. The same types of cold-tolerant food crops that were cultivated by the earlier settlers are still appropriate today: potatoes, turnips, lettuce, carrots, cabbages, onions and peas. Because the soil quickly chills with increasing depth, it is best to select varieties of root crops that grow short and stout. Other plants should also be selected on the basis of a shallow root system.

With the assistance of 18 to 24 hours of sunlight a day, and the addition to the soil of the often-lacking organic material and fertilizers, fruits and vegetables of gigantic proportions and a lot of leafy, green growth can be cultivated. Vegetables, then, are attractive enough to be landscape plants and useful as well (see Chapter 5). The Commissioner of the Northwest Territories, John Parker, and his wife Helen have won several red ribbons at the annual Yellowknife fall fair for the excellent vegetables grown in their backyard. However, it is the story of the *Baby Green Hubbard* squash that tells the tale of the quick growth possible in Northern gardens. One squash plant had vines nearly 18 feet long and another, not to be outdone, decided to climb a nearby Jack pine. Commissioner Parker may be the first gardener, north or south of 60, to produce a squash from a pine. This fast vegetative growth is not always an advantage, but it is useful for the leafy vegetables, always a good bet in the Northern garden. Even unusual greens such as Chinese cabbage, turnip greens and purslane — not everyone considers this plant to be a weed — are frequent inhabitants of the Far Northern landscape.

Gardening exclusively for ornamentation has had a relatively brief history in the North. The nomadic lifestyle of the native Dene and Inuit was not conducive to such enterprises, and the whites, generally posted in the North for only a year or two, could not be bothered to landscape a home in a place where a spruce tree might take a century to attain a 2-inch diameter. Happily, though, there is renewed interest in both edible and ornamental gardening in the North. Relatively stable population centres now exist at Yellowknife (10,000) and Whitehorse (15,000), and there are several other communities numbering a thousand or so. Horticulturists have produced hardier, faster-maturing varieties of fruits, vegetables and ornamentals, and have developed new techniques of mulching and greenhouse construction that improve productivity. Unfortunately, however, Agriculture Canada's only Northern experimental station is now at Beaverlodge, Alberta, the more poleward stations having been closed 12 years ago. Northerners must now look to Alaskan and Soviet experimentation for new, hardy cultivars. For instance, scientists in Yakutia in Eastern Siberia have apparently developed a currant that can cope with permafrost and winter temperatures of minus 94 degrees F. If this currant does indeed yield nearly 25 pounds of fruit per bush, as claimed, it would certainly be a great boon here. There is, however, no ongoing programme of plant exchanges between Canada and either the Soviet Union or the United States.

Fortunately, some horticultural research is still conducted in this region. For instance, Dr. Josef Svoboda, Associate Professor of Botany at the University of Toronto, has worked with others in the Arctic and High Arctic (north of the arctic circle) at Rankin Inlet (63 degrees N) and Alexandra Fiord (79 degrees N). The scientists conducted experiments aimed at increasing the yield of both native and introduced species, and realized 5- to 30-fold increases in the growth of the tested native species arctic dandelion (*Taraxacum lacerum*), mountain sorrel (*Oxyria digyna*), and nodding saxifrage (*Saxifraga cernua*). Like its southern counterpart, the arctic dandelion has edible leaves and flowers. Mountain sorrel, with its refreshing lemon taste, is an excellent source of vitamin C, and has long been used by natives and hikers. Nodding saxifrage is not a prolific herb on the tundra, so was not frequently used by natives, but it is a useful herb in salads. Southern garden vegetables also showed great promise, with radishes reaching table size in 35 days, even at the Alexandra Fiord location.

Dr. Svoboda is convinced that even the High-Arctic ecosystem is capable of higher production if one or more of its limiting factors — lack of heat, nutrients and water — is alleviated. Although some outdoor experiments were done, Svoboda has dealt with all three factors at once, primarily by using greenhouses, not the most attractive alternative for the landscape, but useful for the gardener wanting quantity. Unlike the usual rectangular, glass greenhouses, these were light, low, igloo-shaped units covered in a special fabric, Fabrene, which is tough enough to withstand high winds but translucent enough to admit light and heat. A conical shape allowed

maximum light exposure and permitted even heat distribution, regardless of the sun's position. Because of high transportation and maintenance costs, glass houses are not a viable solution in most communities, especially those not serviced by road. But Fabrene is light and easy to transport, and the whole structure can be taken down in the winter which contributes to a fabric life of about three seasons. Polyethylene can also be used, although it is more vulnerable to tearing and has to be replaced annually.

To increase the distance between the rooting zone and the permafrost table, most of the potatoes and vegetables were grown in black plastic bags arranged in concentric circles in the greenhouses. (If permafrost is more than 3 feet below the ground surface, bags are not necessary,

since at that depth the cold has little effect on the plant roots). The bagging method is soil efficient and results in temperatures around the root zone that are much higher than those of the natural environment. Boxes, cases or cut drums, painted heat-retaining black, could be similarly used. At both the Rankin Inlet and Alexandra Fiord sites, the greenhouse microclimate temperatures rose to resemble tropical rather than arctic conditions, with 80 to 90 degrees F and high humidity so common that zippers had to be installed in the covers to allow the ventilation of overly hot air.

A final note on the constraints of Northern gardening: remember dogs and snowmobiles. Most Yellowknife homes have small fences that bar the passage of such wanderers, but in many other communities there are no distinct property lines at all. If you are serious about a garden, you will have to protect it. Even if you have no trees or shrubs to be damaged or uprooted, snowmobiles will compact the snow and soil. When the snow is compacted, it loses its insulating properties, and the plants beneath are less likely to survive. Also, the soil will take much longer to warm up in spring — and no one in the North has extra days to play with.

What one can play with here, however, are ideas and experiments, the amusements and challenges that have always been the foundation of life in the North.

After earning her degree in Landscape Architecture from the University of Toronto, Karen LeGresley designed landscapes in Calgary, Hamburg, Germany and Caracas, Venezuela before moving to Yellowknife in 1983. She works with the Tourism and Parks division of the Government of the Northwest Territories and is a member of the Alberta Association of Landscape Architects.

Low-growing plants are more weather resistant than taller ones, a restriction exploited by a Northerner who grows annual ground covers in a complex, knot garden configuration.

Acid, acidic or sour soils have a **pH** of less than 7. Good garden soils are slightly acidic, with a pH of about 6.5. Acidic soils are usually made more **alkaline,** when that is desired, by the addition of **lime** compounds or **wood ashes**. Certain plants, such as rhododendrons, mosses and blueberries, thrive only in an acidic soil, which is most common in areas of fairly heavy rainfall, or on acidic bedrock.

Aerate, to supply or impregnate with air. In soil, aeration is important for the health of plant roots, which can die in soil too wet or compacted to permit the presence of air bubbles. Aeration is best achieved by adding **organic matter** to soil, by tilling it, encouraging the presence of earthworms or, in lawns, by plugging the surface with holes.

Alkaline, basic or sweet soil, the opposite of **acid**, has a **pH** greater than 7. Most common garden plants can survive a pH as high as 8, although beyond that, most suffer from a lack of usable nutrients, even though the nutrients may be present in the soil. Alkaline soils, which are most common in dry areas or on alkaline bedrock such as limestone, are usually corrected, when necessary, by the addition of sulphur compounds, gypsum or **peat** to the soil.

Annual plants complete their life cycle within one year. A cornflower, for example, grown from seed one spring, will flower that summer, produce seed and then die in fall.

Biennial plants complete their life cycle within two years. A beet, for example, grown from seed one spring, will form the typical fleshy root that summer and, if it survives the following winter, will produce seeds the next spring and then die.

Biodegradable materials break down into simpler, harmless constituents under natural conditions. Such **mulches** as newspaper, straw and wood chips, and such **pesticides** as rotenone, pyrethrum and sabadilla, are all biodegradable.

Bud, an undeveloped shoot, generally protected by modified scale leaves. It may or may not develop into a leaf, flower or stem when environmental conditions are favourable.

Bulb, a short, flattened or disc-shaped underground stem, with many fleshy scale leaves filled with stored food. Tulips and onions have bulbs, which can be dug up and **transplanted** when **dormant**.

Canopy, the leafy portion of a tree or shrub.

Clay, a soil constituent with extremely fine particles that tend to compact, excluding air and becoming impermeable to water, hindering root growth and even cracking when dry. Clay soils are best improved with the addition of **organic matter** such as **peat**.

Climber, a plant, such as a **vine**, that, though lacking a woody support system to its full height, is capable of staying upright by clinging to or twining around a vertical structure such as a **trellis**, **stake** or tree. This may be done with thorns, **tendrils** or soft, twining stems. Some support, in the form of training or loose tying, may be necessary to keep the entire plant growing upright.

Closure, the state reached when plants have filled in a space as fully as can be expected for those **species**.

Cold frame, a boxlike structure, often bottomless, its top covered with transparent glazing such as glass, polyethylene or fibreglass, that is used to shelter **tender** plants outdoors in cool weather or to hold small **transplants** in one convenient place. It is called "cold" only to distinguish it from a hot bed, whose floor is covered with manure that, as it decomposes, heats the closed frame.

Compost, soil-like material made up of **organic matter** that has decomposed under conditions of warmth, **aeration** and wetness. Frequent compost ingredients include **biodegradable** kitchen scraps, manure, grass clippings and fallen leaves. These are piled in an enclosure or special compost bin and turned occasionally until the mixture is homogenous and crumbly. Compost is an ideal amendment for all garden soils.

Conifer, a cone-bearing tree or shrub, usually evergreen.

Corm, a short, solid, vertical, enlarged underground stem in which food is stored. Gladioli have corms that can be dug up for storage when **dormant**.

Cover crop, a crop grown to protect the soil from erosion and prepare it for a more desired crop, and turned under or removed when no longer needed.

Crown, the place where the above-ground parts of a plant, its stems and leaves, meet the below-ground parts, the roots or underground stems. In **transplanting**, the crown should be left at or just slightly below the previous soil level.

Cultivar, a cultivated variety of a plant with its own designated name – such as *Nelly Moser* clematis, in which *Nelly Moser* is the cultivar name – or at the end of the full Latin name, which usually includes the **genus**, **species** and, if appropriate, **variety**; that is, *Clematis montana Nelly Moser*. The cultivar name is often designated in plain type and single quotation marks; 'Nelly Moser.' Most gardeners know only the cultivar

names and the familiar English names of their plants, and fare quite well, but the knowledge of the full Latin name is necessary for any serious plant study.

Cutting, a piece of a plant taken for the purposes of **propagation**. Depending upon the plant in question, the cutting may be a stem, a leaf or a piece of root, and rooting may be as simple as placing the removed section in soil or water, or as complicated as dipping the base in rooting hormones and keeping the cutting constantly moist until it roots, which may take a year or more.

Deciduous, a plant which loses its leaves in fall and grows new ones in spring.

Dormant, in a state of reduced physiological activity, which, in the North, usually occurs in winter. Plants or parts of plants such as **bulbs** and **corms** are most easily moved without harm to the plant when dormant.

Drift, the traces of spray, especially **pesticides**, that are carried downwind; also an informal planting of a single **species** or **variety** as in a border.

Espalier, to train and prune to grow in a flat, two-dimensional design, and any plant so trained. Espalier plants are best grown against walls or fences.

Fertilize, to allow the male cells from the pollen to contact the female plant organ, the stigma, so that flowering and fruit production can occur; also to add necessary nutrients to the soil, usually in the form of powders and liquids.

Flat, a box about a foot wide, 18 inches long and 3 inches tall, used to hold soil **medium** and seedlings or containers of **transplants**. A flat may be made out of wood, plastic or fibre.

Foundation planting, a row of plants, chiefly **shrubs** such as globe cedars and other variously shaped specimens, used to obscure or interrupt the straight line of a building foundation and thus add aesthetic interest to the landscape.

Genus, a group of structurally or genetically related **species** indicated, in the Latin name of a plant, as the first, capitalized, italicized word. Thus the common lilac, *Syringa vulgaris*, belongs to the genus *Syringa*, as do other lilacs with whom it shares a genus but not necessarily a species.

Granular, any hard, chunky landscaping or building material such as gravel, vermiculite or broken bricks.

Ground cover, a plant or plants that shade the ground directly below them fairly densely, excluding most other plant growth beneath. Ground covers are usually, but need not be, very low-growing, ground-hugging plants.

Hardy, a plant capable of surviving outdoor conditions, especially the winter, in any particular place. Hardiness is a relative term; a plant that is hardy on Vancouver Island may be **tender** in the Yukon.

Herb, strictly speaking, a seed plant that does not develop woody tissues. However, herb has come to have a different meaning, signifying a plant grown for kitchen seasoning. Woody plants such as rosemary and bay are considered herbs as much as are the nonwoody basil and dill.

Herbaceous, plants that do not develop woody tissues. Herbaceous perennials can be expected to die to the ground in winter and reappear in the same spot in spring.

Humus, see **organic matter**.

Hybrid, the offspring of two plants differing in at least one genetic characteristic. The seed of hybrids will produce plants that have the characteristics of the parents of the hybrid and thus may not resemble one another or the hybrid itself. F1 designates a first generation hybrid from a cross of two plants.

Layering, a method of plant **propagation** in which a stem is laid on the ground or buried to induce root growth where soil contact occurs. The new growth can then be cut from the parent plant and **transplanted** elsewhere. Raspberries, currants and thyme are among the plants that can be propagated by layering.

Lime, an alkaline, calcium compound, such as calcitic or dolomitic lime, used to raise the **pH** of **acid** soil. A **soil test** report will include a recommendation about the amount of lime that should be added to a soil to make it suitable for the growth of healthy plants. Depending upon the soil composition, 35 to 80 pounds of limestone per 1,000 square feet will raise the pH one point.

Loam, soil that contains 23 to 52 percent **sand**, 7 to 27 percent **clay**, 28 to 50 percent **silt** and **organic matter**. Although it may vary greatly in texture, from clay loam through sandy loam, it is nevertheless the best garden soil.

Medium, a substance or substances used to support root growth. Growing media may include such ingredients as soil, **peat**, vermiculite, perlite and **sand**, alone or in any combination.

Mulch, a layer of organic or inorganic material placed against the soil to reduce or stop weed growth, to add nutrients and **organic matter** to the soil (in the case of organic mulches), to warm the soil (in the case of plastic mulch) and to hold moisture in the soil. Some typical mulch materials include leaves, grass clippings, newspaper, hay, plastic film and bark chips.

Nitrogen, one of the most important elements needed by plants, and one most frequently lacking in sufficient amounts in garden soils. On **fertilizer** packages, nitrogen is the first constituent noted; that is, 8-12-4 contains 8 percent nitrogen. Among the best **organic** sources of nitrogen are blood meal, livestock manure and fish fertilizer. Nitrogen is needed by plants to produce healthy, green growth, and its lack is manifested in stunted plants with pale or yellow foliage. Too much nitrogen can retard or stop flowering and fruit production and can interfere with a plant's winter hardiness.

Nurse crop, a fast-growing, relatively sturdy crop grown to protect and shade a slower-growing but more desired crop.

Organic, a chemical term that describes carbon compounds, many of which are associated with living organisms. However, in gardening and farming, organic usually describes a style of working that eschews the use of chemical fertilizers and synthetic pesticides, and promotes the use of **biodegradable**, biological materials in the belief that they are better able to produce **humus**-rich soil and healthy, healthful plants.

Organic matter, any animal or vegetable substance, or any substance formed by the breakdown of animal or vegetable material. Organic constituents, such as **compost**, livestock manure, **peat** and hay, are valuable soil additives or **mulches**, increasing **aeration** and enabling plant roots to better penetrate the soil and obtain nutrients.

Peat, peat moss or sphagnum, is plant material that has partially decomposed in water. Collected from bogs and sold in a dried form, it is a slightly acidic soil additive or growing **medium** that will improve virtually any soil's structure.

Perennial plants are capable of living from year to year, provided their basic needs are met.

Pesticide, a substance used to kill any unwanted living organism, including plants (herbicides), fungi (fungicides) or bugs (insecticides or, more properly, pesticides).

pH, a scale of measuring acidity or alkalinity, in which 0 represents the greatest level of acidity, 7 represents neutral, neither **acid** nor **alkaline**, and 14 represents the greatest level of alkalinity. The scale is logarithmic, meaning that neighbouring numbers represent levels 10 times greater (if higher) or lesser (if lower) than one another. Garden soils commonly register between pH 4 and 8. Soil pH can be measured with litmus or pH paper, with a purchased soil test kit or with a **soil test**, available from a commercial or government laboratory.

Phosphorus, one of the elements most needed by plants, and one of the nutrients most commonly lacking in sufficient amounts in garden soils. In the form of phosphates, phosphorus is present in most **fertilizers** in which it is the middle number in the analysis; that is, 8-12-4 contains 12 percent phosphates. Phosphorus is known to contribute to good root growth and is therefore recommended for seedlings and newly planted trees and other plants. Bone meal is an excellent organic source of phosphorus. A lack of soil phosphorus sometimes shows up as a purplish cast to leaves and stems.

Pollination, the transfer of pollen from the male plant organ, the stamen, to the female plant organ, the stigma. It may or may not lead to **fertilization**. Pollination is most often done by wind, animals and insects.

Potassium, the third of the major plant nutrients, along with **nitrogen** and **phosphorus**, is present in the form of potash in most **fertilizers**, where it appears as the third number in the analysis on a fertilizer bag; thus 8-12-4 would contain 4 percent potash. Its role in plant growth is uncertain, but it does contribute to overall plant health. Potassium is a major constituent of **wood ashes**.

Prairie, grassland vegetation with trees essentially absent that can occur wherever conditions are suitable, not only on the central plains of North America; also describes the vegetation that grows in such a site.

Propagation, any means of multiplying a plant that can include growing from seeds, taking **cuttings**, dividing roots or **tubers**, or any other type of sexual (by seed) or asexual reproduction.

Rhizome, an elongated, underground, horizontal stem. Irises and couch grass, for example, produce rhizomes that enable the plant to colonize an increasingly large area and can be used by a gardener who wants to **propagate** the plant.

Rotation, the change of location of a particular type of plant from one year to the next so that plant diseases are minimized and soil nutrients are best utilized.

Runner, a stem that grows horizontally along the soil surface and is capable of rooting where it touches the ground. Plants that form at the ends of the runners can be cut away from the parent plant, such as a strawberry, and placed elsewhere.

Sand, a soil constituent with very coarse particles. A high proportion of sand in soil allows water to penetrate well but also permits fertilizer to pass through quickly. Sandy soils must be watered frequently and should be **mulched** with **organic matter**.

Seedling, a young plant whose first true leaves, the leaves that have the same general shape and appearance as leaves of a mature specimen, have not yet fully developed. It does, however, have its seedling leaf, or cotyledon, its simply shaped first foliage.

Shrub, a woody plant with more than one stem arising close to the ground.

Silt, a soil constituent midway in coarseness between **clay** and **sand**.

Soil test, a soil sample analysis that measures any of several soil constituents, including **organic matter**, **phosphorus**, **potassium**, and **nitrogen**, and soil qualities such as **pH** and texture. A soil test may be performed by the gardener using a purchased test kit, or it can be performed in a commercial or government laboratory for a fee.

Species, a class of individuals usually capable of interbreeding freely and having many characteristics in common. In the Latin name of a plant, the species appears as the second word, in lower case and italicized; the common lilac, *Syringa vulgaris*, is a member of the species *vulgaris*. Tall or short, with blue or purple flowers, different members of the species can freely interbreed.

Specimen plant, a plant chosen for its beauty or interest and planted in such a way that it stands out in the landscape; it may, for instance, appear alone in the centre of the lawn or by a path leading to the front door.

Sphagnum, see **peat**.

Spp, see **species**

Stake, a plant support in the form of a vertical pole, usually wood, placed close to the plant, which is then tied to the stake once or at several intervals; also the process of tying the plant to the stake.

Subsoil, soil that underlies topsoil. It contains less **organic matter** and so has a lighter colour and a more dense structure than topsoil. It may even be so hard that it impedes the passage of water and so is best broken up with a spade before plants are placed in or above it to allow for the penetration of water and roots.

Sucker, a shoot that grows from roots extending outward from the parent plant; also an unproductive, fast-growing vertical branch on a fruit tree; also a suction device that allows some **vines** to cling to walls unassisted.

Tender plants cannot survive very low temperatures and must be protected from frosts — either brought indoors, covered, or, in the case of tender annuals, allowed to die. Tender is a relative term: what is tender in the Yukon may be **hardy** on Vancouver Island.

Tendril, a slender, coiling plant extension that is able to twine itself around a support and so aids the upward growth of **climbers** and **vines**.

Test winter, a winter whose conditions are particularly severe, usually including very low temperatures and poor snow cover. Plants that seem **hardy** enough to survive in a certain zone may succumb during a test winter, which receives its name from that very ability to try plant durability.

Thinning, the removal of a plant or plants from a larger group so that the remaining individuals will have greater space for healthy growth.

Tolerant, a plant able to withstand any of certain adverse conditions, such as cold, drought or disease. The plant is then described as cold-tolerant, fusarium wilt-tolerant, or whatever is appropriate.

Topsoil, the surface layer of soil, which may be only a fraction of an inch to several feet thick. Relatively dark-coloured and high in **organic matter** content, topsoil is the principal rooting medium of plants and is vital to a good garden. The more topsoil and the better condition it is in, the healthier the garden is likely to be — good incentive for adding plenty of organic matter and appropriate **fertilizers**.

Transplant, the act of moving a plant from one growing position to another; also the plant so moved.

Trellis, a vertical plant support, especially for **climbers** and **vines**. A trellis may be made of wood, metal or plastic, but its structural elements, which are narrow, are woven or criss-crossed in order to allow the plants to climb easily. Trellises are often placed against building walls, or they may be freestanding, two joined together into an arch at the top and tall enough to be walked beneath.

Tuber, a much-enlarged, short, fleshy underground stem. A potato has a typical tuber, which may be divided, with at least one eye per piece, to **propagate** the plant.

Variety, an individual or group usually fertile with any other member of the species to which it belongs, but differing from the species in general in at least one reproducible quality. *Brassica oleracea capitata*, the cabbage, differs from another variety that belongs to the same **genus** and **species**, cauliflower, *Brassica oleracea botrytis*, but the plants can interbreed.

Vine, a plant, especially the grape, that is capable of self-support if it is grown close to a stronger, vertical **stake**, fence or tree.

Wood ash, the fine, dustlike remains of wood burning, high in calcium and potash, that can be used as an amendment on **acid** soils, at two or three times the rate recommended for **lime**. Do not overapply wood ashes where food crops will be grown, as they may contain toxic, heavy materials that can accumulate in the soil.

APPENDIX B

GROUND COVERS

The following is a list of suitable ground covers for cool gardens. The letters L, M, or T indicate the plant height: low, to 6 inches (L); medium, 6 to 18 inches (M); or tall, more than 18 inches (T). D is deciduous, E, evergreen. Light requirements are indicated by S for sun or Sh for shade. The zone number refers to the Agriculture Canada climatic zone indicated on the maps on page 20. The number listed is the coolest zone in which the plant is known to be successful. If no number is given, the plant's hardiness has not been ascertained.

Achillea tomentosa (woolly yarrow) — M, E, S. Very hardy, thrives in dry, poor soil; fernlike leaves are topped by flat yellow flower heads; can be mowed and tolerates light foot traffic; spreads rapidly by underground runners. Zone 2.

Aegopodium podagraria variegatum (silveredge goutweed) — M, D, S/Sh. Invasive, tolerates most soils; green leaves are flecked with white; small white flowers; tolerates mowing. Zone 3.

Ajuga reptans (bugle, bugleweed) — L, D, S/Sh. Grows in average soil but prefers moist; rosettes of leaves come in a variety of colours, from green to purple and variegated white; spires of blue or pink flowers appear in spring; quick cover, spreads by surface runners, but easily removed; excellent all-round carpeter. Zone 4.

Alchemilla mollis or *A. vulgaris* (lady's mantle) — M, D, S/Sh. Tolerates most soils; velvety, grey-green leaves shaped like bedding geraniums, sprays of yellow-green flowers in summer; spreads moderately quickly and seeds freely, but easily contained. Zone 4.

Antennaria dioica (pussytoes) — L, E, S. Hardy native good in light soil; greyish basal leaves topped by stalks of pink or white flowers resembling cat's paw; increases by creeping rootstocks. Probably Zone 2.

Anthemis nobilis (Roman chamomile) — L, E, S. Thrives in sandy soil; fragrant when bruised, feathery leaves can be mowed into lawn; white daisies in summer. Zone 4.

Arabis albida (rock cress) — L, D, S. A rockery plant that likes well-drained soil; soft greyish leaves topped with pink, white or lavender flowers in early spring. Zone 3.

Arctostaphylos uva-ursi (bearberry) — M, E, S. Thrives in poor, sandy soil on the acid side; salt tolerant; small, shiny leaves on trailing stems, pink bell-shaped flowers, red berries attractive to wildlife. Zone 2.

Armeria maritima (common thrift) — L, E, S. Prefers sandy soil, tolerates seashore conditions; grasslike foliage forms low mounds; in spring, clusters of pink flowers appear, resembling chives. Zone 2.

Artemisia schmidtiana Silver Mound (silver mound) — M, D, S. Drought-resistent in sandy soil; fragrant, silver foliage forms a mound; flowers are inconspicuous. Zone 3.

Asarum canadense, A. caudatum, A. europaeum (wild ginger) — M, D or E, Sh. *A. canadense*, native to eastern North America, is deciduous, with soft, heart-shaped leaves that hide reddish-brown flowers in spring. *A. caudatum* is native to western Canada and the United States, and, like *A. europaeum*, bears evergreen leaves. All prefer moist soil in shade.

Asperula odorata (sweet woodruff) — M, D, Sh. Thrives in moist shade; good for woodland plantings; whorls of narrow leaves; tiny star-shaped white flowers in late spring. Zone 4.

Astilbe sinensis pumila (dwarf Chinese false spirea) — M, D, S/Sh. Prefers moist soil in semi-shade; magenta plumes rise from divided leaves; makes a good, moderately spreading cover.

Aurinia saxatile (basket-of-gold) also known as *Alyssum saxatile* — M, E, S. Good in light soil; masses of small yellow flowers and greyish leaves; often used in rock gardens; makes a good foil for brightly coloured plants.

Bergenia cordifolia (bergenia) — M, E, S/Sh. Thrives in moist, rich part-shade, but tolerates average conditions; leathery, rounded, shiny leaves turn bronze in winter; in spring, there are pink flower clusters; increases slowly by clumping. Zone 4.

Calluna vulgaris (Scotch heather) — L or M or T, E, S. Small shrub whose height depends on variety. Prefers moist, acidic soil, but tolerates average conditions; tiny, needle-like leaves grow on woody stems; white, pink or purple bell-shaped flowers appear summer to fall; slow growers; clip in spring. Zone 4.

Campanula carpatica (Carpathian harebell) — L, E, S. Well-drained soil and rock garden conditions are ideal. Mounds of small, dense, light green leaves send up white or blue bell-shaped flowers all summer long.

Cerastium tomentosum (snow in summer) — L, E, S. Well-drained soil preferred; invasive, but makes a good ground cover in rocky places; thick mat of tiny, fuzzy, grey leaves with masses of small white flowers in summer. Zone 2.

Convallaria majalis (lily of the valley) — M, D, Sh. Thrives in rich, moist soil; stalks of very fragrant, white, bell-shaped flowers in spring arch from neat, sword-shaped dark green leaves;

excellent dense cover in shade; slow to establish but long-lasting. Zone 2.

Cornus canadensis (bunchberry, creeping dogwood) — M, D, Sh. Native to cool woodlands of the northeast, requires acid, woodsy soil. A relative of the flowering dogwood tree, it bears similar white bracts and rounded, veined leaves that turn rich wine-colour in fall; red berries; spreads by underground shoots.

Cornus stolonifera (red osier dogwood) — T, D, S. One of a number of shrubby dogwoods useful for ground cover; tolerates wet soil; dark red branches for winter colour; clusters of white flowers in spring. Zone 2.

Coronilla varia (crown vetch) — M, D, S. Needs well-drained soil; a very invasive spreader with extensive root system, good for large slopes; light green, pinnate leaves and tiny pink clover-like blossoms. Keep at a distance from all plants less than 6 feet tall. Zone 3.

Cotoneaster dammeri, C. horizontalis (cotoneaster) — M, E, S. A large variety of prostrate shrubs for well-drained soils. Arching stems bear tiny dark green leaves, small white flowers and red berries. Rooting stems increase slowly; graceful cover for slopes. Zone 5.

Cytisus × kewensis (Kew broom) — L, D, S. Needs well-drained soil; good for seaside plantings; dense green stems bear tiny leaves and yellow or cream pea-like blossoms in spring. Zone 6.

Dianthus deltoides (pinks) — M, E, S. Prefers limy soil, but grows in any average well-drained soil; carpets of grassy, grey-green leaves with small, very fragrant red, white or pink fringed flowers. Zone 2.

Epimedium grandiflorum (bishop's hat) — M, D, Sh. Tolerant of most soils, survives even dry shade; smooth, delicate heart-shaped leaves are borne in three lobes on wiry stems, emerge rosy in spring, turn green for summer, then bronze in fall; dainty sprays of yellow, cream, lavender and pink flowers in spring; slow to increase. Zone 3.

Erica carnea (spring heath, heather) — M to T, E, S. Needs well-drained soil; small evergreen shrub bears tiny needles and spikes of pink, white, red or purple bell-shaped flowers in late winter or very early spring; good erosion control. Zone 5.

Euonymus fortunei (winter creeper, euonymus) — M to T, E, S/Sh. Enjoys soil rich in humus; smooth, oval leaves on sprawling or climbing stems; varieties include variegated white or cream; cultivar *Coloratus* turns purplish in winter.

Euphorbia griffithii Fireglow (spurge) — T, D, S. A less rampant spurge than some; available in several cultivars. Tolerates heavy soil; stems are covered with rich green leaves, topped by bright orange bracts in early summer; other varieties often bear yellow-green bracts; grow on infertile soil to prevent rampant growth.

Ferns — Numerous species native throughout the North can be used, usually in moist shade, but also in some sunny areas. Good choices among evergreen ferns include *Polystichum acrostichoides* (Christmas fern), *Polypodium* (polypody), or *Dryopteris marginalis* (marginal shield fern).

Among deciduous ferns, there are *Dennstaedtia punctilobula* (hay-scented fern), which grows in both sun or shade, but can be invasive; *Matteuccia struthiopteris* (ostrich-feather fern), with edible fiddleheads; and *Osmunda cinnamomea* (cinnamon fern). Delicate *Adiantum* spp (maidenhair fern) can be used in very moist shade.

Fragaria chiloensis (wild strawberry) — L, E, S. Native across the continent, its glossy, divided leaves form a dense mat; white flowers are followed by small edible berries; spreads by runners; tolerates seaside conditions; *F. vesca*, the alpine strawberry, prefers semi-shade, and produces small edible berries all summer long. Cultivar *Baron Solemacher* is runnerless.

Gaultheria procumbens (wintergreen) — L, E, Sh. Requires acid soil rich in humus; shiny aromatic leaves form dense carpet; tiny white flowers are followed by red edible berries; excellent woodland cover.

G. shallon (salal) — M, E, Sh. Needs acidic soil; native to the North American west coast; large, rounded, shiny leaves are used in florists bouquets; edible blue berries. Zone 5.

Geranium spp (cranesbill) — M to T, D, S/Sh. Numerous species and varieties generally prefer part shade in average soil; deeply divided leaves form mounds, covered with white, pink, lavender, violet or maroon flowers in summer; shear for denser growth.

Grasses, ornamental — many species, for ground cover. Add movement and grace to the garden. *Phalaris arundinacea Picta* (ribbon grass) with white stripes, can be invasive unless contained; *Avena sempervirens* (evergreen oatgrass), *Arrhenatherum elatius tuberosum* (tuberous oatgrass), *Miscanthus sinensis Zebrinus* (zebra grass), with horizontal golden stripes, and diminutive *Festuca glauca* (blue fescue) are all attractive ground cover additions.

Hedera helix baltica (Baltic ivy) — M, E, S/Sh. One of the hardier ivies, it enjoys a rich soil; trailing vine roots as it spreads, taking a few years to cover an area densely; shear for compact growth. Zone 5.

Hemerocallis spp (day lily) — M to T, D, S/Sh. Versatile plants for most soils. Light green, reed-like leaves form dense clumps; trumpet-shaped flowers, often fragrant, in cream/yellow/orange/ mahogany spectrum. Thousands of cultivars exist, but *H. fulva* cultivars are the best spreaders. Zone 3.

Heuchera spp (alum root, coral bells) — L to M, E, S/Sh. Prefers light, well-drained soil, flat basal leaves in rosettes; arching plumes of tiny pink or red flowers; increases by clumping.

Hosta spp (plantain lily) — M, D, Sh. Enjoys rich soil, but will grow in average soil; many varieties and cultivars with veined, pointed leaves growing from the base, colours from bluish to green, and variegated cream; white or lavender bell-flowers appear on stalks in late summer; several cultivars are fragrant; an excellent cover for shade; increases slowly by clumping.

Hydrangea anomala petiolaris (climbing hydrangea) — M, D, S/Sh. Tolerant of most soils; broad, light green leaves grow on the woody stems of this vine; will climb at any opportunity, therefore good for covering old stumps. Large flat clusters of white flowers appear in summer.

Iberis sempervirens (evergreen candytuft) — M, E, S. Likes well-drained soil; excellent sub-shrub with narrow dark green leaves; clusters of white flowers in early spring; shear for bushy growth; easy to grow from seed; spreads slowly. Zone 4.

Juniperus spp (juniper) — L or M or T, E, S. This genus of shrubs includes many prostrate species and varieties suitable for ground cover; prefers light soil; foliage varies from blue to green; good at the seashore; reliable, maintenance-free cover. Zone 2.

Lotus corniculatus (bird's-foot trefoil) — L, D, S. Tolerant of dry soil; cloverlike leaves and yellow, cloverlike blossoms; invasive, but good for large, steep banks. Zone 3.

Lysimachia nummularia (moneywort) — L, D, Sh. Tolerant of most soils; rounded leaves grow on stems hugging the ground; yellow flowers in summer. Zone 2.

Mahonia aquifolium (creeping mahonia, Oregon grape) — M, E, Sh. One of several shrubby ground covers native west of the Rockies; blue-green holly-like leaves, clusters of yellow flowers followed by edible berries; slow to establish. Zone 5.

Maianthemum canadense (false lily of the valley) — M, D, Sh. This native North American requires woodland soil; leaves similar to lily of the valley; small, white star-shaped flowers.

Minuartia verna caespitosa (moss sandwort) — L, E, S. Moist soil preferred; diminutive plant resembles moss, but has tiny, white, starry flowers in spring; good among stepping stones and rocky crevices. Zone 2.

Nepeta × faasenii (catmint) — M, D, S. Prefers light soil; greyish, fragrant, mint-like leaves and spires of lavender flowers; rapid spreader; good foil for brightly coloured flowers.

Pachistima canbyi (pachistima) — M, E, S/Sh. Prefers acidic soil; excellent small native shrub traditionally planted with rhododendrons; small slender leaves on woody stems; insignificant flowers. Zone 5.

Pachysandra terminalis (Japanese pachysandra or spurge) — L, E, Sh. Light soil preferred, adapts to most; one of the most popular ground covers; glossy, toothed leaves form rosette-like tops; spreads moderately by rootstocks; very good all-round ground cover for shade. Zone 4.

Parthenocissus quinquefolia (Virginia creeper) — M, D, S. This native, rambling vine enjoys rich, moist soil. Large, deeply lobed leaves have bright autumn colouring; good for banks; eager to climb — use with caution near shrubs. Zone 3.

Phlox subulata (moss phlox) — L, E, S. Many varieties and cultivars have been derived from this native; prefers well-drained soil; small narrow leaves; trailing stems are covered in spring with white, lavender, pink or magenta flowers. Very showy, good trailing over rocks and walls. Zone 2.

Pinus mugo mugo (mugho pine) — T, E, S. This dwarf, spreading pine prefers sandy soil, must be pruned in spring to remain shorter than 10 feet in most areas, dependable evergreen. Zone 1.

Polygonum cuspidatum compactum (knotweed) — M, D, S. *P. reynoutria* is the female form, preferred because of its profusion of long-lasting clusters of pink flowers in late summer; leathery, rounded leaves are veined red; prefers moist soil but will grow almost anywhere in sun; other species are often highly invasive — use with care. Useful for moist banks.

Potentilla fruticosa (shrubby cinquefoil) — M to T, D, S. Thrives in rich, moist soil, but tolerates drought; forms a shrub; some derived from native species; downy, deeply divided leaves; depending on variety, covered with cream, yellow, orange or red flowers all summer long; very reliable. Zone 2.

Pulmonaria spp (lungwort) — M, D, Sh. Woodland conditions preferred; long pointed leaves are downy, many with white spots; in early spring, pink, lavender or blue nodding flowers appear.

Rhus aromatica (fragrant sumach) — T, D, S. Good on dry soils, especially banks for erosion control; this native shrub has aromatic leaves that are brilliantly coloured in autumn; lower-growing varieties are available; can be invasive. Zone 2.

Rosa spp (rose) — M to T, D, S. Many species and hybrids lend themselves to ground cover. Notable are *R. Max Graf* with single pink flowers in clusters, and rooting stems; *R. nitida*, a native North American, growing less than 2 feet with small pink flowers; *R. wichuraiana*, also under 2 feet with small white flowers; these make excellent barriers for larger areas.

Salix repens (creeping willow) — T, D, S. This shrub thrives on poor moist soil, and is one of several low willows good for ground cover; narrow, downy, grey leaves, catkins on male plants in spring. Zone 3.

Sedum spp (stonecrop) — L to M, E, S. Many species, all with smooth, fleshy leaves; clusters of small, starry flowers in summer; thrive in poor soil; drought-resistant. Zone 3.

Stachys olympica (lamb's ear) — M, D, S. Appreciates well-drained soil; woolly, silver-grey leaves form a thick carpet; whorls of mauve flowers on fuzzy stems in midsummer; excellent foil of purple-leaved plants. Zone 3.

Symphoricarpos chenaultii Hancock (Hancock coralberry) — M to T, D, S/Sh. Tolerates average soil; prostrate shrub with small soft leaves and pink berries in fall; forms suckers from roots, easily grown. Zone 5.

Taxus spp (yew) — M to T, E, S/Sh. Spreading types provide some of the darkest green in the landscape; slow-growing; tolerates city conditions and thrives in both sun and shade.

Thymus spp (thyme) — L to M, E, S. Several species are suitable for ground cover, all requiring dry, rather poor soil. Tiny leaves, green, yellowish, or variegated, on woody stems form a thick mat; lilac pink flower heads; attractive to bees; culinary herb; withstands shearing. Zone 3.

Tiarella cordifolia (foam flower) — M, D, Sh. This native enjoys woodland conditions; hairy, incised leaves form dense cover; spires of tiny, white flowers in spring; one of the best for moist shade.

Trifolium repens (white clover) — L, D, S. Moist, rich soil preferred; smooth, divided green leaves with clusters of white flowers beloved by bees; use alone or with grass in lawn; nitrogen fixing

capabilities; purple-leaved variety, *T. purpurascens* is very attractive. Zone 2.

Tsuga spp (hemlock) — L to T, E, S/Sh. Prostrate forms of hemlock produce a graceful mound; prefer sandy soil rich in humus; very slow growing; need some shelter from wind.

Vancouveria planipetala (American barrenwort) — M, E, S/Sh. Prefers rich moist soil in part-shade. A relative of *Epimedium*, *V.* is native to northwestern Pacific regions. Its delicate compound leaves resemble maidenhair fern; clusters of small cream flowers in spring. *V. hexandra* is deciduous; slow to establish.

Vinca minor (lesser periwinkle) — L, E, Sh. Tolerates any soil; rapidly spreading, rooting stems with glossy, dark green leaves; varieties with leaves variegated yellow and cream; spring flowers usually blue, but also available in white and burgundy; excellent all-round cover. Zone 4.

Viola spp (violet, pansy) — L to M, D, S/Sh. Well-drained soil preferred; many species, both native and exotic make delightful good cover; heart-shaped leaves; spring flowers white, violet, blue or purple; spreads by creeping rootstocks; also self-seeds.

Waldsteinia ternata (barren strawberry) — M, E, S/Sh. Thrives in moist soil; thick mats of smooth, lobed leaves; yellow strawberry-like flowers in spring.

— *Eva Hoepfner*

The following list of readily available shrubs includes information on the areas in which they are hardy. Not all are totally problem-free, but most have stood the test of time and should present the average gardener with few or no cultural, pest or disease problems.

Amelanchier spp (serviceberry, Saskatoon berry)

These are small trees or large shrubs native to different parts of North America. Small specimens can usually be safely transplanted from wild areas, if they are moved in early spring before they flower. Before the leaves appear, almost all produce welcome shows of small white flowers followed by bird-attracting fruit, some of which is deliciously edible. Several produce good displays of fall colour. The Saskatoons (*A. alnifonia*) grow from 6 to 10 feet tall and are hardy to zone 1. On the Prairies, they are among the most widely known of the indigenous fruit plants and were a staple for native peoples as well as early settlers. The delicious fruit can be eaten fresh or used to make preserves, although the gardener may have to use netting to prevent birds harvesting the crop ahead of time. Saskatoons grow and fruit best in sunny locations with good soil and good drainage. Superior selections such as *Smoky* and *Honeywood* are available from prairie nurseries (see Appendix E). The serviceberry (*A. canadensis*) native to the Northeast and hardy to zone 4, merits greater use in landscaping, where it can grow into a large shrub or a tree (12 to 25 feet) if it is purchased with a single trunk. Masses of small, white spring flowers that may last only a few days if the weather is wet or windy are followed by tiny berries that are edible but not as fleshy as the larger fruit of the Saskatoon. The serviceberry's autumn colour varies from brilliant yellow to orange to red.

Caragana spp (pea shrub)

The various pea shrubs form a diverse group that is among the hardiest available for Northern landscapes. The Siberian pea shrub (*C. arborescens*) has long been used as a drought-resistant hedge or windbreak 10 to 16 feet tall that will survive in zones 2 to 7. It is coarse, however, and recommended only for the coldest, driest areas where other large shrubs will not thrive. The plant does provide some interest in early summer when its yellow, pealike flowers appear. The cutleaf pea shrub, *Lorbergii*, is a more graceful, smaller 8-foot form with deeply cut, fernlike foliage and a more showy abundance of yellow flowers and few seeds. There are other selections that are attractive, compact shrubs for general garden use. The pygmy pea shrub, for instance (*C. aurantiaca*) forms a hardy, dense mound about 36 inches tall and can be used as a specimen in front of other larger shrubs or as a low, informal hedge. It has showy yellow flowers in June. All are hardy to zone 2.

Cornus spp (dogwood)

This is a very diverse and useful group of shrubs and small trees, most of which are noted more for coloured foliage, fruit and twigs rather than for the show of flowers that distinguishes the flowering tree-sized dogwoods such as *C. florida*. Ideal for colour contrast with evergreens or in any shrub border are the silverleaf dogwood (*C. alba Elegantissima*), one of the most striking contrast shrubs, with white and green variegated leaves, and the Tatarian dogwood (*C. alba Gouchaltii*), whose leaves are mottled yellow and pink, with red and yellowish white streaks. Both grow about 6 feet tall and are hardy to zone 2. The Siberian dogwood (*C. alba Sibirica*) is similarly hardy but a bit taller, growing to about 8 feet. It has green foliage but is noted for its vivid red twigs that provide colour throughout the winter. It grows well in dry soils.

Corylus avellana Contorta (corkscrew hazel)

This is a most unusual 8-foot-tall shrub whose branches and twigs, variously twisted into the most unusual configurations, always spark comment. As most plants have been grafted onto standard hazel roots, the gardener must take care to remove any vigorous suckers that appear at the base from below the graft line. It is hardy to zone 5.

Cotoneaster spp (cotoneaster)

This genus (pronounced cottony aster) includes a wide variety of small to large shrubs, some of which are evergreen in the mildest parts of the North. The Peking cotoneaster (*C. acutifolia*) is a vigorous 6- or 7-foot-tall shrub, hardy to zone 2, that is often used for glossy green hedging, but can also be used as a specimen in shrub borders. It has small pink flowers in early summer, followed by black fruit in the fall.

Crataegus spp (hawthorn)

There are many different species of these thorny shrubs or small trees native to various regions of the North. Some selections are occasionally planted for their showy double red or white flowers, and almost all produce quantities of edible but insipid fruit that are the choice diet of various wildlife. Native specimens should not be transplanted, as they are very difficult to move and reestablish.

Daphne spp (daphne)

Low-growing, 12-inch-tall shrubs, daphnes are especially valued for their fragrant flowers. The February daphne (*D. mezereum*) is hardy to zone 3 and is, as its name suggests, one of the earliest shrubs to flower, producing purplish flowers in early spring. Silveredge daphne (*D.* × *burkwoodii Silveredge*) has very fragrant pink flowers in spring and showy small leaves edged with a distinctive cream-coloured band. It is, however, only hardy in gardens in zones 5 to 9.

Elaeagnus spp (eleagnus)

The Russian olive (*E. angustifolia*) is a large shrub or small tree, about 20 feet tall, noted for its bright silver foliage that provides contrast in the landscape throughout the summer. It also has small, sweetly scented yellow flowers in June, followed by silver fruit. It is hardy to zone 2. The autumn olive (*E. umbellata Cardinal*) is less hardy, surviving to zone 5 where it grows about 10 feet tall. It is noted for its bright silver-green foliage and masses of red berries in fall. Both grow well on a wide range of soils, and are ideal for naturalizing.

Euonymus spp (euonymus)

This is a diverse and most useful group, ranging from low, trailing evergreen plants to small, broadleaf, evergreen shrubs to deciduous shrubs and even small deciduous trees. The 8-foot-tall burningbush (*E. alatus*) is noted mostly for its foliage, which turns to a spectacular flame colour in fall. The red berries also add interest, as do the unusual, corklike winged twigs. The dwarf burning bush, *Compacta*, grows only about 4 feet tall, and requires very little pruning when used as a hedge or specimen plant. Both are hardy to zone 3.

Evergreen euonymus (*E. fortunei*) is hardy to zone 5, the hardiest of all larger broadleaf evergreens for the North. Various bushy selections, noted for different leaf colours, are readily available and grow 3 to 7 feet tall. The golden types grow best in full sun, but others will tolerate shade as well.

Emerald Gaiety forms a 4-foot-tall pyramid with silver-edged leaves. It is ideal for colour contrast in sun or shade.

Gold tip, with rich, dark green foliage splashed gold, forms an irregular 4-foot-tall mound.

Sarcoxie is the best dark green selection, growing about 5 feet tall.

Sheridan Gold is spectacular in spring, when the new foliage is brilliant, sunshine yellow. It forms a mound about 4 feet tall.

Forsythia spp (forsythia)

Welcome throughout much of the North, wherever the flower buds are hardy, is the yellow spring bloom of the forsythia. Unfortunately, most of the older selections would not flower if winter temperatures fell below about minus 10 degrees F. Now, thanks to the Agriculture Canada Research Station in Ottawa, gardeners can purchase a much hardier forsythia, *Northern Gold*, which has even flowered in Morden, Manitoba. This is probably the most important new Northern shrub development in the last 20 years. Hardy to about zone 3b, *Northern Gold* grows to about 7 feet tall and is covered in early spring with the usual yellow flowers. In milder areas, zones 6 to 9, the showy forsythia (*F. × intermedia Spectabilis*) flowers well except after the very coldest of winters. The weeping forsythia (*F. suspensa*) can be used throughout zones 6 to 9 as a ground cover or for trailing over walls.

Hippophae rhamnoides (sea buckthorn)

A distinctive, large, 12-foot shrub with narrow silver leaves and masses of bright orange berries in fall on female plants, the sea buckthorn is best used in mass plantings where plants of both sexes can be included. As its name suggests, it does well in seashore plantings, but also succeeds well to zone 2b on the Prairies.

Hydrangea spp (hydrangea)

These are very popular summer-flowering shrubs, some of which have flower heads that dry very well for use in flower arrangements. The Annabelle hydrangea (*H. arborescens Annabelle*) is a decided improvement over the widely known *Snowhill* hydrangea, with much stronger stems and much larger white flower heads. It is hardy to zone 2b and grows about 4 feet tall. Prune the stems to about 8 inches in spring, and cut the flowers in September for use in winter bouquets. Hardy to zone 4 is the peegee hydrangea (*H. paniculata Grandiflora*), a large, 10-foot shrub that, in late summer, produces masses of cone-shaped flower heads which change from white to bronze-pink as the season advances and can be cut and dried. The colourful blue and pink florist type of hydrangea is reliably winter hardy only in zones 7 to 9.

Ilex spp (holly)

Until very recently, evergreen hollies could be grown only in the very mildest Northern landscapes, but recently some new hardy hybrids have been developed in the United States, so that gardeners in zone 6 can plant an evergreen Christmas-type holly with a reasonable assurance that it will prosper and bear fruit. *Blue Princess* is an English holly hybrid that has its typical dark blue-green foliage and masses of red fruit, provided that the male *Blue Prince* is planted nearby to ensure pollination and fruit production. These shrubby hollies will reach a height of 6 to 10 feet. Adventurous gardeners with protected corners in zone 5 may also want to try them. Two additional hardy selections are *China Girl*, a female, and *China Boy*, a male. These American holly hybrids have lighter green foliage.

Juniperus spp (juniper)

This is a variable and versatile group of evergreens that ranges from low creeping selections to massive bushy types to more narrow, upright plants, some of which will reach a height of 25 feet and are recommended in Chapter 10 as outstanding trees. All junipers grow best in sunny locations. The bushy types are excellent for foundation plantings, but gardeners should be sure to use the newer, more compact selections to avoid overcrowding. Many of the junipers can be used in Prairie gardens, but they do need protection from the bright early spring sun. Give them a shade cloth or tepee until growth resumes in spring.

Kolkwitzia amabilis (beauty-bush)

This is a large, arching 10-foot-tall shrub noted for its masses of bell-like pink flowers in early summer. As it is usually bare at the base, it is best used behind shorter shrubs in a mass planting. It is hardy to zone 5.

Ligustrum spp (privet)

Privets are most frequently used for hedging in zones 5 to 9, and some are noted for their colourful foliage as well. For instance, the Vicary golden privet (*L. vicaryi*) has brilliant yellow foliage that keeps its distinctive colour all summer. This privet is hardy to zone 6 and can be easily kept at any size from 3 to 10 feet.

Magnolia spp (magnolia)

Longtime favourites, the magnolias are, unfortunately, reliably hardy only in zones 6 to 9 and in protected gardens of zone 5. The most popular is the saucer magnolia (*M. × soulangiana*) which early each spring is covered with masses of large, chalice-shaped flowers, white flushed with pink on the reverse. The saucer magnolia grows rapidly to a height of 15 to 25 feet, so it should be allowed plenty of garden space. The star magnolia (*M. kobus stellata*) is a dense shrub that, even when quite small, produces profuse crops of white flowers with 12 or 16 petals. In milder zones, the plants will readily reach 10 to 15 feet.

Philadelphus spp (mock-orange)

Mock-oranges are deciduous shrubs noted for their masses of pure white, often fragrant flowers. Unfortunately, neither their foliage nor their fruit is very interesting, although one, the golden mock-orange (*P. coronarius Aureus*) is noted for its golden foliage if planted in a sunny location. It is a compact, 6-foot-tall shrub that is hardy to zone 3. The virginal mock-orange (*P. × virginalis*), hardy to zone 3b, is a popular selection with large clusters of snow white, sweetly scented flowers. *Minnesota Snowflake* is a selection with large, double flowers, while *Waterton* is the hardiest, to zone 2b, and highly recommended for use on the Prairies. All of these specimens are compact and bushy.

Physocarpus opulifolius Luteus (golden ninebark)

This shrub hardy to zone 2b grows to 7 feet tall. Its small, fragrant, pinkish-white flowers are followed by reddish seed pods that can be used in floral arrangements. *Dart's Gold* is a recent dwarf selection, 3 feet tall, with bright golden foliage.

Pinus mugo mugo (Mugho pine)

This is the only readily available dwarf pine for use in Northern gardens and one of the hardiest, surviving in zone 1. The plants are globe-shaped but can readily reach a height and spread of 10 feet if not pruned. To keep them compact, simply prune the candles in late spring, by cutting off one-half to two-thirds of the new growth before the needles begin to expand.

Picea spp (spruce)

Mention spruce to most Northerners, and they think of the native white spruce or perhaps the popular Blue Colorado spruce so widely planted as a specimen. But not as well known are some dwarf selections that are useful for foundation planting. Dwarf Alberta spruce (*Picea glauca Conica*), for instance, is a very slow-growing, dense, conical plant with bright grass-green foliage, hardy to zone 4 and reaching a height of about 7 feet. It does tend to winterburn, so may need protection from the winter sun in exposed plantings. Globe blue spruce (*P. pungens Globosa*) is a dwarf, 5-foot-tall form of the Blue Colorado spruce hardy to zone 2. It is flat and compact when young but gradually becomes pyramidal. Very slow-growing and expensive, it is an aristocrat for special situations. Nest spruce (*P. abies Nidiformis*) is a slow-growing evergreen that forms a mound of dark green foliage about 5 feet wide and 40 inches tall. This is ideal for sunny locations from zone 3 to 9. *Ohlendorfii* is a very slow-growing upright selection that will take 20 years or more to reach a height of 7 feet.

Lonicera spp (Honeysuckles)

These are extremely hardy shrubs, hardy from zone 2 or 3 to 9, long used in flowering hedges. They vary from short to tall, but all flower in midspring. Recently, however, many species have been badly disfigured by the honeysuckle aphid, which is not easily controlled. Honeysuckles should be considered for use only if the insect is not a local problem.

Potentilla spp (potentilla, cinquefoil)

These dwarves, to about 3 feet tall, are among the hardiest Northern flowering shrubs. All grow well in hot, sunny, dry locations to zone 2 and present a profusion of white, cream, yellow or orange with good displays of repeat bloom for the rest of the season. Some of the most popular selections are the bright yellow *Coronation Triumph*, golden yellow *Gold Drop* or *Farreri*, and *Goldfinger*, with large golden yellow flowers.

Prunus spp (cherry, plum, peach, apricot)

This genus contains many of the most economically important fruit trees, all of which are quite showy when in flower in early spring. There are also many shrubby forms such as the native pin cherry (*P. pennsylvanica*) and the choke cherry (*P. virginiana*), both of which are important sources of food for wildlife. The cherry laurel (*P. laurocerasus*) is an evergreen widely used as a specimen or for hedging on the Pacific coast, zone 7b to 9.

Flowering almond (*P. triloba Multiplex*) is a very popular shrub, about 6 feet tall, with masses of double pink flowers early in May. It flowers best in sunny locations to zone 3.

Manchu cherry (*P. tomentosa*) is the hardiest of the flowering cherries, surviving to zone 2, with masses of light pink flowers in early spring followed by small, edible sour cherries on a bush about 10 feet tall.

Pyracantha spp (firethorn)

Where they are hardy, in zone 6 or milder gardens, the firethorns are planted for their masses of showy orange or red berries, which are shown to best advantage if the plant is grown as a specimen shrub or espaliered against a wall. The foliage is semi-evergreen to evergreen in milder zones. *Orange Glow* with bright orange-red fruit, has good resistance to the bacterial disease fire blight, which can destroy some other selections.

Rhododendron spp (rhododendron, azalea)

One of the largest groups of ornamental shrubs in the world, the rhododendron genus, with spectacular flowers and often evergreen foliage, is widely used in temperate countries. Unfortunately, only on the Pacific coast and in southern New England can a good selection be readily used in Northern gardens. In addition, in colder areas where the soil is alkaline, the growing of rhododendrons and azaleas is a real challenge, as they must have an acidic, well-drained yet moist soil. Sandy, gravelly soils are best, although even then, peat moss and well-rotted manure or compost should be incorporated, while in clay soils, a large hole must be dug and filled with a suitably acidic soil mixture. In marginal climatic areas, rhododendrons must be shaded from the afternoon sun throughout the year and protected from cold winds and sun in winter. Deciduous azaleas can be grown in sunnier locations, but they also require an acidic soil. (Evergreen azaleas, so popular as flowering pot plants, can be safely grown outdoors only in zone 7b or milder areas.) In order to be fairly sure of getting sufficiently hardy stock, select only the varieties sold by local nurseries.

Rhus spp (sumach)

The sumach are native shrubs that include poison ivy and poison sumach, plants to be avoided, as well as the ornamental sumachs, which are noted for their colourful fruit and brilliant autumn foliage. As they grow readily in most soils, often spreading by underground suckers, they are very useful for naturalizing on slopes and other difficult areas.

Fragrant sumach (*R. aromatica*) is a useful, low-growing (40 inches) shrub that spreads slowly by suckers. Hardy to zone 3, it turns bright scarlet in fall.

Staghorn sumach (*R. typhina*) spreads rapidly by underground suckers, making it useful where naturalization is desired but a nuisance in a manicured garden. The fall colour is red to orange, and the crimson fruit is useful for attracting wildlife. The cutleaf sumach (*R.t. Laciniata*) has an even more attractive texture, with its deeply divided foliage. Both are hardy to zone 3 and grow about 16 feet tall.

Ribes spp (currant, gooseberry)

Currants are very useful plants that are hardy to zone 2. While there are ornamental types, the fruiting currants and gooseberries can also be incorporated into natural landscape areas that receive full sun. Among the ornamentals is the alpine currant (*R. alpinum*), one of the best dense, dark green, 5-foot-tall hedge plants for shaded or sunny locations, also useful as a specimen plant. The flowering currant (*R. aureum*), a good shrub for sun or shade, is noted for its masses of bright yellow, fragrant flowers in spring and for colourful red fall foliage on a bush about 7 feet tall. Among edible currants, there are red- and black-fruited types, while gooseberries may be pink-, red- or white-fruited. All are delicious fruits especially prized in preserves and pies. Prune out some of the old wood after the harvest each year to keep the bushes open to the sun.

Rosa spp (rose)

While hybrid tea and floribunda roses need a great deal of special care — spraying, pruning and winter protection — that is not the case with shrub roses, many of which were developed by Agriculture Canada in Ottawa and Morden, Manitoba, and so are gratifyingly hardy. These roses are not used in Northern gardens nearly as much as they could be. Many are problem-free and easy to grow, producing attractive foliage as well as masses of colourful flowers and fruit that is an excellent source of vitamin C.

Japanese rose (*R. multiflora*), although a weed in some areas, is still useful in the more northerly parts of its range, such as zone 5b, where it forms a hardy, impregnable hedge up to 8 feet tall that helps control soil erosion. The white flowers are small but profuse, followed by small red fruit.

Redleaf rose (*R. rubrifolia*) is grown as much for its distinctive red-tinted, bluish green foliage, a most unusual colour for the garden, as for its single, deep red flowers followed by bright red fruit. It is hardy to zone 2b.

The rugosa roses (*R. rugosa*) are the best known and most widely used group of hardy shrub roses, ones that can be used as specimens or in attractive informal hedges. Most selections start to flower in June and continue to produce double white, pink or red flowers intermittently throughout the summer. The fruit or hip is large and valued for jellies and wines. It grows 3 to 6 feet tall and is hardy to zone 2.

Salix spp (willow)

Many moisture-loving native plants are included in this diverse genus of shrubs and trees.

Arctic willow (*S. purpurea gracilis*) is a

low, 3-foot-tall shrub with narrow, grey-green foliage that survives on wet, heavy soils to zone 2b.

Laurel willow (*S. pentandra*) grows as tall as 25 feet, qualifying it as a small tree or tall shrub ideal for screening or boundary plantings. The foliage is very attractive, glossy, dark green, but the plant should be pruned severely each year if it is to be kept bushy. Hardy to zone 2b.

The pussy willow (*S. caprea*) is one of the most ornamental willows, with large "pussies" in very early spring. As this is a large shrub, about 12 feet tall, with little interest otherwise, it should be used only in larger gardens, where it grows well in wet soils to zone 4b.

Sambucus spp (elderberry)

Native shrubs that are prized for fruit that makes excellent pies, the elderberries are often noted for their colourful foliage as well. *Adams* is a recent selection of the American elder (*S. canadensis*) that has extra-large fruit, and is hardy to zone 3. *Aurea* (*S. nigra Aurea*), with bright golden foliage, grows best in full sun.

Shepherdia argentea (silver buffaloberry)

This is one of the hardiest of shrubs, surviving even in zone 1. Nevertheless, it is a large plant, about 12 feet tall, with attractive silver foliage and scarlet, edible fruit on the female plants.

Sorbaria sorbifolia (false spirea)

A versatile, hardy (to zone 2) shrub best used in mass plantings, false spirea grows well in sun or shade and on wet or dry soils, reaching a height of about 5 feet. It has delicate, light green foliage and produces masses of creamy white flowers in early summer. As it spreads readily, it is an excellent shrub for slope plantings.

Spiraea spp (spirea)

This is a very popular group of shrubs in the North. Not only do spireas have masses of flowers in spring or summer, but they are able to grow in most conditions. The native species are excellent for naturalizing and should be more widely used in their local regions. Cultivars of *S. × bumalda* are the smallest and should be pruned back hard each spring to encourage strong new growth. *S. × b. Anthony Waterer*, for example, has clusters of crimson flowers for several weeks in midsummer, and grows about 3 feet tall, while the similar *S. × b. Froebeli* grows about a foot taller. *Goldflame* is the most colourful, with bright golden new foliage in spring, turning green by summer. It produces masses of light crimson-red flowers in midsummer.

Bridalwreath (*S. vanhouttei*) is one of the most popular of all Northern shrubs — perhaps too popular and overplanted. It is, however, easy to grow, and has very attractive arching branches that require little pruning. It grows to about 7 feet tall in zones 4 to 9, and has white flowers in late May.

Korean spirea (*S. trichocarpa*) is similar to bridalwreath but is hardy to zone 3, where it is one of the latest of the white spireas to bloom, producing masses of white flowers on arching branches in late spring. *Snow White*, a selection from Manitoba, is hardy to zone 2b and displays its creamy white flowers in mid-June on the Prairies.

Symphoricarpos spp (coralberry, snowberry)

This useful genus produces shrubs noted for their white or red berries and their tolerance of shade.

Coralberry (*S. orbiculatus*) is a compact 7-foot-tall shrub that suckers freely. It is useful as a ground cover in sun or shade to zone 2b. The clusters of small coral-coloured fruit are produced in fall.

Hancock coralberry (*S. chenaultii Hancock*) developed in Ontario, is a prostrate, 3-foot-tall coralberry with graceful, fine foliage. Hardy to zone 5, it is a useful ground cover in sun or shade.

Snowberry (*S. albus*) is hardy to zone 2, and grows about 3 feet tall in shade and in a wide range of soils, where it produces masses of snow-white berries on arching branches in fall.

Syringa spp (lilac)

With their colourful, fragrant spring flowers, lilacs are among the most popular of Northern shrubs, even though some are invasive and most are uninteresting once the flowering season is past. All of the following lilacs are hardy to zone 2.

Common lilac (*S. vulgaris*) is almost synonymous with spring in the rural North, where it was introduced by the earliest settlers. A wide variety of single and double selections, usually known as the French hybrid lilacs, is available, most producing their fragrant blooms in late May. Where possible, dead flower heads should be cut off before the seeds form. Some of the most popular selections are:

Belle de Nancy — bright rose-pink, double
Charles Joly — reddish purple, double
Katherine Havemeyer — blue-purple, double
Ludwig Spaeth — deep purple, single
Madame Lemoine — pure white, double
Mrs. Edward Harding — magenta, double

The dwarf lilac (*S. patula*) is the smallest lilac, about 6 feet tall, and so is most useful in smaller gardens. It grows about as wide as it does tall, however, but can be pruned to size. Covered in late spring with masses of light lilac flowers, it can be used in foundation plantings, shrub borders, and even clipped to make a formal flowering hedge.

Japanese tree lilac (*S. reticulata*) is a large shrub or small tree about 20 feet tall that has masses of creamy white flowers in late June, long after most other spring flowering shrubs have finished.

The late lilac (*S. villosa*) is a large, 10-foot-tall, drought-resistant shrub that can be used as a specimen or screen on large properties. Its dense clusters of rosy lilac flowers appear about a week after the French lilacs.

Preston lilac (*S. prestoniae*) grows about 8 feet tall and flowers in late spring about two weeks after the French lilacs. Many of the selections were developed in Canada and include:

Desdemona — pale lilac-pink
Isabella — large, pyramidal clusters of deep pink buds that open to light pink flowers
James McFarlane — large trusses of deep pink flowers
Minuet — a more compact, 7-foot selection with prolific, light purple flowers

Taxus spp (yew)

Yews are the most versatile and useful of all evergreens. They withstand urban conditions better than most others, grow well in sun or shade, are ideal for planting in a Northern exposure, grow slowly, adapt well to pruning, and make excellent, albeit expensive, hedge plants. Unfortunately, none is hardy on the Prairies. The English yew (*T. baccata*) and most of its selections are hardy only in the mildest areas of the Northwest.

The Japanese yew (*T. cuspidata*) is an upright 15-foot-tall plant that will form a large pyramid of dark green foliage as wide as it is tall in good soil. It does, however, withstand clipping very well and can be shaped into cubes, pyramids or globes with pruning once or twice a year in late spring or early summer. It tolerates sun or shade and is hardy to zone 4. The dwarf Japanese yew, *Nana*, grows very slowly and has very dark green, low-growing, dense foliage, spreading eventually to 5 feet.

Yew hybrids (*T. media*), available in spreading and upright selections are only slightly less hardy than the Japanese yews to zone 5. All adapt well to shaded plantings.

Brown's yew is a compact, slower growing *T. media* type, vase shaped with dark green foliage. It grows about 6 feet wide and is hardy to zone 5.

Dense yew is a broad but compact grower with an ultimate spread of 8 feet. It is also hardy to zone 5.

Hick's yew will form a tall column to 12 feet without pruning.

Hill's yew is a broadly pyramidal, compact variety from 6 to 10 feet tall with very dense, dark green foliage.

Thuja occidentalis (white-cedar or arborvitae)

Native to much of the Northeast, the white-cedar or arborvitae has been widely used for screening and specimen plantings in Northern gardens. It is usually grown from seed for inexpensive, year-round screening. It grows well in sun and partial shade, attaining a height of about 20 feet in areas as severe as zone 3. As only a few selections are hardy on the Prairies, plant only those varieties for that region. All must be planted in a rich soil with a good supply of humus and good moisture levels. Keep the plants mulched with a mixture of peat moss and cattle manure or compost and give them a thorough watering late in the fall. As they are the dog's favourites, arborvitae should be protected by other plants or short fencing.

Brandon, a narrowly pyramidal 12-foot selection that has proven to be one of the best on the Prairies, hardy to zone 2, has good, bright green foliage.

Fastigiata, the pyramid-cedar, is a narrowly pyramidal, 15-foot-tall selection ideal for use in foundation plantings and for narrow screens. It is hardy to zone 3.

Holmstrup is a much slower growing, compact pyramid 12 feet tall, also ideal for foundation plantings.

Little Giant is an excellent, compact globe-cedar with an ultimate height of about 30 inches. Hardy to zone 3.

Smaragd, the emerald cedar, is one of the hardiest, to zone 1b, a recent selection from Sweden that forms a compact pyramid with distinct, bright green foliage.

Woodwardii, the popular globe-cedar, forms a perfect dense, dark green globe to 3 feet tall without pruning. It is hardy to zone 3.

Vaccinium spp (blueberry)

Blueberries are the only edible fruit-bearing shrubs that are regularly considered an attractive adjunct to the ornamental landscape. Not only are their white flowers of note in spring, but many have very attractive foliage that is colourful in fall. Unfortunately, cultivated blueberries (*V. corymbosum*) must have an acid, moist soil, which is not available in many gardens. It is hardy to zone 4, but must be planted in a sunny location. If the soil is not already acid, it must be replaced with a mixture of half loam and half humus that contains additional peat moss and leaf mould or compost. Several selections noted for superior fruit, such as *Bluecrop*, *Blueray*, *Jersey* and *Northland* are readily available; two different varieties should be planted for cross-pollination. The mountain-cranberry (*V. vitis-idaea minus*) is a small-leaved, dwarf, 6-inch evergreen, hardy to zone 1, that is native to northern Canada. It is an attractive shrub that should be planted more frequently on moist, acid soils.

Viburnum spp (viburnum)

This group of shrubs is noted for attractive foliage, sweetly scented flowers and occasionally colourful, edible fruit.

Arrowwood (*V. dentatum*) grows 12 feet tall in moist soils in sun or shade, and produces flat heads of white flowers in late spring, and shiny red foliage and bluish black fruit in fall. It is a North American native hardy to zone 4.

European highbush-cranberry (*V. opulus*) is a vigorous, tall, 13-foot-tall shrub hardy to zone 2b, with flat heads of white flowers in midspring followed by colourful clusters of tart red berries.

Nanum, the hedge viburnum, is a dwarf, 2-foot-tall non-flowering selection that can be used for dwarf hedging or as a small specimen. *Roseum*, the European snowball, has masses of showy, white flower heads in midspring. It is unfortunately frequently attacked by aphids.

Fragrant snowball (*V. carlcephalum*) is noted for its large, 6-inch clusters of fragrant white flowers in early spring. These well-shaped shrubs, about 8 feet tall, are among the most fragrant in the garden. Hardy to zone 6.

Highbush-cranberry (*V. trilobum*) is a native shrub very similar to the European species, but is hardier, to zone 2, and produces edible fruit used to make jelly. The native is 12 feet tall, while *Compactum* is a dwarf fruiting selection that grows about 4 feet tall and is ideal for small gardens.

Nannyberry (*V. lentago*) can be grown as a small tree or large shrub, to 20 feet tall. It has showy flat clusters of white flowers in late spring, followed by blue-black, raisinlike edible fruit. The glossy green leaves turn purplish red in fall. It grows in sun or shade, and is hardy in the Prairies.

Wayfaring tree (*V. lantana*) can grow about 18 feet tall and so is useful as a background shrub to zone 2b, where it produces white flowers in late spring. The red fruit, noted for attracting birds, becomes black in the fall. It tolerates dry soil in sun or shade.

Weigela spp (weigela)

The weigelas are grown chiefly for their colourful pink or red flowers in late spring and early summer. The older branches should be pruned out each spring.

Bristol Ruby is one of the best, attaining a height of 7 feet in zone 5, and producing masses of crimson-red flowers in late May followed by scattered flowers throughout summer and fall.

Dropmore Pink grows 5 feet tall, and is one of the hardiest, to zone 3, producing masses of soft pink flowers in early summer.

Purple-leaved weigela (*W. florida foliis purpuriis*) is most attractive, with purple foliage on a 5-foot-tall bush all summer, plus pink flowers in spring. Hardy to zone 5.

Variegated weigela (*W. florida variegata*) has a colourful green foliage edged with yellow on a bush about 5 feet tall. The flowers are light to deep pink in spring. Hardy to zone 4.

Yucca spp (yucca)

Decidedly exotic, with their large clumps of spearlike leaves, the yuccas must be planted in hot, sunny, well-drained areas.

Adam's needle (*Y. filamentosa*) makes spectacular displays with its towering spikes of bell-shaped, creamy white flowers in summer. The basal clusters of leaves are soft and flexible. The plant grows about 3 feet tall, and is hardy to zone 4.

Spanish bayonet or soapweed (*Y. glauca*) is a striking sword-leaved plant the same height as Adam's needle, but producing 4-foot-tall spikes of creamy white flowers in summer. This is an excellent barrier plant that is indigenous as far north as southeastern Alberta.

— Lawrence C. Sherk

APPENDIX D

ORNAMENTAL TREES FOR NORTHERN LANDSCAPES

The following trees are particularly valuable for landscape use and many are widely grown in Canada.

Included with the botanical name are the height, the coldest zone in which the tree can be grown, and, if there is one, the common name or names. The botanical names are in accordance with the *International code of botanical nomenclature* and the *International code of nomenclature of cultivated plants* – 1969. (Invalid names, often still used in Canada, are included in parentheses after the name presently accepted.)

In addition to botanical and common names, many cultivar names are given. Cultivars are plants that have originated and persisted under cultivation. In the past, they were known mainly as varieties or forms. In the following list, cultivar names are capitalized, for example *Crimson King,* which is a cultivar of *Acer platanoides.* Cultivars are listed under the species to which they belong, except when they cannot be assigned to a particular species, as in *Malus Hopa.*

The term variety is now usually reserved for a botanical division of a species. In this checklist, varieties are set in the same type as the species name. For example, in *Fraxinus pennsylvanica subintegerrima, subintegerrima* is a variety of *Fraxinus pennsylvanica.*

Interspecific hybrids, or hybrids whose parents belong to the same genus, are treated as species and are designated by the multiplication sign × immediately preceding the specific epithet, as in *Aesculus* × *carnea,* the red horse-chestnut. Intergeneric hybrids are listed with the multiplication sign × immediately before the hybrid genus name as in × *Cupressocyparis leylandii,* a hybrid of *Cupressus macrocarpa* and *Chamaecyparis nootkatensis.* In most cases hybrids, like cultivars, must be propagated by cuttings, grafts, or other vegetative means.

Each height given is the maximum usually expected under ideal cultural conditions in Canada. Many references list only the maximum height for a species when it grows in its native habitat. However, such a height is usually not attained under cultivation, although some plants grow larger in cultivation. A range is also given, as in 60 to 100 feet for *Picea abies,* the Norway spruce. The minimum height is the one to be expected under ideal conditions in areas where the species is growing at the limit of its hardiness range. The maximum is the height to which the plant will grow in more favourable climates. Heights in parentheses are for trees native to Canada (indicated by *) as found in native stands.

The hardiness zone ratings refer to those on the Agriculture Canada Map of Plant Hardiness Zones in Canada, page 20.

On the map each zone bears a number; numbers have been alotted in decreasing order of severity. Most zones are subdivided into sections a and b, also in decreasing order of severity. In the zone column in the following list for each item there is a number or number and letter, which represents the most severe zone in which the tree can be expected to survive and grow satisfactorily. The plant will also be hardy in all zones with a higher number. A zone number alone indicates that the tree should grow throughout that zone. A tree listed with a b zone should be hardy in the milder half of the one, but cannot be expected to survive satisfactorily in the a section.

Botanical Name	Height (Feet)	Zone	Common Name(s)
Abies amabilis *	50-80	7b	Pacific fir
A. balsamea *	30-60	1	balsam fir
A. cephalonica	70	5	Greek fir
A. concolor	60-100	4	Colorado fir
A. grandis *	50-120	7	giant fir
A. holophylla	30-80	3b	needle fir
A. homolepis	80	5	Nikko fir
A. koreana	50	4	Korean fir
A. lasiocarpa	50-80	2b	alpine fir
A. nordmanniana	60-100	6	Nordmann fir
A. pinsapo	66	8	Spanish fir
A.p. Glauca	60	8	blue Spanish fir
A. procera (A. nobilis)	60-150	8	noble fir
A. sibirica	40-80	2	Siberian fir
A. veitchii	70	5	Veitch fir
Acer buergeranum	20	7	trident maple
A. campestre	20-30	5b	hedge maple
A. cappadocicum Aureum	33	6	golden coliseum maple
A.c. rubrum	33	6	red coliseum maple
A. carpinifolium	30	7	hornbeam maple
A. circinatum *	10-30	6	vine maple
A. davidii	40	7b	David maple
A. ginnala	20-30	2b	Amur maple
A. glabrum douglasii *	10-23	5b	Douglas maple
A. griseum	23	6	paperbark maple
A. japonicum	23	6	fullmoon maple
A. macrophyllum *	50-70	8	bigleaf maple
A. mandshuricum	30	6	Manchurian maple
A. monspessulanum	20-30	7	Montpellier maple
A. negundo *	30-50	2	box-elder, Manitoba maple
A.n. Variegatum	33	7	silverleaf box-elder
A. palmatum	10-30	6	Japanese maple
A.p. atropurpureum	10-16	6	purple Japanese maple
A.p. Bloodgood	10-16	6	bloodgood Japanese maple
A. pennsylvanicum *	10-30	2b	striped maple, moosewood
A. platanoides	50-75	5	Norway maple
A.p. Cleveland	40	6	Cleveland maple
A.p. Columnare	40-50	5	columnar Norway maple
A.p. Crimson King	40	4b	crimson king maple
A.p. Drummondii	30	5	harlequin maple

Botanical Name	Height (Feet)	Zone	Common Name(s)	Botanical Name	Height (Feet)	Zone	Common Name(s)
A.p. Emerald Queen	40	6	emerald queen maple	A. glabra	20-60	2b	Ohio buckeye
A.p. Faassen's Black	40	5	Faassen redleaf maple	A. hippocastanum	75	5b	horse-chestnut
A.p. Globosum	15-20	5	globe Norway maple	A.h. Baumannii	60	5b	Baumann horse-chestnut
A.p. Goldsworth Purple	40	5	Goldsworth purple maple	A. × mutabilis induta	6.5-10	5	arboretum buckeye
A.p. Olmsted	40	5	Olmsted maple	A. sylvatica (neglecta)	23-60	5	painted buckeye
A.p. Royal Red	40	5	royal red maple	Ailanthus altissima	30-40	6	tree of heaven
A.p. Schwedleri	50-66	5	Schwedler maple	Albizia julibrissin	26	8b	silk tree
A.p. Summer Shade	60-75	5	summer shade Norway maple	A.j. Rosea	20	7b	
A. pseudoplatanus	40-70	5b	sycamore, sycamore maple	Alnus cordata	40	6	European alder
A.p. Erectum	40	6	columnar sycamore maple	A. glutinosa	20-50	4	black alder
A.p. Leopoldii	40	5b	Leopold sycamore maple	A.g. Imperialis	10-30	4b	royal alder
A.p. Spaethii	30	5b	Spaeth maple	A. hirsuta	10-30	5	Manchurian alder
A.p. Worleei	40	5b	golden sycamore maple	A. incana	13-50	4	European white alder
A. rubrum*	60	3	red maple, swamp maple	A.i. Aurea	30	5	yellowleaf white alder
A.r. Morgan	50	4	Morgan red maple	Amelanchier arborea*	33	4b	downy serviceberry
A.r. October Glory	50	5	October Glory maple	A. canadensis*	26	4	shadblow, serviceberry
A.r. Red Sunset	50	5	red sunset maple	A. × grandiflora	26	4	apple serviceberry
A.r. Schlesingeri	50-60	5	Schlesinger red maple	A. × g. Robin Hill	20	5	
A. saccharinum*	60-90	2b	silver maple	A. laevis*	30	3b	Alleghany serviceberry
A.s. Wieri (Laciniatum)	70	3	cutleaf silver maple	Aralia elata	6.5-26	5	Japanese angelicatree
A. saccharum	60-90	4	sugar maple, hard maple	A. spinosa	10-33	6	Hercules' club
A.s. Green Mountain	50	4	green mountain maple	Araucaria araucana	60	8	monkey puzzle tree
A.s. Newton Sentry	40	5	sentry sugar maple	Arbutus menziesii*	30-46	8	Pacific madrone
A. nigrum*	60	4	black maple	Asimina triloba*	20-33	6	pawpaw
A.n. Temple's Upright	40-50	5	Temple's upright maple	Betula albo-sinensis	40-70	3	Chinese paper birch
A. spicatum*	13-23	2	mountain maple	B. alleghaniensis*	50-70	3b	yellow birch
A. tataricum	13-20	2b	Tatarian maple	B. lenta*	40-50	4b	sweet birch
A. truncatum	20	4	purpleblow maple	B. nigra	40-70	3b	river birch
A.t. mono	30-50	5	mono maple	B. occidentalis*	20-40	2b	water birch
Aesculus × carnea	40-50	5b	red horse-chestnut	B. papyrifera*	50-80	2	canoe birch
A. × c. Briottii	40	5b	ruby red horse-chestnut	B.p. commutata	33-82	2	western white birch
				B. pendula (B. verrucosa)	60	2	European white birch
				B.p. Fastigiata	33-46	2	columnar European birch

Botanical Name	Height (Feet)	Zone	Common Name(s)	Botanical Name	Height (Feet)	Zone	Common Name(s)
B.p. Gracilis (Laciniata)	40	2	cutleaf weeping birch	C.l. Stewartii	15	7b	Stewart golden false-cypress
B.p. Purpurea	30	3	purpleleaf birch	C. nootkatensis*	80-100	6b	Nootka cypress
B.p. Tristis	40	2	slender birch	C.n. Pendula	20-82	5b	pendulous Nootka cypress
B.p. Youngii	30	2b	Young's weeping birch	C. obtusa	23-75	5	Hinoki cypress
B. populifolia*	20-30	3	grey birch	C. pisifera	16-82	4b	Sawara false-cypress
Calocedrus (Libocedrus) decurrens	40-82	8	California incense-cedar				
Carya cordiformis*	50-66	4	bitternut hickory	Chionanthus virginicus	10-30	5b	white fringetree
C. glabra*	33-66	5	pignut	Cladrastis lutea	30-40	4b	American yellowwood
C. illinoinensis (C. pecan)	40-70	5b (Fruit-7b)	pecan				
C. ovata*	60-82	4b	shagbark hickory	Cornus alternifolia*	16-30	3b	pagoda dogwood
C. tomentosa*	50-66	6	mockernut hickory	C. controversa	20-40	6b	giant dogwood
Castanea dentata*	60-82	5	sweet chestnut, American chestnut	C. florida*	20-40	6b	flowering dogwood
C. mollissima	33-66	6	Chinese chestnut	C.f. Cherokee Chief	10-20	7	
Catalpa bignonioides	40	6	southern catalpa, common catalpa	C.f. Rubra	20	7	red flowering dogwood
C.b. Nana	16	5b	umbrella catalpa	C. kousa	20	6b	Japanese dogwood
C. ovata	33	5	Chinese catalpa	C.k. chinensis	20	6b	Chinese dogwood
C. speciosa	40-60	5b	western catalpa	C. mas	10-23	5b	Cornelian-cherry
Cedrela sinensis	50	7	Chinese toona	C. nuttalii*	20-40	8	Pacific dogwood
Cedrus atlantica	80	7b	atlas cedar	C.n. Eddiei	30	8	variegated Pacific dogwood
C.a. Glauca	80	7b	blue atlas cedar				
C.a. Pendula	40	7b	weeping atlas cedar	Corylus colurna	30-50	5	Turkish hazel
C. deodara	100	8	Deodar cedar	Crataegus arnoldiana	25	2b	Arnold hawthorn
C. libani	60-100	8	cedar of Lebanon	C. Autumn Glory	13-20	6	
Celtis occidentalis*	34-70	2b	common hackberry	C. chlorosarca	13-20	2	blackfruit hawthorn
Cercidiphyllum japonicum	40-60	5	Katsura tree	C. crus-galli*	13-30	2b	cockspur hawthorn
Cercis canadensis	10-30	6	eastern redbud	C. erythropoda	16-26	4	chocolate hawthorn
C. chinensis	16-30	7b	Chinese redbud	C. × grignonensis	20	3b	
C. siliquastrum	26	8	Judas tree	C. laevigata (oxyacantha)	20	6	English hawthorn
Chamaecyparis lawsoniana	80	7b	Lawson false-cypress	C.l. Paulii	20	6	Paul's scarlet hawthorn
C.l. Allumii	30	7b	scarab Lawson false-cypress	C.l. Plena	20	6	double English hawthorn
C.l. Fletcheri	12-20	7b	Fletcher false-cypress	Cryptomeria japonica	30-100	6b	cryptomeria
				Cunninghamia lanceolata	16-50	7	common China fir
				× Cupressocyparis leylandii	40-50	7b	Leyland cypress

Botanical Name	Height (Feet)	Zone	Common Name(s)
Cupressus macrocarpa	50	8b	Monterey cypress
C. sempervirens	50	8b	Italian cypress
Davidia involucrata	20-50	7b	dovetree
Diospyros virginiana	30-50	7	common persimmon
Elaeagnus angustifolia	20-33	2b	Russian olive
Eucommia ulmoides	40	7	hardy rubbertree
Euonymus europaeus	16	4	European spindletree
E.e. Aldenhamensis	16-20	4	Aldenham spindletree
E.e. Red Cascade	16-20	4	red cascade spindletree
E. hamiltonianus maackii	20-30	2	maack euonymus
E.h. yedoensis	16-20	4	Yeddo euonymus
Evodia danielii	16-30	6b	Korean evodia
E. hupehensis	23-40	6	
Fagus grandifolia*	60-80	4	American beech
F. sylvatica	50-80	6	European beech
F.s. Asplenifolia	40-50	5b	fern-leaved beech
F.s. Atropunicea (Cuprea)	33	6	purple beech
F.s. Fastigiata	30-40	6	pyramidal European beech
F.s. Laciniata	30	6	cutleaf European beech
F.s. Pendula	40-50	6	weeping beech
F.s. Purpurea-pendula	20	6	weeping purple beech
F.s. Riversii	33-50	6	Rivers purple beech
F.s. Spaethiana	40	6	Spaeth purple beech
F.s. Tricolor	40	6b	tricolor beech
Ficus carica	20	7b	common fig
Franklinia alatamaha	16-30	7	franklinia
Fraxinus americana*	50-66	3b	white ash
F.a. Kleinburg	50	4	Kleinburg ash
F.a. Manitou	40	4	Manitou ash
F. excelsior	30-60	4	European ash
F. holotricha	40	6b	Kimberly blue ash
F. mandshurica	50-66	3b	Manchurian ash
F. nigra*	50-66	2b	black ash
F. ornus	40	7b	flowering ash
F. pennsylvanica	40-60	2b	red ash
F.p. lanceolata (subintegerrima)	50	2b	green ash
F.p. Marshall's Seedless	46	4	Marshall's seedless ash
F.p. Summit	50	2b	summit ash
Ginkgo biloba	40-60	4	maidenhair tree
G.b. Autumn Gold	50	4	autumn gold ginkgo
G.b. Fastigiata	50	5	fastigiate ginkgo
Gleditsia triacanthos*	50-66	4	common honey-locust
G.t. Imperial	50	4	imperial honey-locust
G.t. inermis	60	4	thornless honey-locust
G.t. Moraine	50	4	Moraine honey-locust
G.t. Rubylace	40	4	rubylace honey-locust
G.t. Shademaster	50	4	shademaster honey-locust
G.t. Skyline	50	4	skyline honey-locust
G.t Sunburst	40	4	sunburst honey-locust
Ilex aquifolium	10-30	7	English holly
I. opaca	10-34	7	American holly
Juglans ailanthifolia cordiformis	30-50	4b	heartnut
J. cinerea*	50-75	3	butternut
J. mandshurica	40-60	3b	Manchurian walnut
J. nigra*	50-90	3b	black walnut
J. regia	60	7	English walnut, Persian walnut
J.r. Carpathian	50	4	Carpathian walnut
Juniperus chinensis	20-40	5	Chinese juniper
J.c. Ames	10	5	Ames juniper
J.c. Fairview	16	5	fairview juniper
J.c. Mountbatten	13	4	Mountbatten juniper
J. scopulorum	10-30	2	western red cedar, rocky mountain juniper

Botanical Name	Height (Feet)	Zone	Common Name(s)	Botanical Name	Height (Feet)	Zone	Common Name(s)
J.s. Grey Gleam	10	3	grey gleam juniper	M. × atrosanguinea	20	5	carmine crab apple
J.s. Greenspire	13	4	greenspire juniper	M. baccata	16-30	2b	Siberian crab apple
J.s. Springbank	13	3	springbank juniper	M.b. Columnaris	20	2b	columnar Siberian crab apple
J. virginiana	23-30	3	eastern red cedar, red cedar	M.b. mandshurica	20	2b	Manchurian crab apple
J.v. Burkii	16	3	Burk red cedar	M. floribunda	26	5b	Japanese flowering crab apple
J.v. Canaerti	20	2b	Canaert red cedar	M. Garry	26	2b	Garry crab apple
J.v. Skyrocket	16	3	skyrocket juniper	M. Golden Hornet	20	4b	golden hornet crab apple
Kalopanax pictus	20-40	5	castor-aralia	M. Hopa	30	2b	Hopa crab apple
Koelreuteria paniculata	16-30	6b	goldenrain tree	M. hupehensis	26	5	tea crab apple
Laburnum alpinum	16-26	6b	Scots laburnum	M. ioensis Plena	30	4b	Bechtel's crab apple
L. anagyroides	20	6b	goldenchain tree	M. Prairie Rose	30	4	prairie rose crab apple
L. × watereri Vossii	26	6	Waterer laburnum	M. Katherine	20	4	Katherine crab apple
Larix decidua	50-82	3b	European larch	M. Kelsey	16	2	Kelsey crab apple
L. × eurolepis	60	3	Dunkeld larch	M. Makamik	30	2b	Makamik crab apple
L. kaempferi	40-82	2b	Japanese larch	M. Maybride	13	4	maybride crab apple
L. laricina*	60-90	1	American larch, tamarack	M. × moerlandsii Liset	20	4	
L. sibirica	50-82	2	Siberian larch	M. × m. Profusion	20	4	profusion crab apple
Liquidambar styraciflua	60-82	7	sweet-gum	M. Nipissing	23	4	Nipissing crab apple
Liriodendron tulipifera*	40-80	5b	tulip tree, yellow-poplar	M. Radiant	26	3b	radiant crab apple
Maackia amurensis	23-30	3b	Amur maackia	M. Red Jade	16	5	red jade weeping crab apple
Maclura pomifera	20-40	6	Osage-orange	M. Red Silver	30	4b	red silver crab apple
Magnolia acuminata*	40-66	5b	cucumbertree	M. Red Splendor	26	2b	red splendor crab apple
M. cordata	33	8	yellow cucumbertree	M. Renown	30	2b	renown apple crab
M. × soulangiana	13-26	5b	saucer magnolia	M. Rescue	26	2b	rescue apple crab
M. × s. Alba Superba	13-26	5b	white saucer magnolia	M. Royalty	20	2b	royalty crab apple
M. × s. Alexandrina	13-26	5b	Alexander saucer magnolia	M. Rudolph	23	2b	Rudolph crab apple
M. × s. Brozzonii	13-26	5b	Brozzoni saucer magnolia	M. sargentii	10	5	Sargent's crab apple
M. × s. Lennei	13-26	6	Lenne saucer magnolia	M. × scheideckeri	20	5	Scheidecker crab apple
M. × s. stellata	10-20	5b	star magnolia	M. Selkirk	30	2b	Selkirk crab apple
M. virginiana	10-50	7b	sweet bay	M. Sissipuk	33	2b	Sissipuk crab apple
Malus Almey	20	2b	Almey crab apple	M. Snowcloud	23	4	snowcloud crab apple
M. American Beauty	23	5		M. Strathmore	23	2b	Strathmore crab apple
M. Arctic Dawn	26	2b	arctic dawn crab apple	M. Sundog	30	2b	sundog crab apple
M. × arnoldiana	20	5	Arnold crab apple	M. Sutherland	30	2b	Sutherland crab apple
				M. Tanner	23	2b	Tanner's crab apple
				M. Thunderchild	23	2b	thunderchild crab apple

Botanical Name	Height (Feet)	Zone	Common Name(s)	Botanical Name	Height (Feet)	Zone	Common Name(s)
M. Van Eseltine	20	2b	Van Eseltine crab apple	P.d. Umbraculifera	10	5	Japanese umbrella pine
M. White Angel	23	5	white angel crab apple	P. flexilis*	23-50	2b	limber pine
M. × zumi calocarpa	20	4	redbud crab apple	P. jeffreyi	60-100	5	Jeffrey's pine
				P. koraiensis	82	5	Korean pine
Metasequoia M. glyptostroboides	60	6	dawn redwood	P. monticola*	100	2b	western white pine
				P. nigra	33-66	4b	black pine
Morus Alba	30	3	white mulberry	P. nigra (austriaca)	40-66	4	Austrian pine
M.a. Pendula	16	4	weeping mulberry	P. parviflora	82	5b	Japanese white pine
M. nigra	30	6	black mulberry	P. peuce	50	4	Macedonian pine, Balkan pine
M. rubra*	16-33	6	red mulberry				
Nyssa sylvatica*	30-60	5b	black gum, sour gum	P. ponderosa*	60-82	2b	Ponderosa pine
				P. resinosa*	50-100	2b	red pine, Norway pine
Ostrya virginiana*	23-33	3	American hop-hornbeam, ironwood	P. rigida*	33	5	pitch pine
				P. strobus*	66-100	2b	eastern white pine, white pine
Oxydendrum arboreum	20-40	7	sorrel tree, sourwood	P. sylvestris	33-82	2	Scotch pine
				P. thunbergiana	66	5	Japanese black pine
Parrotia persica	16-33	7	Persian parrotia	P. wallichiana	66-100	7	Himalayan white pine
Paulownia tomentosa	40	7	paulownia, princess tree				
				Platanus × acerifolia	60	6	London plane
Phellodendron amurense	33-50	3	Amur cork tree	P. occidentalis*	66-82	5b	sycamore, buttonwood
Photinia serrulata	16-33	7b	Chinese photinia	P. orientalis	33-66	7b	oriental plane
Picea abies	66-100	2b	Norway spruce	Platycladus (Thuja)			
P. brewerana	66	7b	Brewer spruce	P. orientalis	20-50	7	oriental arborvitae
P. engelmannii*	66-100	3	Engelmann spruce				
P. glauca*	66-100	1	white spruce	Poncirus trifoliata	13-26	7	hardy orange
P.g. albertiana*	66-100	1	western white spruce	Populus alba	50-82	2	white poplar
				P.a. Nivea	82	2	silver poplar
P.g. Densata	82	1b	black hills spruce	P.a. Pyramidalis	33-50	4	Bolleana poplar
P. omorika	66-100	3b	Serbian spruce	P.a. Racket	40	3	rocket poplar
P. orientalis	66-82	6	oriental spruce	P. angustifolia*	23-40	2	willow-leaved poplar
P. pungens	33-82	2	Colorado spruce				
P.p. Glauca	33-82	2	blue Colorado spruce	P. balsamifera*	50-66	1	balsam poplar
				P.b. subcordata (P. candicans)	66-100	3b	balm of Gilead
P.p. Hoopsii	33-66	2	Hoopsi blue spruce				
P.p. Koster	33-66	2	Koster blue spruce	P.b. trichocarpa*	66-82	2	black cottonwood
P.p. Moerheimii	33-66	2	Moerheim blue spruce	P. × bernardii	66-82	2b	northwest poplar
				P. × berolinensis	50-82	2	Berlin poplar
Pinus aristata	10-33	3	bristlecone pine	P. × canadensis Aurea	50-82	3b	Van Geerte poplar
P. banksiana*	33-82	1	jack pine	P. × c. Eugenei	66-100	2	Carolina poplar
P. cembra	33-66	2	Swiss stone pine	P. deltoides occidentalis* (P. sargentii)	33-82	2b	plains cottonwood
P. contorta*	16-50	6	shore pine				
P.c. latifolia*	50-82	1	lodgepole pine	P. grandidentata*	50-66	2b	large-toothed aspen
P. densiflora	66	5	Japanese red pine				

166

Botanical Name	Height (Feet)	Zone	Common Name (s)	Botanical Name	Height (Feet)	Zone	Common Name (s)
*P. tremuloides**	30-40	1	aspen poplar, trembling aspen	*Pterostyrax hispidus*	16-33	6	epaulette tree
P. tristis	40-60	2b	browntwig aspen	*Pyrus calleryana*	30	5	Callery pear
Prunus amygdalus	20	7	flowering almond	*P.c. Bradford*	50	5b	Bradford pear
P. armeniaca	25	7	flowering apricot	*P. ussuriensis*	20-40	2b	Ussurian pear
P.a. sibirica	20	2b	Siberian apricot	*Quercus acutissima*	40-60	7	sawtooth oak
P. avium Plena	30	4b	double-flowered mazzard cherry	*Q. alba**	50-90	4	white oak
P. × blireiana	20	6	flowering plum	*Q. bicolor**	40-60	4b	swamp white oak
P. cerasifera Atropurpurea	20-30	5b	pissard plum	*Q. coccinea*	40-82	4	scarlet oak
P.c. Thundercloud	20	5	thundercloud plum	*Rhus typhina**	10-26	3	staghorn sumach
P. Hally Jolivette	13	6		*R.t. Laciniata*	10-16	3	cutleaf staghorn sumach
P. × hillieri Spire	23	6	Hillier spire cherry	*Robinia × ambigua Decaisneana*	40	4	Decaisne locust
P. lusitanica	10-30	7b	Portugal laurel	*R. × a. Idahoensis*	26	4	Idaho locust
P. maackii	20-30	2b	Amur choke cherry	*R. boyntonii*	6.5	5	Boynton's locust
P. padus	33	2	European bird cherry	*R. fertilis Monument*	10-20	4	monument locust
P.p. commutata	20-40	2	May Day tree	*R. hispida*	5-6.5	5	rose acacia
P. Pandora	20	6	Pandora spring cherry	*R. pseudoacacia*	30-50	4	black locust
*P. pennsylvanica**	13-26	1	pin cherry, wild red cherry	*R.p. Pyramidalis*	30-50	4	pyramidal black locust
P.p. Stockton	23	2b	Stockton double pin cherry	*R.p. Umbraculifera*	20	4	mop-headed black locust
P. persica	20	6b	flowering peach	*Salix acutifolia*	50	2	ashleaf willow
P. sargentii	30-46	5	Sargent cherry	*S. alba*	60	4	white willow
P.s. Columnaris	33	5	columnar Sargent cherry	*S.a. chermesina*	40	3	redstem willow
P.s. Rancho	26	5	Rancho cherry	*S.a. Dropmore*	50	2	Dropmore willow
*P. serotina**	40-66	2b	black cherry	*S.a. sericea*	60	2	silver willow
P. serrulata	20-26	6	Japanese cherry	*S.a. tristis*	43-60	4	niobe willow
P.s. Amanogawa	26	6	Amanogawa Japanese cherry	*S.a. vitellina*	50	3	yellowstem willow
P.s. Kiku-shidare-sakura	20	6	weeping Japanese cherry	*S. babylonica*	30	7b	Babylon weeping willow
P.s. Kwanzan (Hisakura)	26	6	Kwanzan Japanese cherry	*S. × blanda*	60	4	Wisconsin weeping willow
P.s. Pink Perfection	20	6	pink perfection cherry	*S. caprea*	13-26	5	goat willow
P. virginiana Shubert	13-26	2	Shubert choke cherry	*S. × elegantissima*	33	5	Thurlow weeping willow
P. × yedoensis	20-40	7b	Yoshino cherry	*S. matsudana Tortuosa*	30	5	corkscrew willow
P. × y. Akebono	26	7	Akebono flowering cherry	*S. pentandra*	23-40	1b	laurel willow
Pseudolarix kaempferi (amabilis)	20-50	7	golden larch	*Sassafras albidum**	30-40	6	sassafras
				Sciadopitys verticillata	10-40	7	umbrella pine
*Ptelea trifoliata**	13-26	3b	hop tree	*Sophora japonica*	23-60	6b	Japanese pagoda tree
				S.j. Pendula	30	6b	weeping Japanese pagoda tree

Botanical Name	Height (Feet)	Zone	Common Name(s)
Sorbus alnifolia	23-40	4b	Korean mountain ash
S. americana*	10-30	3	American mountain ash
S. aria	13-33	4	white beam
S.a. Lutescens	13-33	4	goldbeam
S.a. Majestica	13-33	4	Decaisne mountain ash
S. aucuparia	23-43	3	European mountain ash, rowan
S.a. Edulis	23-33	4	Moravian mountain ash
S.a. Fastigiata	23-30	4	upright mountain ash
S.a. Pendula	23	3	weeping mountain ash
S.a. Rossica	23-33	3	Russian mountain ash
S. decora*	13-33	2	showy mountain ash
S.d. Rowancroft Pink Coral	23	4	
S. intermedia	40	5	Swedish white beam
S. scopulina*	23	2	Greene's mountain ash
S. × thuringiaca Fastigiata	26	5	oak-leaved mountain ash
S. × t. Leonard Springer	30	4	Springer mountain ash
Stewartia koreana	10-20	7	Korean stewartia
S. pseudocamellia	13-26	7	Japanese stewartia
Styrax japonicus	10-26	6b	Japanese snowbell
S. obassia	10-26	7	fragrant snowbell
Syringa reticulata (amurensis japonica)	20-26	2	Japanese tree lilac
S.r. Ivory Silk	26	2	ivory silk tree lilac
S.r. mandshurica (amurensis)	10-16	2	Amur tree lilac
Taxodium distichum	23-80	5b	bald cypress
Taxus baccata	30	7	English yew
T.b. Fastigiata	13-26	7	Irish yew
T. cuspidata	13-50	4	Japanese yew
Thuja occidentalis*	13-43	3	arborvitae, white cedar
T.o. Brandon	10-20	2	Brandon cedar
T.o. Elegantissima	13	3b	goldtipped cedar
T.o. Ellwangeriana	10-20	3	Ellwanger's arborvitae
T.o. fastigiata	16	3	pyramid cedar
T.o. Holmstrup	13	3	Holmstrup cedar
T.o. Nigra	16	4	black arborvitae
T.o. Robusta (Wareana)	16	2	Siberian cedar
T.o. Smaragd	10-20	3	Smaragd cedar
T.o. Techny	16	3	Techny cedar
T. plicata*	50-180	6b	giant arborvitae
T.p Atrovirens	50	6	
T.p. Aurea	33	6	golden arborvitae
T. standishii	40	5	Japanese arborvitae
Thujopsis dolabrata	33	7b	hiba arborvitae
Tilia americana*	60-66	2b	basswood, American linden
T. cordata	40-50	3	littleleaf linden
T.c. Morden	50	3	Morden linden
T. × flavescens Dropmore	50	3	Dropmore linden
T. mongolica	43	3b	Mongolian linden
T. petiolaris	60	5	pendant silver linden
T. platyphyllos	50-82	4	bigleaf linden
T.p. Orebro	50	4	Orebro linden
T. tomentosa	40-60	6	silver linden
Tsuga canadensis*	60-75	4	Canadian hemlock
T. caroliniana	50	7	Carolina hemlock
T. diversifolia	50-75	7	Japanese hemlock
Ulmus americana*	60-120	2	American elm
U. carpinifolia	60	5	smooth-leaved elm
U.c. Umbraculifera	23	5	globe elm
U. glabra Horizontalis (Pendula)	23	4b	table top elm
U. parvifolia	30-40	5	Chinese elm
U. procera	80	6	English elm
U. pumila	60	3b	Siberian elm
U.p. Dropmore	60	2	Dropmore elm
U. × vegeta Camperdownii	40	4b	Camperdown elm
Viburnum lentago*	10-20	2	nannyberry
Zelkova serrata	60	6	Japanese zelkova

— from Agriculture Canada publication 1343, *A Checklist of Ornamental Trees for Canada.*

APPENDIX E
MAIL—ORDER SOURCES

The use of mail-order nurseries and seed houses enables most landscape gardeners to obtain a far greater selection of plants than could be purchased locally. The following source list has been divided into two sections: first, companies that specialize in plant materials — that is, anything other than seeds, including bulbs, rhizomes, tubers and whole plants — and those companies that specialize in seeds, whether from trees, shrubs, vegetables, herbs or flowers, wild or domestic. While seeds can be moved relatively freely across most borders — only beans, corn and peas are not sent by some companies — plant materials, potential disease carriers, are not as freely exchanged. Some plants, including all *Prunus* (such as cherries), *Pyrus* (such as pears) and *Malus* (such as apples) species cannot be sent to Canada from the United States at all.

Cooperating United States nurseries, including those in the following list, must comply with Agriculture Canada restrictions and complete a phyto-sanitary certificate in order to ship permissible plant materials to Canada. A Canadian customer wanting to buy plant materials from the United States must first request an "application form for permission to import" from the Permit Office, Plant Health Division, Agriculture Canada, Ottawa, Ontario K1A 0C6, obtaining one application form for each American company that will be patronized. The permit is completed and sent back to Agriculture Canada for approval. It is then returned to the customer, who sends it along with his or her foreign order. In paying for imported goods, consider using a money order for foreign funds, which can be purchased at any bank or post office. International Postal Reply coupons, needed for some catalogues, are also available at all post offices.

Each company description includes the 1985 catalogue price, which may change in subsequent years. A self-addressed, stamped envelope or, if foreign, an International Postal Reply coupon, sent to the company will encourage it to advise the customer about the current catalogue price.

PLANT MATERIALS

ALBERTA NURSERIES & SEEDS
Box 20
Bowden, Alberta T0M 0K0
Hardy fruit trees, ornamental trees, shrubs, berry bushes, perennial flowers. Also flower, vegetable seeds. Catalogue free in Canada, $2 elsewhere.

ALPENGLOW GARDENS
13328 King George Highway
Surrey, British Columbia V3T 2T6
Hardy alpines, perennial flowers, rock garden plants including several thymes, dwarf ornamental shrubs, heathers, rhododendrons, dwarf conifers. Catalogue $1.

APPALACHIAN WILDFLOWER NURSERY
Route 1, Box 275A
Reedsville, Pennsylvania 17084
Wildflower plants. Catalogue $1 (U.S.).

ASHBY'S
RR 2
Cameron, Ontario K0M 1G0
Organically grown herb plants, ground covers, perennial flowers to Canada and the United States. Catalogue $1.

AUBIN NURSERIES LTD.
Box 1089
Carman, Manitoba R0G 0J0
Hardy ornamental and fruit trees, berry bushes, hedge plants, shrubs. Catalogue free.

BEAVERLODGE NURSERY LTD.
Box 127
Beaverlodge, Alberta T0H 0C0
Hardy fruit trees, ornamental trees, shrubs, berry bushes, climbers, hedge plants, perennial flowers. Catalogue free.

BLACKTHORNE GARDENS
48 Quincy Street
Holbrook, Massachusetts 02343-1989
Lilies, wildflowers, alliums, hostas.

HOPESTEAD GARDENS
6605 Hopedale Road
RR 4
Sardis, British Columbia V0X 1Y0
Hardy perennial plants. Catalogue free.

BOUGHEN NURSERIES VALLEY RIVER, LTD.
Box 12
Valley River, Manitoba R0L 2B0
Hardy fruit trees, ornamental trees, shrubs, berry bushes, climbers, hedge and windbreak plants, roses, perennial flowers. Catalogue free.

BOUNTIFUL RIDGE NURSERIES
Princess Anne, Maryland 21853
Fruit trees and berry bushes, hardy and tender. Catalogue free.

LEONARD W. BUTT
Huttonville, Ontario L0J 1B0
Gladiolus corms, rare and exotic bulbs. Price list free.

CALIFORNIA NURSERY COMPANY
Niles District
Box 2278
Fremont, California 94536
Fruit trees including dwarf citrus, figs. Price list free.

CATNIP ACRES FARM
Christian Street
Oxford, Connecticut 06483
Herb plants. Catalogue $1 (U.S.) refundable.

COOK'S GERANIUM NURSERY
712 North Grand
Lyons, Kansas 67554
Geranium plants. Accepts Canadian orders greater than $15. Catalogue $1 (U.S.) refundable.

CORN HILL NURSERY
RR 2
Anagance, New Brunswick E0E 1A0
Fruit trees, especially apples, berries, hardy roses, shrubs, climbers, ornamental trees. No foreign orders. Catalogue free.

CRAWFORD'S COUNTRY GARDENS
RR 3
Milton, Ontario L9T 2X7
Perennial flowers, herbs, miniature roses, shrubs. Catalogue $1.

C.A. CRUIKSHANK LTD.
1015 Mount Pleasant Road
Toronto, Ontario M4P 2M1
An extensive list of popular and exotic bulbs, corms, rhizomes for perennial flowers. Catalogue $1 refundable.

EDIBLE LANDSCAPING
Route 2, Box 343A
Afton, Virginia 22920
Eight types of kiwi (*Actinidia* spp), other fruits. Price list free.

FARLEIGH LAKE GARDENS
Box 128
Penticton, British Columbia V2A 6J9
Perennial flowers, herb plants. Send self-addressed, stamped envelope or International Postal Reply coupon for price list.

FERNCLIFF GARDENS
SS 1
Mission, British Columbia V2V 5V6
Gladioli, dahlias, irises, peonies. Canada only. Catalogue free.

FORESTFARM
990 Tetherow Road
Williams, Oregon 97544
Native and permaculture plants, herbs, trees. Catalogue $1.50 (U.S.).

DEAN FOSTER NURSERIES
Hartford, Michigan 49157
Fruit trees, berry bushes, some shade

trees, evergreen seedlings. Catalogue free.

FOUR WINDS GROWERS
42186 Palm Avenue, Box 3538
Mission San Jose District
Fremont, California 94538
True dwarf citrus trees, many types, suitable for pots. Price list free.

GARDENIMPORT, INC.
Box 760
Thornhill, Ontario L3T 4A5
Day lilies, dahlias, cannas, gladioli, lilies; also vegetable, flower seeds. Catalogue $1 refundable.

GILBERT'S PEONY GARDENS
Elora, Ontario N0B 1S0
Peony plants. Catalogue $1.

GLADSIDE GARDENS
61 Main Street
Northfield, Massachusetts 01360
Gladioli, dahlias, cannas, rare bulbs. Accepts Canadian orders over $20. Catalogue $1 (U.S.).

GOLDEN BOUGH TREE FARM
Marlbank, Ontario K0K 2L0
Hardy ornamental trees, fruit trees, shrubs, berry bushes. Catalogue $1.

GREER GARDENS
1280 Goodpasture Island Road
Eugene, Oregon 97401
Azaleas, rhododendrons, bonsai plants, conifers. Catalogue $2 (U.S.).

HALLMAN ORCHARDS & NURSERY
Box 1218
Ganges, British Columbia V0S 1E0
Fruit trees on various rootstocks. Catalogue free.

HARBORCREST NURSERIES
4634 West Saanich Road
Victoria, British Columbia V8Z 3G8
Perennial flowers, house plants, herb plants. Catalogue $1.

THE HERB FARM
RR 4
Norton, New Brunswick E0G 2N0
Herb plants, perennial flowers. Price list $1.

170

LES HERBES FINES DE SAINT-ANTOINE
480 Chemin l'Acadie
Saint-Antoine-sur-Richelieu
Quebec J0L 1R0
Herb plants to Canada only. Catalogue $1 refundable.

HONEYWOOD LILIES
Box 63
Parkside, Saskatchewan S0J 2A0
Lilies, peonies. Price list free. Lily catalogue $1.

JACKSON & PERKINS CO.
Box 1028
Medford, Oregon 97501
Ornamental fruit trees, berries, bulbs, rose specialists. Accepts Canadian orders over $50. Catalogue $2 (U.S.).

K & L CACTUS NURSERY
12712 Stockton Blvd.
Galt, California 95632
Cactus plants. Catalogue $2 (U.S.).

LAKESHORE TREE FARMS LTD.
RR 3
Saskatoon, Saskatchewan S7K 3J6
Hardy fruit trees, ornamentals, berries, shrubs, climbers, hedge plants, perennial flowers. Catalogue $1.

MAKIELSKI BERRY FARM & NURSERY
7130 Platt Road
Ypsilanti, Michigan 48197
Raspberries, other small fruits. Catalogue free.

McFAYDEN SEED CO. LTD.
Box 1800
Brandon, Manitoba R7A 6N4
Fruit trees, berry bushes, perennial flowers; also flower, vegetable seeds. Catalogue free.

McMATH'S DAFFODILS
6340 Francis Road
Richmond, British Columbia V7C 1K5
Narcissus, daffodil bulbs. Price list free.

JOHN McMILLEN'S IRIS GARDEN
RR 1

Norwich, Ontario N0J 1P0
Irises, day lilies. Catalogue free.

MOORE WATER GARDENS
Port Stanley, Ontario N0L 2A0
Water Plants. Catalogue free.

MORDEN NURSERIES LTD.
Box 1270
Morden, Manitoba R0G 1J0
Hardy fruit trees, berries, ornamental trees, shrubs, roses, vines, hedge plants. Catalogue free.

MUSSER FORESTS
Indiana, Pennsylvania 15701
Conifers, flowering shrubs, hedge plants, ground covers, vines, ornamental trees; seedlings, rooted cuttings. Catalogue free.

NEW YORK STATE FRUIT TESTING CO-OP
Geneva, New York 14456
Fruit trees, small fruits, grapes. Catalogue by donation.

NORTHSTAR PLANTS AND HERBS
Box 2262, Station A
London, Ontario N6A 4E3
Herb plants. Catalogue 50 cents refundable.

P.F.R.A. NURSERY
Indian Head, Saskatchewan S0G 2K0
Trees for farm shelterbelts in Alberta, Saskatchewan and Manitoba. Write for free information.

PACIFIC TREE FARMS
4301 Lynnwood Drive
Chula Vista, California 92010
Conifers, ornamental and fruit trees, many exotic. Catalogue $1.50 (U.S.).

CARL PALLEK & SON
Box 137
Virgil, Ontario L0S 1T0
Roses. Catalogue free.

PATMORE NURSERY SALES
Box 582
Brandon, Manitoba R7A 5Z7
Hardy fruit trees, berries, ornamentals.

PEDLINGHAM'S TREE FARM
RR 2

Thornton, Ontario L0L 2N0
Seedlings of Scotch pine, Austrian pine, mugho pine, blue spruce. Price list free.

W.H. PERRON & CO. LTD.
515 Labelle Blvd. Chomedey,
Laval, Quebec H7V 2T3
Landscaping plants to Montreal area. Also flower, vegetable, herb seeds. Catalogue $1.

PRAIRIE NURSERY
Box 365-A
Westfield, Wisconsin 53964
Native perennial plants, wildflower seeds. Catalogue $1 (U.S.) refundable.

RED'S RHODIES & ALPINE GARDENS
15920 S.W. Oberst Lane
Sherwood, Oregon 97140
Rhododendrons, azaleas, sempervivums, sedums. Catalogue 50 cents (U.S.).

LE REVEIL DE LA NATURE
RR 1
St-Philibert, Quebec G0M 1X0
Hardy fruits, berries, ornamental trees, shrubs, perennial flowers. French language catalogue $1.

RICHTER'S
Box 26
Goodwood, Ontario L0C 1A0
Herb plants and an extensive listing of herb, wildflower seeds. Catalogue $2.

ST. LAWRENCE NURSERIES
RD 2
Potsdam, New York 13676
Hardy fruit trees, nut trees, berries. Catalogue free.

SEARS-McCONNELL NURSERIES
Port Burwell, Ontario N0J 1T0
Ornamental trees, shrubs, hedge plants; fruit trees, berries. Some flowers, vegetable seeds. Catalogue free, can be ordered through any Sears outlet in Canada.

SIMPLE GIFTS FARM GREENHOUSES
RR 1
Athens, Ontario K0E 1B0
Perennial flowers, herbs. Catalogue $1.

KEITH SOMERS TREES LTD.
10 Tillson Avenue
Tillsonburg, Ontario N4G 2Z6
Low cost landscaping shrubs, trees. To
Canada only. Catalogue free.

SPRINGWOOD MINIATURE ROSES
Box 255H
Port Credit P.O.
Mississauga, Ontario L5G 4L8
Miniature roses. Catalogue free.

SUNNYBROOK FARMS NURSERY
9948 Mayfield Road
Box 6
Chesterland, Ohio 44026
Perennial flowers, herbs, houseplants.
Catalogue $1 (U.S.).

SURSUM CORDA
Scotstown, Quebec J0B 3B0
Hardy fruit trees, berries. Catalogue $1.

T&T SEEDS LTD.
Box 1710
Winnipeg, Manitoba R3C 3P6
Ornamental trees, shrubs, perennial
flowers, fruit trees, berries, flower,
vegetable seeds. Catalogue 75 cents.

TANSY FARMS
RR 1 – 5888 Else Road
Agassiz, British Columbia V0M 1A0
Herb plants, many types of thyme,
Artemisia, geraniums. Catalogue $1.50.

VINELAND NURSERIES
Box 98
Vineland Station, Ontario L0R 2E0
Dwarf and unusual evergreens, bamboo.
Catalogue 50 cents.

WEST KOOTENAY HERB NURSERY
RR 2 Bedford Road
Nelson, British Columbia V1L 5P5
Herb plants. Catalogue free.

**WESTERN ONTARIO FRUIT
TESTING ASSOCIATION**
Agriculture Canada Research Station
Harrow, Ontario N0R 1G0
Hardy fruit trees. Membership $10 year.

LANDSCAPING SEEDS

W.R. AIMERS LTD.
Cotswolds, The Green Lane
RR 1
King, Ontario L0G 1K0
Wildflower seed mixtures for various
regions and conditions. Price list free.

THOMAS BUTCHER LTD.
60 Wickham Road
Shirley, Croydon, Surrey CR9 8AG
England
Seeds for flowers, trees, shrubs,
vegetables and herbs. Catalogue, two
International Postal Reply coupons.

JOHN CHAMBERS
15 Westleigh Road
Barton Seagrave
Kettering, Northants NN15 5AJ
England
Seeds of wild and cultivated plants,
grasses, vegetables. Catalogue, two
International Postal Reply coupons.

ESP WILDFLOWERS
Box 5125
El Monte, California 91734
Wildflower seed mixtures for
landscaping, and individual types of
flower seeds in bulk. Catalogue free.

**FRIENDS OF THE TREES SEED
SERVICE**
Box 1064
Tonasket, Washington 98855
Seeds for native shrubs, trees, vines,
flowers. Catalogue $1.50 (U.S.).

GARDEN MAGIC SEED CO.
310 Main Street
East Haven, Connecticut 06512
Vegetable, herb, houseplant, tree and
shrub seeds. Catalogue $1 (U.S.).

LARNER SEEDS
Box 60143
Palto Alto, California 94306
Seeds of native plants of California and
New England. Catalogue 50 cents (U.S.).

McLAUGHLIN'S SEEDS
Buttercup's Acre
Box 550

Mead, Washington 99021-0550
Three tabloid catalogues for flowers,
vegetables, wildflowers. Catalogue $1
(Can.). Canadian currency at par.

MELLINGER'S INC.
2310 West South Range
North Lima, Ohio 44452
Seeds for flowers, shrubs, trees,
vegetables, herbs. Catalogue $1 (U.S.) to
Canada, free to the U.S.

MIDWEST WILDFLOWERS
Box 64
Rockton, Illinois 61072
Wildflower seeds. Catalogue 50 cents
(U.S).

NORTHPLAN SEED PRODUCERS
Box 9107
Moscow, Idaho 83843
Seeds of native plants. Price list 50 cents
(U.S.).

GEORGE W. PARK SEED CO.
Box 31
Greenwood, South Carolina 29647
Seeds of vegetables, flowers,
wildflowers, herbs. Catalogue free.

RECOR'S TREE SEED
640 El Paso
Denver, Colorado 80221
Tree seeds. Catalogue free.

REDWOOD CITY SEED CO.
Box 361
Redwood City, California 94064
Worldwide collection of flower, shrub,
herb, vegetable seeds. Catalogue 50
cents (U.S.).

**ROCKY MOUNTAIN SEED
SERVICE**
Box 215
Golden, British Columbia V0A 1H0
Seeds for British Columbia native
flowers, shrubs. Catalogue $1.

SEEDS BLUM
Idaho City Stage
Boise, Idaho 83706
Non-hybrid flowers, vegetables, herbs,
and suggestions for epicurean
landscaping. Catalogue $2 (U.S.).

SOUTHERN SEEDS
The Vicarage
Sheffield, Canterbury, New Zealand
Seeds of native alpine plants. Catalogue
$1 (U.S.).

STOKES SEEDS LTD.
39 James Street
Box 10
St. Catharines, Ontario L2R 6R6
or
28 Water Street
Fredonia, New York 14063
Vegetable, flower, herb seeds. Catalogue
free.

SUNRISE ENTERPRISES
Box 10058
Elmwood, Connecticut 06110-0058
Oriental vegetable, herb seeds.
Catalogue free.

THOMPSON & MORGAN INC.
Box 1308
Jackson, New Jersey 08527
A worldwide collection of flowers, wild
plant, vegetable, herb seeds. Catalogue
free.

TIMBERLINE TREE SEEDS
9100 Abbey Road
Pueblo, Colorado 81004
Evergreen and wildflower seeds. Price
list free.

THE URBAN FARMER, INC.
Box 22198
Beachwood, Ohio 44122
Vegetable, herb seeds for confined
gardens. Catalogue $1 (Can.).

A.J. WOODWARD FLORIST
635 Fort Street
Victoria, British Columbia V8W 1G1
Imported English flower and vegetable
seeds. Catalogue $1.

A WORLD SEED SERVICE
Box 1058
Redwood City, California 94064
A worldwide collection of wildflower,
shrub, domestic flower, vegetable, and
herb seeds. Catalogue $1.

Index